CAN'T KNOCK THE HUSTLE

CAN'T KNOCK

THE HUSTLE

Inside the Season of Protest, Pandemic, and Progress with the Brooklyn Nets' Superstars of Tomorrow

MATT SULLIVAN

DEY ST.
An Imprint of WILLIAM MORROW

HarperCollins books may be purchased for educational, business, or sales promotional use. For information, please email the Special Markets Department at SPsales@harpercollins.com.

FIRST EDITION

Designed by Michelle Crowe

Emojis in text by Carboxylase/Shutterstock, Inc.

Library of Congress Cataloging-in-Publication Data

Names: Sullivan, Matt (Sports editor) author.
Title: Can't knock the hustle : inside the season of protest, pandemic, and progress with the Brooklyn Nets' superstars of tomorrow / Matt Sullivan.
Description: First edition. | New York : Dey St., An Imprint of William Morrow. [2021] | Includes bibliographical references. | Summary: "An award-winning journalist's behind-the-scenes account from the epicenter of sports, social justice, and coronavirus, Can't Knock the Hustle is a lasting chronicle of the historic 2019-2020 NBA season, by way of the notorious Brooklyn Nets and basketball's renaissance as a cultural force beyond the game"—Provided by publisher.
Identifiers: LCCN 2021012801 (print) | LCCN 2021012802 (ebook) | ISBN 9780063036802 (hardcover) | ISBN 9780063036819 (paperback) | ISBN 9780063036826 (ebook) | ISBN 9780063036833 | ISBN 9780063036840
Subjects: LCSH: Brooklyn Nets (Basketball team)—History—21st century. | Basketball players—United States. | Social justice—United States. | COVID-19 Pandemic, 2020—United States. | Sports—Political aspects—United States.
Classification: LCC GV885.52.B76 S85 2021 (print) | LCC GV885.52.B76 (ebook) | DDC 796.323/640974723—dc23
LC record available at https://lccn.loc.gov/2021012801
LC ebook record available at https://lccn.loc.gov/2021012802

ISBN 978-0-06-303680-2

21 22 23 24 25 LSC 10 9 8 7 6 5 4 3 2 1

FOR DAD

CONTENTS

CAN'T KNOCK THE HUSTLE

AUTHOR'S NOTE

KEVIN DURANT SAT ALONE beside his locker, at a social distance. He'd finished working out his ruptured Achilles on the court here at Barclays Center for the afternoon, and he was feeling healthier by the day. A few weeks earlier, back when the world was slightly less upside-down, he had shown me the progress of this rehabilitation on his iPhone, outside one of several living rooms at his $38 million penthouse. In the video, KD looked like KD again, sprinting all over the gym and dunking with glee. "I just gotta get that muscle memory back," he exclaimed, on his way to smoke a joint in the car. "But I felt great! That shit happened *fast.*" KD snapped his fingers, remembering the last time he played basketball at relatively full strength, in the 2019 NBA Finals, on the Golden State Warriors. "It's really been damn near a *year.*"

In the Brooklyn Nets locker room, beat writers clustered six feet away from the superstar, and not because of the virus. Not yet. The sports media had grown scared of the one-time most valuable player, two-time champion, four-time scoring leader and ten-time All-Star, knowing that he preferred to communicate on his terms, on social media. So the reporters continued asking a 21-year-old center named Jarrett Allen about how the team might adapt its defensive coverages for the day's upcoming game against the Chicago Bulls, since the Nets had just—spoiler alert—fired their head coach. This seemed, at the time, to be the last dramatic episode that the franchise could possibly endure in the year 2020, after Brooklyn got mixed up in a geopolitical disaster on a preseason trip to China, then reeled from the sudden death of Kobe Bryant. It was, however, only March. A lone bottle of hand sanitizer stood unused in the corner. There was not a mask in sight.

As KD turned his back to wriggle into his jeans, a longtime sportswriter whispered to me that KD and "that piece of shit" Kyrie Irving had only begun to detonate the team—that he couldn't believe I'd picked the 2019–2020 NBA season, of all seasons, to embed with the Nets, and that my book was about to get spun on its axis again, by matters of the hardwood. But I walked right up to KD, as he pulled a T-shirt over his wire of a frame, and reminded him that the real story was beyond the game. We agreed that, no matter what fresh hell got in Brooklyn's way, this book could offer an unfiltered look at power and fame, precisely because I was not another sportswriter.

"No offense," I told KD, "but I don't care much about your on-court stuff."

"Yeah, for sure," he said, glancing down toward a memorandum, crisp and unread, on the leather chair to his right: . . . *your chances of getting the coronavirus are currently low.*

This risk assessment, the memo continued, *can change rapidly.*

Less than eighty hours later, the National Basketball Association shut down, as soon as one of its players tested positive for Covid-19. As usual, the rest of the culture followed the NBA. But tectonic events were approaching, and the Nets would be at the epicenter: At the White House, Donald Trump was asked if the team, having procured exclusive access to elusive coronavirus testing, represented a class of the rich and famous that went to the front of the line. "Perhaps that's been the story of life," the president said. After yet another video of the death of yet another unarmed Black man, George Floyd, went viral for all the wrong reasons, Brooklyn's arena became the most recognizable gathering place in a new civil rights movement sprouting quickly across the globe. Basketball managed, in a miracle of leadership and science, to revive an entertainment economy that the virus had disposed of, as the NBA sequestered thousands of people in Disney World to play and protest at the same time. By then, the Nets roster included even more radical disruptors than when the year-long season began.

This book was reported contemporaneously, revealing how everyone from LeBron James and James Harden to shifty billionaires and calamity-stricken Brooklynites were forced to adapt as frantically as the world did. In my own shadow beat, I attended all the Nets games at Barclays Center—a mile from my house, and from the penthouses of many players themselves— and I witnessed the mid-practice moments that make a team coalesce or combust. I traveled from Washington to San Francisco, from Staples Center in Los Angeles to NBA All-Star Weekend in Chicago, conducting more than four hundred interviews with players who shaped the season and with generational thought-leaders in every facet of the game: Hall of Famers, All-Stars, owners, executives, coaches, doctors, agents, influencers, politicians, activists, friends and family. When the Utah Jazz star Rudy Gobert's single test result forced a nation to confront a pandemic, my mother worried that I had Covid-19, since I'd been the only reporter walking the court with players at Jazz practice in Manhattan the week before. One day during the season when hoops culture never stopped, I'd be meditating with a Nets star on video chat; another, I'd be marching through the streets of Brooklyn with his teammate. I would interview a player about the virus, then he would go viral for contracting it. I would chat with a player about his or her ideas for activism, in private (many central characters spoke freely—very freely—so long as they weren't quoted), only for a politician to chastise the NBA and the WNBA, in public, for being too political. Such were the upended and even more influential lives of athletes in 2020.

I have taken the players at their word, piecing together details, conversations and memories in fast-forward and rewind, accompanied by previously unpublished documents and audio, as well as years' worth of reporting by the many dedicated NBA journalists cited in the endnotes. But this is the players' story, devoid of scoop-hunting while full of fresh hell.

As KD and I discussed in the locker room back in March, his power moves from Silicon Valley to Hollywood were part of a vanguard in the footprints of LeBron. And we agreed that Kyrie, his friend and fellow Nets superstar, was grossly misunderstood—perhaps more than any athlete since Colin Kaepernick—while remaining highly secretive: an untold story on purpose, in an age of living extremely online. Kyrie called himself a prisoner of his own fame; another teammate called him "the enigma of the century." In one of our final exchanges, Kyrie sent along a 67-page Supreme Court ruling on Indigenous land rights and encouraged me to *Keep the truth Alive.*

KD peered up from his seat, past the beat writers, to the other corner of the locker room, where his teammates Garrett

Temple and Wilson Chandler talked politics throughout the election year. We recalled how, two seasons earlier, Garrett had found himself in the middle of a police-killing protest that shut down an NBA arena—and how many players on this team in particular had, before they all came together in Brooklyn, experienced the cross-pollination of basketball with the American scene, a decade-long season in bloom right as the plague, and a worldwide resistance against racism and the cops, began to spread. I told KD about my experience overseeing an investigation of every police killing in America, before I started covering sports as an outsider on the inside, and lamented how the killing hadn't stopped. "No," he said, "and it won't."

But Kevin Durant was busy preparing to get back in the gym with his teammates during the off-season. "Shit," he reminded himself. "Summer's comin' up!" We imagined what the world might look like when this book was published: He and Kyrie would be healthy, they would have a new coach, America could have a new president, and the Nets should be in first place— sixty wins and then some, perhaps, making a run at the NBA title. KD was thinking more like three championships in a row, with a few former colleagues in tow. But first, Brooklyn would have to withstand the most unimaginable and unforgettable season of anyone's lifetime, until the world spun right round again.

I asked KD if he'd be joining the Nets that week in California. He was indeed, which meant a spotlight return to visit the Warriors, albeit on the bench, where he'd been watching the NBA go by all season long, so far. Pulling on his favorite Balenciaga hoodie, KD prepared to head out. He didn't care to stick around for the afternoon's game itself. Not really. He had a plane to catch—and he was about to catch the virus, too, if the pandemic hadn't caught up with him already.

1

DECISIONS, DECISIONS

MAY 21, 2019 ▶

Malibu, California

THE SUPERSTAR BURST into a bedroom of his temporary mansion, searching for keys. He grasped at them and swooshed back out the door with that same tornado zoom he could summon on a basketball court, picking up speed toward the garage and the Range Rover and the road. He hoped to keep his flight from waiting. He hoped to keep his secret. He hoped. "I'm about to go see a hero," Kyrie Irving said, then clambered aboard the helicopter of Kobe Bryant.

He'd been flying in Kobe's chopper for nearly half the decade, since he'd sought out the five-time NBA champion as a frustrated phenomenon with the Cleveland Cavaliers in 2015. Kobe had challenged Kyrie to confront the anxieties of modern fame: *Do you really care what other people think about you?* Kyrie did not, or so he claimed at the time. *Are you afraid to be different?* Kyrie was not, certainly, and his ensuing apprenticeship helped the young point guard deliver the title that his teammate

LeBron James promised to a hometown crowd. Kyrie had felt an awesome kind of balance when his clutch three-pointer won the 2016 Finals—an equilibrium of power earned, power left to bestow—and now he hovered forward once again, fluttering high and clear over the coast. It was the dawn of a new season, of a new decade, and he could breathe.

Kyrie touched down in Orange County, then got straight to work. At the office of Kobe's budding multimedia company, Granity Studios, the student and the teacher talked hoops. They broke down how Kyrie's most recent season, with the Boston Celtics, had fizzled two weeks earlier in the second round of the playoffs, how his attempt to demand his own contender had failed. But Kyrie was a free agent this summer—and he'd already chosen a new team, keeping his decision on the low as he assembled the rest of his squad. The next move for Kyrie, they agreed, was to get the most out of the people around him. "That's really hard," Kobe had said recently. "How do you find an emotional connection with each player? Figure out what their fears are, and help turn those fears into strengths. And to do that, you have to put *time* in. I don't mean time in the gym."

So they talked about real life, too, about their shared mistakes and pains, about business. Kyrie admired his mentor's second act, during which Kobe had won an Oscar, written children's books and found joy in coaching his daughter's basketball team. Except Kyrie did not aspire to be cutthroat like The Black Mamba, a personality of killer instincts with hoops on the mind all the time, which Kobe had invented to refashion his public image after a sexual assault accusation in 2003. And Kyrie continued to despise the game's showmanship for entertainment value—the high-school soap-operatics and Instagram-demonium of the NBA—as mere shadow-puppeteering on the walls his country built to divide. "It's hatred and oppression all around us, all the time," Kyrie would say, "but I believe we are the generation to change it."

This being another week in 2019, in the allegedly United States of America, fear and distraction reigned: A child had died under quarantine in the negligent custody of the border patrol. The reality-show president was preparing for a photo op with cops. An actual billionaire had surprised graduates of an historically Black university by pledging to pay off their student debt, but Americans preferred to obsess over the finale of a television show about dueling kingdoms in a fantasy world and the march of the dynastic Golden State Warriors into the NBA Finals.

Kyrie was a rebel by nature, and he made every effort, as did so many athletes in America's new pastime, to be more than famous. Like Kobe, he sought the meaning of influence. "I saw what he was creating," Kyrie explained to me, "and I knew that I wanted that same structure: He had his own company, he had his own belief system, he had his own principles that he lived by. He didn't give a fuck what anyone said. And I think that having that type of strength, he was just that type of leader of a *movement* that so many people want to follow."

The Mamba Mentality was its own brand of advice that Kobe delivered to basketball superstars, to almost-stars and to teenagers alike, often by way of text-message affirmations that even Kyrie, his prized pupil, could admit were pretty corny. *Be who you are! Be aggressive! Shoot 'till your arms fall off! The best shot is the NEXT shot!* But Kobe advised Kyrie to find something inside of himself, during the season ahead, that he knew was there, that was bigger than basketball—a revolution *off* the court, if he could unlock it.

First, Kyrie would have to return Kobe's favor, with an hour of skills training in a sweat-stained old gymnasium that Vanguard University students called The Pit.

Sliding in the side door, Kyrie could hear the bounces and footsteps echo louder, as the girls of The Mamba Basketball Club finessed to impress the master of the crossover dribble. Kyrie and Kobe dapped-up—closer than ever, into a special handshake, into a hug—and turned back toward practice.

Kyrie found three orange cones and set them down, like his father had in the driveway lights of Jersey, where he'd played against Kobe in his imagination. Team Mamba had learned from guest coaches at practice before, like Giannis Antetokounmpo, who was expected to win the NBA's Most Valuable Player Award in a few weeks, and Anthony Davis, the versatile big man whom LeBron was in the process of acquiring to play alongside him on the Los Angeles Lakers. But nobody had balled with the girls like this. Kyrie went up and down the floor, toughening up on defense, especially against Gigi Bryant. "Whaddaya got?!" He blocked her shot and pretend-bullied, but on the next possession, she went directly at him, one-on-one. Kobe's daughter had just turned 13.

"Damn, this girl is *exactly* like you were," Kyrie joked with her dad, laughing at a familiar and fearless determination, as full of life as the hero himself. "She's an asshole!"

This was, in the frequently delusional grandeur of basketball players, a compliment.

MAY 31, 2019 🎥

West Orange, New Jersey

KYRIE HAD BEEN MAKING power moves, on his new company, on his new house, on his new roster, even though the 2019 NBA free-agency window hadn't opened yet, officially. He traveled solo through the empty streets of gingerbread suburbia, Manhattan hiding below the tree line, to his old middle school, where he was already planning to host a contract-signing ceremony, out of sight, so that his secret decision might remain safe.

This was the same hedge-trimmed Jersey where Kyrie had stepped out in disguise as Uncle Drew, a prosthetically aged character he embodied for a series of wildly popular Pepsi commercials. Uncle Drew looked a bit like Bill Russell and talked even more trash on the neighborhood blacktop. The undercover shoot had worked in 2013, but Kyrie became too recognizable, so his fellow All-Stars cameoed in camouflage instead, leaving Uncle Drew to operate in the background of his own advertising as a recruiter of elderly teammates. Pepsi's campaign trailed off the next year while Uncle Drew was in the midst of "searching for the big man." Filmmakers hoped this mysterious character could be played by the Los Angeles Clippers center DeAndre Jordan in a Fu Manchu costume, or perhaps by the Oklahoma City Thunder superstar Kevin Durant, until plans for production in China shut down once Kyrie got hurt, yet again, with the Cavaliers.

But Kyrie was back where his real-life legend had begun, all Hollywood effects aside. He was 27 years old, with a couple hundred million to his name. And he appreciated that he could still, on the same wandering stroll between his childhood home and his homeroom class, run into the neighborhood crossing guard.

When school let out at Roosevelt Middle School those days, Black kids and white kids wore Kyrie's signature Nike sneakers, in white and black and so many flavors of the rainbow. An Indian American boy sprinted to catch the bus in a sky-blue pair. A purple-haired girl rode her purple skateboard in her purple Kyries. There were Kyries with the logo from the TV show *Friends*, Kyries dedicated to the cereals he ate; if Michael Jordan's face covered every Wheaties box on every kitchen counter in the '90s, then Kyrie would put his symbol of impact upon the feet of the teenagers of his time.

And there it was, in the dirt at the front door to his junior high, imprinted from the sole of the Nike Kyrie 5s: the all-seeing eye, trapped inside a pyramid—the symbol of the Illuminati, and the unofficial logo of Kyrie Irving's peculiar brand of headiness. Kyrie was, as influencers went, a pretty heady dude. He wanted to challenge the foundational lies of America and his private-school upbringing: He'd been rediscovering his late mother's Sioux heritage, and he'd been reading, at the suggestion of the late rapper Nipsey Hussle, *The Spook Who Sat by the Door*, about a Black revolutionary who uses his government training to expose police brutality and political corruption. And in 2017, on a show hosted by his teammates, Kyrie had traveled, quite notoriously, a bit too far out there: "The Earth is flat."

Kyrie didn't actually believe this conspiracy theory, he reminded friends and colleagues. Thing is, teenagers paid more attention to @KyrieIrving than to their teachers, and at times even to the great American attention vacuum itself, @realDonaldTrump: Kyrie had the third most online fan engagement of any athlete in the NBA, and, in 2019, Instagram's most followed NBA players drove more engagement to the leading social-media platform than did the most followed politicians in the land.

"People want to hear from the personas that they look up to—they want to hear from people who they feel are being authentic and real with them—and that's hard to come by in politics," the head of Instagram, Adam Mosseri, told me. "So Kyrie can have his theories and say what he wants, and that's good—it's actually a good thing for people who we disagree with to express themselves—but fans are gonna self-select the voices that they care about and that resonate with them."

Or, as Myles Price, the seventh-grade star of the Roosevelt

Middle School Rough Riders, said: "All of Kyrie's IG posts are inspiring—even the weird ones."

When Kyrie was in middle school, he was inspired enough to, immediately after his father took him to watch their New Jersey Nets at the 2003 NBA Finals, scratch a home-team daydream into the sheetrock of his bedroom closet: *I AM GOING TO THE NBA!! Promise.* Kyrie could still smell the popcorn from the nosebleeds, sixteen years later, as he pulled up to Roosevelt Middle School and headed straight for the principal's office, to settle his unfinished business.

He liked to chop it up with Principal Hush, who was a Knicks fan—"Boston is Boston," they agreed—and who did not pry too hard on Kyrie's free-agency window.

"Still," Principal Hush reminded his famous alum, "there's a lahhhhhhtta talk . . ."

The reverb surrounding the school, out there in the humming echo of sport, was as infuriating as it had become impossible to ignore. *LeBron "likes" Kyrie in a Lakers jersey,* offered *SportsCenter*'s analysis on Twitter, about a post on Instagram. On the radio, pundits were closing in on Kyrie's destination: *It's going to be in New York—and whether it's going to be the Knicks or the Nets remains to be seen.* On TV: *When you start to connect the dots, it says Nets. But . . . REALLY?*

"Lahhhhhhtta options," Principal Hush continued.

Kyrie looked up behind the principal's desk, at portraits of Obama and MLK, and looked his elder in the all-seeing eye.

"I'm comin' home."

"Aight!" Principal Hush called out, already beginning to ask himself the obvious next question: *Which* home? Madison Square Garden, with the Knicks? Or Barclays Center, in Brooklyn? He left his curiosity at a piqued eyebrow and led the graduate to the court. Kyrie's mission in visiting here, besides the walk down memory lane, was to make sure he could use the school gym in a month or so, for a celebration with his friends, alongside dignitaries from his new team—whichever uniform its players might wear—plus, well, yeah, with Jay-Z, the boss of his new agency, who'd just been named the first billionaire rapper. Kyrie wanted to mark the moment, for himself and for his thirteen million followers, with a carefully orchestrated act of authenticity.

"Oh," Kyrie said on his way out, "I'll be wearing all-black."

"Oh-*KAY!*" The principal knew what that meant: Legend had it, Jay-Z had designed the black-and-white jerseys for the Nets. They'd look pretty slick on the kids around here, Principal Hush thought, and quickly got back to nodding again, to keep Kyrie's choice at a whisper.

Kyrie promised to return to Roosevelt Middle School, maybe even to work out on the court they were trying to name after him. He didn't care if the blue paint was chipping on the walls, because he'd promised Kobe and his new private shooting instructor, Kobe's friend Alex Bazzell, that he would grind with an open mind, at any gym in town, to become even better than he knew he was. Kyrie was impatient, but he would commit to the long game.

Later that week, laying out his vision for his basketball future, Kyrie told Alex that he wanted to be remembered as one of the greatest point guards in NBA history, and he wanted to win multiple championships in the next few years, back home.

As for the best-ever part, the trainer gently replied, "You know . . . right now, we're at the point where, um, people view you as probably the second- or third-best point guard in the *current* league, not even all-time. Just . . . right *now.*" Steph Curry, the boy-prince of the Warriors, had two MVP awards to go with three rings and counting, starring on Golden State's near-perfect lineup of all-time hoopers.

Kyrie nodded heavily.

And on the whole championship thing, uh, "If you don't mind me asking . . ."

"Oh, yeah," the trainer remembered Kyrie adding, "we got, you know, Kev's coming, too."

Kev as in Kevin, as in Kevin Durant, as in KD—the greatest basketball player on this round Earth—who was about to play in the NBA Finals for the Golden State Warriors. And who was—apparently, already, if things kept going according to Kyrie's plan—destined for the Nets. The *Brooklyn* Nets.

⏮ JULY 1, 2010

Cleveland

LEBRON JAMES WAS FINALLY a free agent in the summer of 2010, when the NBA's increasingly flexible salary cap could allow a single team to sign multiple superstars at the same time, changing the course of a city, a culture, a generation of followers across the planet. Los Angeles had the reigning champion in Kobe, but the other big-market franchises had long been plotting their pitches for why LeBron, the biggest name in the game, should leave Cleveland after seven seasons straight out of high school. Along came this ultimate off-season, and with it a murmur inside the rebrand meetings of the New Jersey Nets—still two seasons away from moving to Brooklyn, and still the worst team in the league: *We're gettin' Bron.*

The Russian financier Mikhail Prokhorov, who was preparing to run against Vladimir Putin for president, had just completed his $223 million deal to take ownership of the Nets, and he wanted a face of the franchise. But the group from Moscow didn't initially understand that in American basketball, ownership could not pay for the best athletes they desired; the franchise players chose you. What the Nets *did* have working for them was a superstar with supreme clout and a 0.15 percent stake in the team: not simply a minority owner or even just a *minority* owner but Mr. Shawn Carter, the Roc-A-Fella founder, Jay-Hova himself, H-to-the-izzo, Jay-mothafuckin'-Z.

Jay-Z had met a 15-year-old LeBron while looking down the staircase of a penthouse at the Four Seasons—two years before *Sports Illustrated* proclaimed him The Chosen One—and LeBron was mesmerized by the 30-year-old mogul, suit-free in a Jordan jersey and Jordans on his feet. By the summer of LeBron's free agency in 2010, Jay-Z was 40, and when he met the Nets new majority owner, he discovered that Prokhorov, a fellow self-made oligarch, had that extra *extra* suite at the Four Seasons— the *super*-penthouse—that he'd never seen before.

"Now there's something else to shoot for," Jay-Z said. "There's always an extra level you don't know about."

This would be the maxim of the Nets delegation as they stepped off Prokhorov's Gulfstream G550 in Cleveland and approached the office of LeBron's marketing agency. Over the next hour and a half, New Jersey's slender Russian did most of the talking, about how Brooklyn was a diversifying city unto itself, a gateway to a globalized economy for media and fashion, and how the Nets were a bare scaffolding of a franchise on which LeBron could begin, even at 25, to spray-paint his place in history. The iPad presentation did not feature basketball players so much as Tiger Woods, Roger Federer and David Beckham, their gross earnings and endorsement deals wholly separate from any team, any team sport, any sport whatsoever. "In the same way Jay has transcended being a rapper into being a global brand and a major business and cultural influence," Prokhorov told me, "we laid out to LeBron what we saw as his potential to transcend sports."

Next up, Jay-Z and the Nets CEO, Brett Yormark, reminded LeBron and his business partner Maverick Carter that there was simply no place like New York to build a personal enterprise: Brooklyn was rooted in sports but, they said, had been underserved since 1957, when the Dodgers left town. LeBron's appeal, though, was strong enough to procure marketing deals without proximity, and the Knicks were about to walk in the room promising the same thing. LeBron was already worth $120 million, so a reminder from the Nets president, Rod Thorn, that Prokhorov could pay salaries up front, spending wildly for a champion, didn't sell LeBron either. The head coach, Avery Johnson, asked LeBron to imagine a superstar duo, in a brand-new arena, without appreciating that Miami and Chicago would encourage him to make it a Big Three.

On the way out of the boardroom, Jay-Z stopped LeBron. He believed his friend should exercise his right to freedom and agency, to play with his best basketball friends, to win as many rings as he could. The minority owner knew that the New Jersey Nets were a team of temporariness, and that LeBron didn't need them; he needed a coronation. Deep down, Jay-Z knew they didn't stand a chance.

LeBron, of course, chose to play for the Miami Heat alongside Dwyane Wade and Chris Bosh, announcing his decision a week later on an ESPN special called *The Decision*, which began as a well-intentioned effort to raise money for charity and was remembered for the hubristic nervousness of the words "I'm gonna take my talents to South Beach."

The Decision was the first domino in a decade-long deal-a-thon known as The Player Empowerment Movement. This meant, to the NBA media and smaller-market fans who often resented such personal freedoms while judging from afar with Capitalized Misperception, that franchise players could create their own lawless, disloyal, ring-stealing rosters together, controlling the message and the means to upheaval however they saw fit, whenever free agency hit and, increasingly, whenever else they demanded.

"He paved the way," Kevin Durant would tell *Bleacher Report*'s magazine, of LeBron's 2010 move to Miami. "As time goes on, and the changes start to become normal, people will start looking at it as normal—a decision that's best for them, and nobody else." One day before *The Decision*, KD announced his five-year contract "exstension" with the Oklahoma City Thunder, typo and #Thunder hashtag included on Twitter, so that he could skip over the frenzy of free agency—a period of time which professional basketball players also refer to as, you know, looking for a job.

The boldness of LeBron and KD's generation of so-called Player Empowerment Movement superstars was greeted with a swelling everywhereness of skepticism from the outside. Around 3 a.m. on the night of *The Decision*, LeBron slumped off a quiet jet ride to Miami, crying—former fans were burning his jersey back in Ohio, and all-new haters were venomizing his two-day-old account on Twitter. By the time he and his business partners arrived at the W Hotel, they'd read the open letter from the Cavaliers owner, a mortgage marauder named Dan Gilbert, to the city of Cleveland, in the childish font Comic Sans: *This shocking act of disloyalty from our home grown "chosen one" sends the exact opposite lesson of what we would want our children to learn. And "who" we would want them to grow-up to become.* LeBron absorbed the instant villainy of launching a dynasty on purpose, but he felt, too, the racism still smashing away at even the pinnacle of Black excellence: "I think that had a lot to do with race at that time," he told *GQ*. "And that was another opportunity for me to kind of just sit back and say, 'OK, well, how can we get better? How can we get better? How can I get better?' And if it happens again, then you're able to have an even more positive outlook on it. It wasn't the notion of, I wanted to do it *my way*."

As Barack Obama said in his State of the Union address that year, it is tempting to assume that progress is inevitable. But the march toward true free agency in American sport had been one of generational struggle, with more losses than wins for freedom, and more symbolism for the culture than action on behalf of it.

In 1969, the St. Louis Cardinals outfielder Curt Flood refused a trade to Philadelphia, declaring that the Major League Baseball system of limitless allegiance that forbade him from doing so "was the same system used in the South where the plantation owner owned all the houses that you live in." He risked his career by sitting out the 1970 season and suing the league, and lost. But Curt Flood's sacrifice laid the groundwork for an athlete's very right to test the open market of free-agency decisions in the first place and, he said, "to give every ballplayer a chance to be a human being."

Two years later, Julius Erving was stuck with a bad agent and an even worse contract. He'd been permitted to play professionally a year early out of college because of Spencer Haywood, who was both a serious baller and rule-breaking trailblazer, which Julius, too, would soon become. Even on a bunk deal for the Virginia Squires in the soon-to-be-defunct ABA league, he soared, eyes beyond the rim, to earn the name Dr. J.

With the twelfth pick in the 1972 NBA Draft, Dr. J was chosen by the NBA's Milwaukee Bucks. Except he wanted to play with the superstar Pete Maravich in Atlanta, so he reported for training camp there instead. He sued, and lost, getting stuck back in Virginia, until he was traded to the ABA's New York Nets. Dr. J led the Nets, often single-handedly, to two championships. But when the National Basketball Association subsumed the American Basketball Association in the summer of '76, the NBA was so concerned that the Nets were "invading" New York City that the league demanded its new franchise pay the Knicks more, and Dr. J. less, for the privilege to play in the big leagues in The Big Apple. Julius Erving, having none of this, found a way to Philadelphia and, with trampoline trajectory, toward the NBA Hall of Fame.

Wilt Chamberlain had requisitioned a trade to live in Los Angeles. So would Kareem Abdul-Jabbar. But Dr. J's relentless power moves were an early flex of player empowerment: unapologetically individual, precedent-setting and, he admits, selfish. "There's a responsibility that comes with the territory," Dr. J told me. "The building of the super-teams—what happened in Miami, what exists now—is definitely player-driven and very self-serving. I'm not hating on it, but there's a difference: service to yourself, and service to the game. So it's probably a very short list of people—and Curt Flood would be one of them—who were fighting for the rights."

You didn't have to be born a *super*star to fight for agency *and* freedom—the more rebellious athletes often weren't, and LeBron had resisted joining those truth-seekers, so far.

The *real* player empowerment was always available, less an earned inheritance of the wealthy and the gravity-free among us—a legacy—than an evolving responsibility of each generation of talent to push it forward to the next one, wielding influence for inexorable good. But the methods of communication in the twenty-first century were shifting faster than the rulemongers or haters could keep up with, and sometimes the moment calls out for our role models to hurry things along. In the decade following The Decision, LeBron and his generation of basketball stars became our best available hope, onward to a fast break of better fortunes. "He's empowered himself to empower other people, so he's been very generous with his platform," Dr. J concluded. "He can say and do things that, at one time, there was a consequence to say and do. Understanding that, and kind of *reveling* in that, he's like, 'Well, I'm going to say and do these things, and so be it.'"

Miami threw a pep rally to welcome LeBron and D-Wade and Chris Bosh in July 2010, and the three friends laughed together onstage, reveling in the smoke machines and championship predictions. The knee-jerk reaction of sports fans and sportswriters was to hate it; Jay-Z, watching from home, couldn't help but smile. Partly because he liked how LeBron had counted off his imaginary rings ("Not two, not three, not four, not five, not six, not seven . . .") with lyricism. But mostly because he didn't see an antihero so much as a successor, a role model on a mass, memorable scale. A hero yet, perhaps.

"In the midst of our demands, we forgot that LeBron James is human," Jay-Z said. "Why would we ever deny him, or anyone, the moment of hubris or vulnerability, given all that we asked of him to put the NBA on his shoulders? But it's in these moments that we've witnessed the humanity, and the leadership, and the growth."

Miami's Big Three got booed everywhere during Year One of The Player Empowerment Movement, including on Halloween 2010 in Newark, where the Nets were stranded and starless—except for the reality-TV star Kim Kardashian, who was dating their power forward and taking selfies courtside. "Could've ended up *here*," LeBron told Chris Bosh on the team bus to the game. In the hinterlands of the New York City media that night, LeBron was forced to reflect on *The Decision*. "If I had to go back on it, I probably would do it a little bit different," he admitted before beating the Nets by twenty-three, and added: "We want them to boo us." The Heat did make the Finals that season, only for LeBron to go off at the haters within minutes of losing to Dallas: "All the people that was rooting on me to fail, at the end of the day, they gotta wake up tomorrow, have the same life that they had before they woke up today."

The coronation of King James, as champion and hero both, would have to wait. Billionaire NBA owners, who wanted their players to stop making so much money and their stars to stop leaving for bigger cities, used what leverage they still had to allow their collective bargaining agreement with the players' union to expire in the summer of 2011, thereby forcing a "lockout" of their employees after the first season of the Miami experiment.

Displaced from franchises and disassociated from rivalry, LeBron and KD worked out one-on-one back in Ohio. Fellow All-Stars teamed up on exhibition squads in undersize gyms across the country, live and in-person for all to see, by word-of-mouth and 'round-the-block lines for free entry. The NBA as it had been known ceased to exist, but as Nike's campaign for Kevin Durant went: *BASKETBALL NEVER STOPS*. And KD absolutely dominated the summer of the lockout, on a nomadic North American tour, each and every place without a camera crew in sight: L.A., Long Beach, Miami, D.C., Baltimore . . . and New York City streetball's center court—Rucker Park in Harlem—for one sweltering night in August. At 23, KD had already been the NBA's leading scorer for two years in a row. But he got so hot that evening, with so many ecstatic fans gathered around him, chasing his greatness up and down the sideline and over it and back again, as he made four three-pointers in a row and scored sixty-six points in total, that they had to blow the whistle early. KD felt a burst of energy like he'd never felt before. He loved New York, its up-close-and-personal exchange between fandom and fame, without any socially polite distance whatsoever.

"That feeling, that's why he plays basketball," said Mike Beasley, KD's oldest basketball friend and fellow No. 2 NBA draft pick from growing up in Maryland, who went at it with him on the court, and then with a fan who called him a bitch during a free throw, three nights later at nearby Dyckman Park. "It's like that old fuckin' *Cheers* song: We want somewhere familiar, where everybody knows our name. And for Kevin Durant, that place has always been a basketball court . . . even if it's in OKC, or if he was in Miami, if he was in fuckin' Timbuktu."

After one hundred and sixty-one days without official NBA basketball, organized play resumed under an ownership-friendly deal. And Miami showed up in full force that truncated season, blowing out KD and the Oklahoma City Thunder for LeBron's first title in June 2012. KD wept his way off the Finals court into his parents' arms—his teammate James Harden offered the family a brief hug and a prickle of his increasingly lush beard—while LeBron, D-Wade and CB headed to the Heat locker room for champagne and a sigh of relief.

"Man, we're glad we got OKC this year," head coach Erik Spoelstra said in a private celebration with Miami's Big Three. "Little pups."

Oklahoma City had cultivated a Big Three of its own in Kevin Durant, the point guard Russ Westbrook and James "The Beard" Harden—they were all under 24, and, if the Thunder could sign The Beard to an extension that summer, they would all be working under ownership-friendly contracts for that rare foreseeable future in professional basketball. "You could see, not necessarily that they had three future MVPs, but that was top-of-the-food-chain talent," Spoelstra told me. "We thought this could be a cool rivalry. The Celtics-Lakers of the 2010s."

The Heat were convinced that the Thunder had what they had: elite athleticism, excellent timing and an expanding awareness for how to manage the itinerant dramas, egos and economies of sport. No matter the superstar multiplicity—whether one, two or ten, uprooted or homegrown—that was a super-team.

KD knew the Heat would have fizzled out soon enough—sports dynasties, like presidencies, have age restrictions and term limits—so that he could subsequently be entitled to the NBA franchise that cast the shadow. But his team didn't know how to fit the league's reigning Sixth Man of the Year into its starting lineup or the Thunder payroll: Three days before the 2012–2013 season, OKC traded 23-year-old James Harden and his beard to the Houston Rockets. "It just didn't work," KD said, "but it worked out perfectly, individually, for us all."

JUNE 12, 2019

Manhattan

KD CAME TO, tubes up his nose, panicking about blood clots. Despite the eight-inch gash in the back of his right leg, doctors told him that the surgery had gone smoothly. Just thirty-six hours earlier, he'd been showing off pregame dance moves to his teammates on the Golden State Warriors, returning from injury straight into the middle of the 2019 NBA Finals. After a month away from the postseason to nurse a calf strain, he'd dropped three-pointer after three-pointer over the Toronto Raptors. He'd talked shit, confidently and comfortably, and lollygagged all the way up the court to drop another one, and played pretty good defense, too, until along came the *thwap*, and KD's best-laid plans hung together as flimsily as his torn Achilles tendon. His foot felt slanted, like an entire side of him was twirling clockwise down a hill. As if everything wrong hadn't gone wrong enough already, now the doctors said he might have fuckin' blood clots?

Achilles recovery could take a year, said the surgeon, who

was also the Brooklyn Nets orthopedist, and even then he might never be the same player again. KD felt powerless without the game, insisting that his talent *was* his platform. But the NBA spotlight shined brighter on a superstar's persona than upon even the shadow of his skill. The game would still be there, KD assured himself, just maybe not at 7:30 every night, in front of nineteen thousand people. Rehab started in thirty-six hours.

The good news was that he didn't have blood clots after all. And he had much bigger repercussions to worry about: Free agency would begin, at least officially, in two weeks or so, at the end of June.

Since January, KD and Kyrie had been talking seriously about teaming up in Brooklyn. After months of lobbying for KD to take his talents to BK, too, Kyrie was furious that Golden State had placed KD "on a national stage to end up selling a product that came before the person." Kyrie felt he had been forced to play through pain in the 2015 Finals by Cleveland's staff, and he was—if not entirely distrustful of all traditional corporate systems—certainly protective of his best basketball friend.

The friends had grown close in 2016 on Team USA in Rio, where a couple dozen pro hoopers lived, sequestered, on a mega-yacht with room enough for three hundred—a kind of Vegas–Disney World hybrid, docked across town to keep the richest and famousest away from the Olympic Village, which had been contaminated by raw sewage. Government scientists warned that the plebeian quarters reserved for the rest of Team USA were a petri dish prone to viruses and superbacteria that might kill those with vulnerable immune systems and, in any case, would leave non–USA Basketball athletes "swimming in human crap." Aboard the five-hundred-fourteen-foot boat, though, cards and cabernet ruled. The poolside air smelled not of shit but of expensive marijuana. A co-captain of the cruise liner's party was DeAndre Jordan, who stands six-foot-eleven but is so down-to-earth that he might have sunk a smaller ship with laughter and a foot-stomping love for rock 'n' roll. DeAndre was everyone's favorite teammate. And Team USA's banter in the summer of 2016, naturally, turned to how Kyrie had just bailed out LeBron in the Finals, how best basketball friends squading-up in The Player Empowerment Movement had become so very common-place, so out-in-the-open while behind-closed-doors, that KD had just signed with Golden State and could be—maybe, already, as the Jay-Z song goes—on to the next one.

DeAndre recalled, in the last days of The Anti-Crap All-Star Pleasure Cruise, a toast.

"Hey," Kyrie told him and KD, "this would be cool to do for real."

"What you mean by that?" DeAndre asked him.

"Let's all get on the same team," Kyrie said, "and play together."

As the summer of 2019 and his thirty-first birthday approached, KD told his agent and business partner, Rich Kleiman, that he didn't want free-agency PowerPoint slideshows like LeBron had welcomed in 2010. He didn't need the courtships that he and Rich had sat through, holed up in the Hamptons in 2016, on the way out of OKC. He understood that Kyrie was coming home to his childhood team, and for the first time in their careers, KD and Kyrie felt the employee-employer power dynamic recalibrated toward something closer to fair.

KD texted his dad: *What you think about Brooklyn?*

Like his agent, KD's occasionally estranged father, Wayne Pratt, was a Knicks fan. When Wayne told his son that he'd taken a video-conference call from the Knicks executives Steve Mills and Scott Perry, and that the Knicks were trying to turn away KD's interest from Brooklyn before free agency had officially begun, the father-son text chain blew up with expletives. KD didn't think it was on anyone else to mess with his personal freedom. Plus, this Knicks meeting seemed to be a violation of the NBA's rules against tampering, to "entice, induce or persuade" one player under contract to sign somewhere else. The regulations had long been ignored by most executives, but the league office had been cracking down on tampering over the past two years—when he ran the Lakers, Magic Johnson got fined repeatedly for *speculating* on TV how stars from small-market franchises would look in the purple and gold—and the summer of 2019 was thought to be something of a last splash before the commissioner might start collecting iPhones for his culture of "compliance." The NBA's balance of power was as sensitive as Kevin Durant, and he did *not* want his pops fucking with the plan.

Let me explain one fucking thing to you, his dad responded. *Don't you ever question my integrity. There's nobody more important in this world when it comes to you THAN YOU.*

Well, why can't I do something different?

The Knicks is Mecca, KD's dad declared. *If you want to do it, do it big! If you want to be a New Yorker, be a Knick!*

New York *City* was the Mecca of basketball, and KD wanted to live there. But he felt like Brooklyn was his vibe: "chill, on the low, all-black everything." He'd been eyeing the Nets for years now, and they him.

Dad shot back: *Are you doing this just for Kyrie cuz he your buddy?*

No, KD replied. He was making this decision for himself.

KD and his guy Rich agreed to make the announcement, once it was allowed, on the Instagram account of their sports-business TV show, *The Boardroom,* which was about The Player

Empowerment Movement itself. @TheBoardroom had only thirty thousand followers and had some catching up to do, to KD's ten million. Why waste any opportunity presented by fame? Why just do it for the fans, when you could do it for the 'Gram?

2

THE CLEAN SWEEP

JUNE 30, 2019 ▶▶

Brooklyn

THE REST OF THE NETS waited on the rooftop lounge of their practice facility, scanning the waterfront: Lady Liberty's flaming fist, the towering shimmer of Manhattan and, emerging to the east, out toward their arena and swaying in a hard summer wind, Brooklyn's cranes in the sky. Up here, fifty-five blocks away, they claimed as headquarters yet another ex-warehouse in the old neighborhood that new developers had named Industry City, after all the startups trying to expand in the borough and disrupt their businesses as usual—startups not entirely unlike the Brooklyn Nets.

About an hour earlier, the reporter Adrian Wojnarowski had broken the news on Twitter . . .

Brooklyn is making a clean sweep tonight: Brooklyn will sign Kevin Durant, Kyrie Irving and DeAndre Jordan, league sources tell ESPN.

. . . but the Nets—their existing young players and holdover coaches, their franchise proprietors and front-office operators, their wives and children, their agents, all manner of experts in the human body—still couldn't quite believe who was about to arrive downstairs.

Kevin Durant's small entourage drove by the body shops and the strip club and, passing through the green-light threshold of gentrification, rumbled onto the cobblestone street with the high-end furniture store on the corner, the minimalist coffee shop at ground level and the NBA franchise inside. He knew the organization on the roof was still in what he later called "the garage stage," but arrive he did, prepared for a public offering. "A championship would be a whole other level," KD had ventured, "but injecting a new energy into a city through basketball would be even cooler."

KD zoomed into the party one-legged on a trike and found Kyrie. There were *Woo!*s and *Yessir!*s and *Oh-KAY!*s, but the friends embraced in an exhale. They'd been trying to solidify this partnership for so long, since they were up shit's creek in Rio, since they had sipped wine on it back in the Bay, then dined vegan together in Boston, and finally: *Clink.* KD and Kyrie would make $164 and $141 million, respectively, over four years—maximum-value contracts for maximum-profit men. DeAndre Jordan, their Olympian amigo, was 30 years old in a league that had become less dependent on centers, and executives no longer valued him as a max guy, but DeAndre's powerful friends viewed him as a starter and an essential presence in the revamped Nets locker room. KD and Kyrie told their agents to go get him $10 million a year, even if they had to take a pay cut for a Big Two-and-a-Half.

Giraffing around the rooftop of Nets HQ, as if chaperoning prom, was a six-foot-ten-inch New Zealander named Sean Marks. He was the general manager who'd inherited one of the

NBA's worst teams in 2016, a franchise not even close to established enough to entice KD when he was a free agent *that* summer, even though impressing KD with an emergent contender was exactly why the previous GM had traded away so much of Brooklyn's future to Boston for an aging Big Three, in a 2013 deal that failed spectacularly. So the Nets relied upon a roster of burnouts and castaways to survive twenty- and twenty-eight-win seasons until they became a forty-two-win playoff team by 2019, the foundation built for a skyscraping dynasty heading into 2020 and beyond. Marks introduced himself to the friends and loved ones of his new players—there were nine in all, on a roster of fifteen, arriving one by one as the sun went down—because, he believed, when you had a chance to add future Hall of Famers who wanted to play together, you jumped at it, you healed them, and you kissed the ring.

Kenny Atkinson was not so sure. The Nets head coach had spent three seasons transforming the castaways into near-All-Stars with an eighteen-hour-a-day combustion of chips on shoulders, analytics and the spacious European game, which he'd played professionally before becoming an assistant with the Knicks a decade earlier. Atkinson had never made the NBA as a player, and he worried that his value would be questioned in the presence of superstars. But KD, in his perfunctory research for accompanying Kyrie to Brooklyn, had loved watching Atkinson's fun, free-flowing offensive schemes on YouTube, as the coach went brilliantly berserk along the sideline. Kenny Atkinson looked like one of those bad guys from *The Matrix*, in the same black suit and tie every night, his smirk bending into a scowl.

Atkinson had been doing his own scouting of the NBA's best available franchise players. Seconds after KD crumpled to the floor in the Finals three weeks back, Atkinson had freaked out and talked to Marks: "This could change things," he said, and considered if maybe it should have. The head coach knew there'd been other options in free agency. There was the muted superstar Kawhi Leonard, who'd just won the title with Toronto over the KD-less Warriors. Atkinson thought he would fit his system, and Kawhi had a relationship with Marks, but Kawhi had indicated to Brooklyn management through back channels in the spring that he was headed home to L.A., to the Clippers. There was also the explosive guard Jimmy Butler, who had included the budding Nets on his wish list when demanding trades in the past, but he was headed for Miami. Coaches especially understood that personnel decisions could be forced upon them nowadays, that the whole point of The Player Empowerment Movement was for franchise players to control the options. Atkinson thought this was unfair, but the first CEO of a successful startup often had to trade his vision for the vision of his ambitious talent, or else get out the way.

Spencer Dinwiddie, Brooklyn's 26-year-old backup point guard, had many, many, *many* thoughts on this dilemma of the next-wave NBA super-team. Which was to say nothing of larger economic trends in the decentralization of corporate power, on which he had many thoughts as well.

But team basketball, Spencer insisted, had become *pretty* boring to your average sports fan. He believed this problem dated back to the days of Dr. J, when the NBA, in a television war with college hoops, began embracing generation after generation of *personalities* on its way toward becoming a superstar-driven league. Spencer marveled at the arc of history: Magic Johnson and Larry Bird as Black and white, not Lakers and Celtics; Jordan's perfection giving way to Allen Iverson's hip-hop infusion and Kobe's "reincarnation of MJ"; LeBron and then KD, arriving to "undo some of the hip-hop damage and spotlight business ventures"; Steph Curry as "the man every woman could bring home." And then there was Kyrie, who was "a polarizing star—not necessarily one that walks the line like a LeBron James and is a media darling like Steph. He kinda does things his own way, so it gives pundits ammo to attack him." The by-product, Spencer wasn't afraid to say, all day and night on his Twitter account, was that nobody outside of a certain radius cared all that much about *teams* like the Nets, or even the regular season, anymore. The internet, by collectively rooting for individual stars in GIFs and highlights and a loop-de-loop of debate, had completed the arc of teamlessness, simultaneously depleting television ratings for the game itself and dividing locker rooms from the outside in.

Near a low-slung cabana couch on the roof, Spencer searched for his remaining teammates from the previous season, his fellow members of Brooklyn's "player development" system, which Atkinson occasionally referred to as The Program: a college basketball–style regimen of improvement built for non-star players that was becoming more popular among new-school NBA franchises. In addition to Spencer leveling up under Atkinson, The Program had nurtured the introverted scorer Caris LeVert, the second-year center Jarrett Allen and the sharpshooter Joe Harris, who was the only non-European white guy on the full-time roster. The incubated reclamation projects needed to play with exclamation this season, if they were ever going to step foot on a court with KD and Kyrie.

Rushing upstairs with late notice, from *The Lion King* on Broadway and the NBA players' union summit on real-estate and tech investing, were Garrett Temple, the 33-year-old guard whom Kyrie had told Nets management would bring balance to the locker room, and his girlfriend, Kára McCullough, a scientist for the U.S. Nuclear Regulatory Commission, who just so happened to have won the Miss USA pageant. She specialized in disaster preparedness for power reactors, and this Brooklyn sunset was a much better way to end this first day of free agency than the way it had begun, with the American president and the North Korean supreme leader shaking hands.

By nightfall, toasts had been made and, as some players got ready to leave for the club, DeAndre Jordan finally strolled in with his model girlfriend. Chopping it up with Spencer, he looked down from the six-foot-eleven view of things and remembered one night on the Clippers, when he ended up guarding the six-five Spencer by accident. "Don't worry," DeAndre had hollered out to his then-teammates. "I got this Richard Pryor–looking motherfucker!"

Spencer rejoiced with his familiar colleagues and laughed with these newly arrived, slightly older prom kings. "We did it," he said, knowing that he had a leg up with the three amigos running the show. Especially with Kyrie.

He and Kyrie had hit it off in early 2018, at NBA All-Star Weekend, when Spencer won the Skills Challenge, a human arcade-game undercard to the Slam Dunk Contest, staged as an excuse for the NBA to market its not-yet-household names in primetime. He'd been recruiting Kyrie to Brooklyn ever since, Spencer told me. "The NBA wants to act like I called him the night before and was like, *Yo, you better come to the fucking Nets! Or I'm gonna release the tape! You and Trump!*—and then he committed. And now it's like tampering or whatever: *Come over!*

"But," he added, "a *lot* can happen in a year and a half."

Kyrie had brought up his impending free agency on a call in December 2018: "New York might be real fun next year." By then, Spencer knew priorities had shifted for Kyrie in Boston; by winter, Kyrie kept bringing up his Jersey connection and asking questions: Did the Brooklyn Nets culture—the systematic basketball buy-in, the luxury lifestyle pampering—really work as well as it looked from the outside? Spencer gathered from their conversations a maxim of warfare: There must be one or two consistent voices of direction in battle—too many agendas, and you end up with Brutus, not Cassius Clay. They both understood, at that point in their late twenties, that nothing was ever perfect, especially in the business of basketball. But there was very little beef on these new-school Nets, and a family you could depend upon, before The Clean Sweep. "Bro, it's perfect for you," Spencer replied. "And Kenny gonna let you *rock*."

A lot *could* happen in a year and a half.

⏮ SEPTEMBER 28, 2012

Brooklyn

ALL THE SUBWAYS STOPPED here: the 2 and the 3, whether fans were arriving from Harlem or Flatbush; the N, Q and R, from Central Park to Coney Island; the 4/5, the B/D and the C, and Fort Greene's very own G. The damn G, slowest and slimiest of all mass transport in NYC. Exiting the station up the escalator, New Yorkers could sense the ambitions of the oculus—a swirling hulk of steel overhang that hollowed out in the middle, as if the Nike swoosh had met a rusty bridge inside a fifty-six-by-one-hundred-and-seventeen-foot pottery wheel. Rimming the skylit canopy, a billboard luminesced so brightly with sponsorship that passengers reaching the top of the staircase might need sunglasses at night. This wasn't Times Square, not quite, but in case you missed it, there were lasers spitting into brownstones and condos all across the neighborhood, out from the neon-glow branding on the front of Downtown Brooklyn's new billion-dollar arena: *BARCLAYS CENTER*.

The outdoor plaza at the corner of Flatbush and Atlantic Avenues, at this triangular intersection of neighborhoods, would *quickly become one of Brooklyn's great public spaces*, declared Bruce Ratner, the former New Jersey Nets owner and New York City's most divisive real-estate baron since one Donald J. Trump. This was after The Great Recession forced him to adapt: Ratner and Co. had promised affordable housing, local apprenticeships and seventeen thousand construction jobs for towers built in part on public subsidy, and for an estimated billion dollars in private profit. By the arena's debut, as one investor put it, "the Nets are owned by a Russian industrialist, the property sold to a Chinese conglomerate, and the public officials who advanced the project are nowhere in sight."

Most of what the New Yorkers *did* see on the plaza that Friday night in September 2012, approaching Barclays Center at the meeting point of increasingly vertical Brooklyn and its One Percent–approved Wonder Wheel of fun, were protesters defying the existence of the grand hulking mass in the first place, cursing every symbol of class and greed it had come to stand for. A local reverend reminded the attendees of a candlelight vigil outside that Barclays, the bank that had paid $400 million for the naming rights, "was the same Barclays that financed the trans-Atlantic slave trade." As security gathered at sunset, gun-violence activists from the not-so-shimmering neighborhoods to the east carried a coffin across the plaza, its stonework barely dry. An NYPD scooter squad had eyes on a group blocking the view from the subway exit—a group from Occupy Wall Street. This resistance stood up for "the ninety-nine percent," and its activists were still upset that Jay-Z's clothing brand, Rocawear, had co-opted their movement against sell-outs and economic inequality to sloganize and sell T-shirts: *OCCUPY ALL STREETS*. "The One Percent that's robbing people and deceiving people," Jay-Z explained to the writer Zadie Smith, "that's criminal, that's bad.

Not being an entrepreneur. This is free enterprise. This is what America is built on."

Barclays Center was where the action was, for better or worse. Jay-Z wanted everyone who walked into the arena to feel like a celebrity, and he was kicking things off with eight sold-out shows starting that night—opening night—in a Brooklyn Nets jersey of his own design.

Jay-Z had "created" the Nets' identity, went the narrative— even though the Barclays Center brass paid off its logo designers $20,000 to say that he did. And the suits backstage still weren't sure, with minutes until showtime, if he was even going to rock the Nets' new look. Jay-Z was willing to endure and manipulate the whiteness of the entertainment industry for progress, but he was no walking billboard. He had been adamant that the Nets jerseys be black and white, and NBA negotiators wanted to get black out of the uniform. Dark blue looked better on television, apparently. Multiple officials involved in the approval process sensed a subtext emanating from the office of NBA commissioner David Stern, who seven years earlier had instituted a dress code prohibiting players from wearing do-rags and chains to games. As Irina Pavlova, a Barclays executive who helped lead redesign plans, told me: "You say that to Jay-Z, and you get, *Excuse me? What do you mean that doesn't look good on Black players?* All of a sudden, it goes from being a marketing thing to being a race thing." The Nets brought in Mr. Shawn Carter, the closer, to call out Adam Silver, then the deputy commissioner, and break the rules for good. Silver said yes: Black was OK.

"Ultimately, they placed a bet on Jay," said Brett Yormark, then the CEO of Barclays Center and the Nets. "Adam said, 'Jay, if you feel *that* strongly about it, given who you are in the culture, we're gonna defer to you.'"

The second Jay-Z took to the stage and revealed that jersey, marketers went live with merch sales down the block, with merch sales online, with merch sales like the NBA hadn't seen in years. Even players on other teams rocked Brooklyn gear. Kevin Durant loved that all-black jersey. Jay-Z, the keeper of the real, was right: Blacker the better, build for the future, break a few rules and maybe Brooklyn would stand a chance at changing the game.

Now when I bring the Nets, Jay-Z flowed onstage that night, *I'm the Black Branch Rickey.* It was a reference to the Dodgers executive who signed Jackie Robinson. A month after his run of shows to open Barclays Center for business, Jay-Z was supposed to commemorate opening night for basketball—the Nets home opener, on November 1, 2012—with Jackie's widow. Then Hurricane Sandy, a superstorm that New York City was utterly unprepared for, swept in. The subways stopped everywhere, and a creeping catastrophe landed three days before tip-off. Some of the Barclays brass believed for a moment that playing on—against the Knicks, on national TV—could serve as a rallying cry for the city, a sequel of sorts to the Mets' Mike Piazza hitting a game-winning home run after 9/11. Executives thought about playing without fans, then thought it unthinkable, and began drafting emails with directions for New Yorkers to try taking alternative transportation toward the center of the storm. Mayor Mike Bloomberg and the NBA thought otherwise, once organizers of the New York City Marathon hoarded precious generators and food for an inevitably cancelled sporting event, and the Nets postponed their festivities.

The delayed opening night came and went—T-shirts got saved for later in the season, the mascot got stuck while descending by wire from the ceiling—but the suits had one last ceremony they'd been putting off, before an exhausting 2012 was through: Jackie Robinson and the flagpole. Bruce Ratner, the tycoon who'd bought off at least one minority leader to gin up neighborhood support for the arena and its surrounding condos, had purchased a metal rod off a local church. This flagpole once stood in center field at Ebbets Field, the home of the Brooklyn Dodgers, until real-estate developers like him demolished the house that Jackie built. The former Nets owner insisted on dragging out the Robinson family once more, to raise the American flag, in the middle of the Barclays plaza. Only Sharon Robinson, Jackie's daughter, could make the rescheduled photo op. She listened to "The Star-Spangled Banner" play through a mid-afternoon New York City breeze and stared at the flagpole just as her father had, when he played in the 1947 World Series. "I must tell you that it was Mr. Rickey's drama and that I was only a principal actor," Jackie wrote in his autobiography. "I cannot stand and sing the anthem. I cannot salute the flag; I know that I am a black man in a white world."

It pained Jay-Z to see people of color treated as product. From baseball to basketball, football and soccer and boxing, he heard stories of predominantly white sports agents signing athletes to commission-laden contracts, only for the average pro athlete to go broke within four years. The super-broker Scott Boras had built a reputation in the business of baseball on avarice and greed; Jay-Z began talking with friends about learning how to help athletes stay rich while making sure that money changed hands with purpose. Jay-Z had failed to close the previous year's recruitment of Carmelo Anthony, the Brooklyn-born sensation itching out of Denver, which effectively left Brooklyn without a franchise superstar other than himself. But Mr. Carter, the most legit self-made mogul in the modern entertainment business, would now become a sports agent. And by NBA rule, that meant Jay-Z's partnership with the Nets would have to end: Satisfied with the rebrand, he sold his minority stake and teamed with the behemoth Hollywood deal makers at Creative Artists Agency to get his player-first shop, Roc Nation Sports, off the ground. Roc's first major NBA recruit, to the establishment's shock, was Kevin Durant. *Scott Boras, you over, baby,* Jay-Z flowed on his next record. *It's a new day, hit up KD.*

JULY 9, 2019 📷

Los Angeles

BK IN L.A. WAS a vibe. Most of the Nets had places out here for the summer of 2019. Most players across the NBA did, it seemed. But KD's off-season cribs were always the spot for isolationist, almost-teamless basketball chill. Housemates would stumble down the grand staircase as their private chef drizzled syrup over waffles and their personal trainer came in from the guest house. A blunt might be sparked; the TV was always on. This was how KD got to live, whether he could or could not hoop. For weeks into his rehab there *was* no hoop, except for the one hanging over the infinity pool. He compared scars with Breanna Stewart, his friend and one of the best players in women's basketball, who'd torn her Achilles two months before him, and she texted him to follow up: *Don't rush it! Slow grind!*

The party line was that KD would miss at least "a good portion of the season" and that the Nets did not "expect" him to return for a year. But the door remained open. He couldn't physically go much of anywhere in the meantime, and he didn't have to—everything came to KD, in his personal quarantine by entourage.

A garden of barbells sprouted along the Beverly Hills cliffside. Next to his palatial window, KD stood on an anti-gravity treadmill sent west by the Nets, which let him run again. The team shipped a hyperbaric chamber for the living room, too, although KD's best friend and housemate, Randy Williams, couldn't get it to work. It was presumed by NBA front offices that franchise players came with unforeseen costs, but when the Nets built in a budget cushion for the whims of KD's rehab and Kyrie's lifestyle—another private trainer, another house rental for another friend—they would blow through it, with a new surprise every week. "It was," said a high-ranking Brooklyn official, "a blank check."

The Nets spent more than almost any other team in the league on "basketball operations," both for player salaries and a concierge culture but also for the nerd-bros who made personnel decisions and the sports scientists from the "human performance" group who micromanaged fifteen of America's healthiest bodies. Kyrie was on vacation with Spencer and their families in Hawaii, but he was preparing to gather his teammates for a series of informal, players-only pickup runs at a high school close enough to KD's place that KD could scoot by to watch, then maybe pick up the tab for a team dinner. Later in the summer, the franchise would descend upon L.A. First, though, management sent the physiotherapist Stefania Rizzo out west, to keep an eye on the most expensive right ankle in the world.

Stef was tough but very laid-back; she had broken through to Nets players without pissing them off, by treating them with humanity. But she was taken aback that basketball players in particular had such a stubborn threshold for trust. Where NHL players were happy to let experts fix their bodies, these NBA guys had layer upon layer of their personal staffers and longtime workout partners, their gurus and yoga instructors, second and third and fourth opinions. "It takes them a while to study, to really kind of see what your value is to them," Stef said. "We get buy-in through osmosis." She had to explain the benefits of using a tourniquet to restrict blood flow and fatigue muscles on purpose, of sticking needles around an injury to create "micro-trauma," even though the treatment wasn't technically legal in some states, and of doing extremely boring exercises in the infinity pool, between KD's flamingo jump shots, so that the human body could heal itself.

"Yeah, that shit took a while—that shit was every day," KD told me. "That shit felt like: I *dread* gettin' up goin' to work."

In the evenings, KD's teammates and friends from around the NBA and the top of the hip-hop charts would come over to blaze, to mess around with the at-home recording studio, to play a *lot* of video games. When the new Nets forward Taurean Prince pulled up one night for some *Call of Duty* on PlayStation 4, he couldn't figure out which of KD's twelve bathrooms to choose from. One month's rent for this place had to be more than he'd pay all year on his lease back in Brooklyn, where Taurean would be expected to hold down KD's role in the starting lineup. Here at KD's crib in L.A., it was dim enough to have to squint through every hallway, like an art gallery after closing. And, *man*, the art! An eight-foot photo of a serpent in the kitchen, big-ass eyeball in the den, a marble bust at the stairs and a graceful sprinting sculpture that, when he was box-training in the yard, KD could join off the blocks in stride.

At 25, Taurean had never been a homeowner, but he'd been in houses like this before, when he played three seasons for the Atlanta Hawks. Yet every time he saw a bed—there were seven of them at KD's place—he would go jump on it, to feel how big the mattress was, to test the softness. Just the feedback of a box spring was enough sometimes. He'd grown up in a split-level house with his grandmother in San Angelo, a two-street West Texas cattle town, until she died of breast cancer when he was 12. His parents split up, but he chose to stay with his father, who was transitioning back to civilian life after doing time. Taurean and his dad would couch-surf, or stay with girlfriends and uncles, but mostly they lived at the Salvation Army. Neither his mom nor his classmates knew this. Taurean would brush his teeth in the communal bathroom, rush to school for the free breakfast, then linger after class and often well past basketball practice. But if he didn't make it back to the Salvation Army by sundown, entry was barred. "Just be grateful to have a place to sleep," his father told him. A few nights, they didn't, so the two Princes stayed on the street. Taurean finally revealed his homelessness to his mother, since remarried, once he moved in with her for high school. She was pregnant, and he was helping around the house, when her boyfriend was shot and killed. Taurean had to skip practice to look after his siblings. He was 16 going on 40.

When the Nets traded for Taurean in June, he'd been labeled as part of a "salary dump": He was entering the final year of a contract for $3.5 million, compared to the $18.5 million man headed back to Atlanta, Allen Crabbe. This would save money, allowing the Nets to afford both Kyrie and KD, the max guys, under the NBA salary cap, before Taurean's agents at CAA began negotiating a two-year, $29 million contract extension. He would try to build a house for his mother, Tamiyko, from the ground up, then purchase a crib fit for an NBA champion, his girlfriend, his two-year-old daughter and his five-month-old son—for the generational wealth of Princes. But Taurean still felt like an acquisition, arranged by a front office full of white staffers he'd never even met.

"They look at us as assets," Taurean told me. "What can we do to help their team for however long that is? Whether it be six months, and then they plan to do something else with you, or it be long-term, that's exactly what we are: assets."

Nearly 75 percent of NBA players identified as Black or African American, and 83 percent were people of color. Yet there were only nine head coaches of color from the thirty teams, and people of color held just 36 percent of staff jobs for teams in the league. The Brooklyn Nets had the most diverse fan base in all of the major American team sports, and while Sean Marks, the general manager, had been lauded for hiring an Australian-rules rugby therapist and an ex–Navy SEAL, his trusted staffers represented primarily white dudes who liked to play golf together. Of the fifty-eight people on the Nets' basketball-operations staff, only thirteen were Black—three were brought on personally by KD and Kyrie, and one was an intern.

"That was shocking: Sean saw diversity, in his mind, because he had international individuals," Maurice Stinnett, who ran diversity and inclusion efforts for the Nets' parent organization, told me. "Culturally, you're disconnected—you need to reflect the culture that you're situated in, and it didn't quite meet the mark. It was a disconnect with the people in Brooklyn, with Barclays, with the Brooklyn Nets."

AUGUST 19, 2019 📺

Los Angeles

BEFORE HE ARRIVED at Brooklyn's two-day preseason workouts at UCLA, Kenny Atkinson sought advice on how to mesh his newly signed superstars, Kyrie above all, with The Program—an operation three years in the making that the head coach perceived as accommodating to lighter loads and shorter practices, as determined by literally listening to the human body, while emphasizing an old Phil Jackson maxim of player development, to coach the last guy off the bench as hard as the first one.

"Put them in with everybody else who's been doing it," Mike

Budenholzer, the Milwaukee Bucks head coach and Atkinson's mentor when they worked together in Atlanta, remembered telling him. "Those guys are kinda gym rats—they wanna grow and develop."

Atkinson loved to get out there on the floor, jumping in at point guard during practice. He'd played the point at Richmond University, where he bulldozed his pickup truck across the quad and honked until the freshmen were ready for the first day of workouts. And one day in 2017, during his second season as head coach of the Nets, Atkinson subbed himself in at the top of the key for some three-on-three with his younger players. He hollered at Brooklyn's new six-foot-ten draft pick, Jarrett Allen, who was not used to defending the perimeter, to guard him. This was a skill expected of leaner, quicker centers in the modern NBA—if you couldn't keep up with Steph Curry on a pick-and-roll, you weren't going to get minutes, despite the Nets' data-led efforts to avoid such situations in the first place. So the bashful big man got right up in his 50-year-old coach's face, as Atkinson launched a heavily contested three.

A pop sounded across the floor. The human-performance staffers sprung over: "Who's down?! Who's hurt?"

"It's Kenny."

Atkinson, red in the face after falling awkwardly on his way down from the shot, waved off his own experts. He'd grown up on Long Island, surrounded by pressure in what one of eight brothers described as "full-contact living from the time you woke up until the time you hit the pillow," and he thought he'd been through worse, including an Achilles tear that ended his professional playing career at 37. Atkinson the coach may have been a new-school advocate of sports science, but the player inside him preferred the old-school, original-gangster virtues of working hard, walking it off and the coach always being right that the game must go on. Atkinson the hard-ass OG wanted it both ways, so that the worst didn't have to be true. "Yeah," he admitted, "I fucked up my knee pretty bad."

Heading into the 2019–2020 season, Atkinson wondered how hard he should really push The Program on Kyrie, and he solicited more advice from Mike D'Antoni. They'd both coached Carmelo Anthony when Atkinson came up on the Knicks staff— Melo had become an all-time scorer at Madison Square Garden after Brooklyn missed its chance—and D'Antoni had his hands full as head coach of the Houston Rockets, juggling KD's former teammates Russ Westbrook and James Harden—he of the by-now Santa-worthy beard and the league-leading thirty six points per game, a Sixth Man no more at almost 30 years old. "Not all the rules are the same for everybody," D'Antoni said. "You might not like it—it's not the old-school, where the coach says, *That's the way it is*, it's not like that anymore—and you better get along with him. But in the end, it can be great." He told Kenny Atkinson to give Kyrie Irving the damn ball.

It remained important to Atkinson that there be buy-in from players and coaches, not just to the offensive playbook or the franchise luxuries but to his existing culture—The Program's principle that even a franchise player could get better all the time, including with the guidance of a wearable, biometric player-tracking device called Catapult. This was a dashboard stickered between the shoulder blades, which the performance staff brought along to the L.A. workouts to monitor every athlete's every second of play, every change of direction, even when a future Hall of Famer went to take a leak.

Kyrie's message, as soon as the players-only summer camp of blunts and pickup games and video games turned into summer school with coaches and systemic systematism, was clear: "I'm not doing it." None of the max guys were. Kyrie believed the culture of Brooklyn basketball had yet to be defined and that the players themselves would cultivate its championship mentality.

"I don't think there was a moment when Ky took it over from us," a Nets executive involved in his recruitment told me. "We all understood—basically everybody who is following the NBA understands—he's a personality. But we were at a point where we thought the organization is strong enough, and the culture is strong enough, to survive or absorb different personalities. Whether that assumption is true remains to be seen."

Before the head coach and management showed up, DeAndre would recall fondly, "it was us hanging out, *without* it being mandatory." Kyrie and Spencer would throw alley-oops to him and Blake Griffin, his old teammate from the "Lob City" Clippers who had jumped over a car in the 2011 Slam Dunk Contest and could still jump out the gym on a friendly morning pickup run at the prep school. Even Melo, New York's last great basketball superstar, showed up for a while, getting in runs and coaching up the team's young talent in what became an unofficial, and ultimately unsuccessful, tryout. To maintain the player-first vibe, DeAndre added each player on the roster—*not* the coaches or the front-office suits or the lab coats—to a group text chain. It had heretofore been used to organize practice times and team dinners, but the Nets were beginning to form an attitude all their own—protective, progressive, pretty funny, too—and so they gave the Brooklyn group chat a name: *DEATH ROW*.

Death Row as in Death Row Records, the West Coast hip-hop label that had, out of nowhere, been everywhere, with Dr. Dre's *The Chronic* and, one year later, Snoop Doggy Dogg's *Doggystyle*. Death Row was home to Tupac Shakur—the poet, the prophet, the revolutionary, who, with apologies to Jay-Z, represented more of Brooklyn's low-key brazenness these days than Roc-A-Fella boardroom compromise. "No shade," DeAndre explained to me. "It's us keeping that mind-set that we gotta have each other's back out there, no matter what—us versus everybody else . . . together."

DeAndre counted down in the huddle: *Us against everybody. Death Row on three. One . . . two . . . three . . . DEATH ROW!* And with that, Brooklyn left L.A. to the Lakers and Clippers, who had title expectations for the first time since Kobe and DeAndre both starred there more than half a decade earlier. The Nets had formal training camp in a month, back at HQ, before a week abroad for exhibition games that several players saw as an unnecessary international disruption to their personal lives and regimens. KD bounced to Sicily, and even with his rehab progressing through every milestone, Brooklyn had what Kyrie and Spencer agreed was a silver lining of tempered expectations without him: Playoffs, *definitely.* Rings? Later. But the journey, they agreed, was the reward.

Before he traveled back east again, Kyrie owed another skill session to the teacher, and he wanted some more quality time after their night with the Mamba girls in The Pit. So he journeyed up northwest of Los Angeles, through the too-misty hills of Calabasas, past the aircraft supply store and left into a strip-mall parking lot in Thousand Oaks, California, to a genuine sanctuary: Kobe's gym.

The Sports Academy is California's most elite neighborhood workout space, with alien-aircraft pods off one hallway and performance laboratories down another, and, oh yeah, some serious hoop, too. Kobe put his name on it, slapped the snake-charmed *M* on the wall and called it The Mamba Sports Academy.

This is where Kobe still coached his daughter's team, where he would welcome prospects to train alongside local NBA and WNBA players who were shooting around in the back, and, for two days in late August, where The Black Mamba re-empowered the real ones. These invite-only sessions were dead-serious: 8 a.m. start, All-Stars lined up doing push-ups, no sponsor shit, no tweets. Big-name summer pickup had become a thing again the last few off-seasons, as Instagram-famous trainers gathered their clients on-camera for the followers and the likes, but Kobe only wanted true hoopers who were willing to put in the work, in stealth mode.

At Kobe's gym, Kyrie *had* to do the high-tech testing, just like everybody else. The Sports Academy's cognition lab examined reflexes and, while they were wired to an iPad, gamified an athlete's ability to mentally recover from a failed mission with a sudden boost of confidence. Kyrie's cognitive pendulum was off the charts; he finished first.

During the lunch break on the first day of the invitational, Kobe stood in front of his class at a wheeled-in whiteboard. He drew up basic-enough plays for the second-year guy to understand—the same approach he used with his eighth-grade girls' squad—but these were franchise-player tactics never meant for mere role players. Kobe referred to himself and his students with a royal *we* and insisted that players like these could read defenses just fine: "That's not a problem. The problem is your fuckin' teammate. 'Cuz *that* motherfucker don't know what to do when he catch the fuckin' ball, right? So you gotta be able to explain it to 'em."

Many of the assembled All-Stars-in-the-making, though disarmed by F-bombs and that distinctly Mamba confidence, were busy taking mental notes in a hushed humility. But Kyrie began chirping up almost as soon as the thirty-minute session began, asking questions about how to prepare for isolation and create for oneself on the attack, once enough of a coach's prepared plays had been run early in a game. Kyrie approached the whiteboard with a towel around his neck, pointing at Kobe's

X and *O*, which made Kobe draw another *X* as they finished each other's sentences. They designed plays together for Kyrie's new Nets teammates, DeAndre and Taurean; on their canvas, coaches and unwelcome teammates were imaginary.

Kobe began diagramming a play from his final NBA game, when he scored sixty points at 34 years old, then cut himself off, to ask what else his dozen-plus students needed help with.

Kyrie chirped up again: "denying pressure." He returned to Kobe's whiteboard and complained how, in his final games with the Celtics, defenders on the Bucks had apparently focused solely on him, all playoff series long. "Just like fuckin' reckless as fuck, just chasing behind you like the *whole* entire time, man," he moaned. "Everywhere I went, bro!"

"This is why the most important thing for you," Kobe said to Kyrie, "and most of y'all in this room, is not so much how *you* figure out how to handle the pressure, but how do you communicate to your *team*mates to *help* you handle the pressure? It's about communication, right? So that's our responsibility: You got to have your teammates *support* you. That's how they can fuckin' help you. You tell 'em, 'Listen, man, I'm helping you get all these wide-open goddamn shots. The least you can do is help me get a fuckin' layup.' Right? So you've got to *use* them."

Kobe talked shit, and Kobe told stories, mostly at the same time. About how he'd been double-teamed by defenders assigned to Shaquille O'Neal: "There's a reason why *you* are open, motherfucker: 'cuz you won't let *me* be open!" About how he'd complained to Michael Jordan for twenty minutes when Kobe couldn't connect with a then-young Lakers teammate, Dwight Howard, even after accompanying him to Bible study: "Well," MJ finally told Kobe, "you still gotta figure shit out. You ain't got no excuses. Don't tell me how rough the water is; bring the fuckin' boat in."

The conversation turned to coaches—and how superstars had no excuse to settle for mediocre ones asking for help. "I've had a handful of those," Kyrie muttered. But Kobe talked over him, about how Phil Jackson had ultimately succeeded with a figure-it-out creativity among players in Chicago and L.A. "If it's the coach giving you strict rules," Kobe said, "rules are easy to beat."

As players broke off to eat lunch, Kyrie stayed close to Kobe, like Kobe had stayed close to MJ. Kyrie, over a vegan sandwich, grumbled about how his most recent head coach in Boston, Brad Stevens, "has a bunch of rules, and I'm like, 'OK, *this* is what we're running, and we gotta be great within this.'" Kobe said that it was OK for the talent to overrule the boss—that Jackson had gotten credit for a matchup switch that helped the Bulls get to the Finals once, and MJ didn't care. "At the end of the day, *you* do it, *you* figure it out, *you* win . . . and the coach gets paid. You're welcome."

Kobe dapped-up stars like Kawhi and Tobias Harris, as some players prepared to continue the day's on-court drills downstairs and others headed back to the business of stardom before returning to Kobe's gym again the next day.

"Ky! Hey, Ky! I'll teach you tomorrow, brother," Kobe said.

Except Kyrie had another flight to catch. Before he headed out, he at least made sure to snag some merch. The Mamba Pro Invitational backpack was stuffed with swoosh-branded swag and a pair of just-released Kobe AD NXT kicks. Stitched on the front pocket of the gift bag was a proverb that sounded older than basketball but was straight outta Kobe, from an unfinished series of fantasy novels he was writing for young adults. The backpack was like a briefcase to Kyrie, and he would carry its epitaph with him throughout Brooklyn's never-ending season of hope and dread: *VICTORY HAPPENS IN THE MIND FIRST.*

3

FIGHT FOR FREEDOM

NEW YORK TO SHANGHAI still took fifteen hours on an NBA team's private flight, so Wilson Chandler did what most athletes liked to do when they were bored: check Twitter. He'd seen a tweet in his feed two nights earlier, a message of solidarity posted by the general manager of the Houston Rockets: *FIGHT FOR FREEDOM—STAND WITH HONG KONG.* Wilson had read about the young pro-democracy activists who'd been taking to the streets of Hong Kong for months, seeking transparency into police tactics imposed by the Chinese government, which was cracking down. He'd suggested to a few of his new Brooklyn teammates, as they prepared for a week of bonding on a preseason trip in China, that the GM's one tweet might shake the NBA's tightrope between its liberal American values and its worldwide economic ambitions. "You seeing that?" he asked. "China's a proud country. They care about that shit."

Wilson used Twitter to follow politics more than basketball.

But those followings had commingled more and more throughout his career and especially since Adam Silver, a former media and antitrust lawyer and Democratic congressional aide, took over as the league commissioner in 2014, encouraging players, coaches and team executives to talk publicly about the news, not merely hoops, with the media in locker rooms and at press conferences and directly to their fans on social media. The NBA fashioned itself as a barometer of progress, down with hope and change and *very* socially conscious—*très* woke. The players felt politically empowered by the league's values, Wilson said, "but to a certain extent, when you need us to be."

As the Nets charter cleared the western seaboard, feeds collided: The Rockets GM, Daryl Morey, walked back his already deleted tweet, which seemed pro-democracy at worst—but then the NBA put out a statement that his views "have deeply offended our friends in China, which is regrettable." Wilson's eyelids, which could Dalí-droop toward his hardened cheekbones, popped open, and he refreshed his timeline. This tweet, he realized, was going to be a big deal. *China is trying to use its market power to silence free speech and criticism of its conduct*, posted Elizabeth Warren, the senator leading the Democratic presidential primary. *In response, the NBA chose its pocketbook over its principles—and our values. We should all be speaking out in support of those protesting for their rights.* The Republican senator Marco Rubio questioned just how socially aware basketball could be: *I thought the @NBA was proud to be the "wokest professional sports league"?*

After all, it was The Woke NBA that had welcomed the first openly gay active male athlete in the four major American team sports, when Jason Collins signed with the Nets in 2014. In his first game, against the Lakers, he'd been the first player out for warmups, like absolutely nothing had changed, and been made

Brooklyn's honorary co-captain before tip-off. "You're just one of the guys," Kobe told him. Three years later, the NBA moved its All-Star Game from Charlotte when the state of North Carolina forced transgender people to use public restrooms according to their birth-assigned gender. After the state repealed and replaced its law with a softer one that still otherized transgender people, the league also moved the game *back* to Charlotte. Commissioner Silver believed sports could change attitudes, not laws. Activists said the league was "doubling down on discrimination."

The Woke NBA was OK with the Warriors head coach, Steve Kerr, calling the president of the United States, Donald Trump, "a vile person" with "a lack of humanity" in passing conversation with me. When I asked Gregg Popovich, the head coach of the San Antonio Spurs and Team USA, how he'd look back on basketball's role as a force for progress in the Trump years, he said the NBA had a chance to restore honor from an administration that was "dangerous" and a president who was a "coward" for disavowing free speech. "Weak people who are basically demagogues at heart make those kinds of arguments: If you protest something, if you're disloyal, you're unpatriotic," Popovich, who served five years in the Air Force, continued. "We don't want to be embarrassed by what our country does on an international basis, and especially don't want to be part of a situation where government *really* doesn't care about people."

The NBA's self-styled wokeness wasn't limited to domestic politics: The Canadian superstar point guard Steve Nash wore a T-shirt to All-Star Weekend in 2003 that read *NO WAR, SHOOT FOR PEACE*, then called the American invasion of Iraq a mistake, and got ostracized for his stand. "I never said, 'Go out and believe what I believe,'" he said. The point of amplifying politics from his platform, he explained, "was 'Go out and decide for yourself.'" By 2010, Steve Nash was agreeing with a suggestion from his team's owner—The Woke NBA calls them "governors"—that the Phoenix Suns should wear their *LOS SUNS* uniform in response to Arizona's "very misguided" anti-immigration law. And by 2019, the commissioner directly supported the Celtics center, Enes Kanter, who got detained abroad after his pro-democracy tweets about the strongman Recep Erdoğan being "the Hitler of our century," and supported Enes as he kept tweeting about authoritarianism ever since, including at that very moment midair, in Wilson's feed: *The @NBA stands with me for freedom and democracy.*

But did it? "The NBA is politically correct," Wilson told me. "They always have one foot in, one foot out. They're gonna say enough to make people feel like, *Oh, we're progressive!* But they're not going to do too much to piss off the establishment. It's kinda like how players play both sides. Like, I *kinda* want to be vocal, but I still want to kind of keep my job, too. So we all tiptoe."

Wilson, who was 32, knew a thing or two about the sensitivities concerning Hong Kong and mainland China, because he'd been the first of several NBA stars to sign with the Chinese Basketball Association during the 2011 lockout. He even got his name tattooed in Mandarin on his elbow. The NBA had been striking deals in China ever since the former commissioner, David Stern, delivered a demo tape of sorts to the state broadcaster in 1987 and began trading highlights of Wilson's childhood role models for a foothold in the world's fastest growing fanbase. Stern was troubled by China's human rights record—mass restriction on free expression and then whole swaths of the internet, mass surveillance of dissidents and demonstrators, mass gender discrimination and, eventually, the mass detention of a million people in an ethnic minority. "But at the end of the day, I have a responsibility to my owners to make money," the commissioner said. "I can never forget that."

Brooklyn's trip to kick off the 2019–2020 season seemed to be the climax of the NBA and China's special relationship: Joe Tsai had finished buying out the Nets and their arena from the Russians eighteen days earlier for what would be a grand total of $3.5 billion, the most ever paid for a sports franchise—Wilson heard that this new owner, a co-founder of the e-commerce empire Alibaba, was like the Chinese Jeff Bezos. Two months earlier, Commissioner Silver had announced a $1.5 billion rights deal for China's tech behemoth Tencent to stream NBA games. And Nike grossed more than $5 billion a year in China, powered by basketball shoes from Kyrie and LeBron, who sold more sneakers there than they did in the States. Word on Brooklyn's Crystal AirCruises flight to Shanghai was that five hundred million people were expected to watch Kyrie's Nets and LeBron's Lakers play in less than four days, in a meaningless exhibition contest that mattered a whole lot to rich people who still thought they owned the game.

Wilson looked at his iPhone: China's state-run TV and the Chinese Basketball Association were cutting ties with the Rockets over their GM's single political tweet, despite a claim from the team's owner, a Trump-supporting restaurant magnate and reality-show host named Tilman Fertitta, that *we are NOT a political organization.*

He looked around the Nets plane: Franchise executives huddled toward the back, reviewing the final draft of a political memo sent to them and to the commissioner's office by Tsai, who identified as Chinese, who had business interests to protect in the middle of a trade war and who was very heated about this lone tweet concerning protest, very heated indeed.

Wilson searched for his fellow veteran leaders—Kyrie Irving

and Garrett Temple stretching out in their leather pods up front, DeAndre Jordan checking the flight-status map—and wondered if Brooklyn could turn around midair. But their owner was headed to meet them in Shanghai. The commissioner wasn't far behind. Neither was LeBron James, en route to the most urgent global test yet of what the NBA and its outspoken employees stood for.

⏮ **APRIL 24, 2014**

San Francisco

DEANDRE LAUGHED, AT FIRST. So did his teammates. The Los Angeles Clippers were gathered at the team hotel, in the middle of their 2014 playoff series against the upstart Golden State Warriors, to rewatch some game tape from on the court. Their head coach, Doc Rivers, gave the fifteen men before him a heads-up that the celebrity website TMZ was about to publish something, from off the court. Something vile. They were waiting for the link to drop online to find out what it was. Maybe a sex tape, Doc thought. The Clippers all laughed again. "*Nah*," DeAndre said. "Donald always says crazy shit."

DeAndre had played on the Clippers his entire six-year career, and he knew that Donald Sterling—the owner, a slumlord with a documented bias against Black and brown tenants—was profoundly bizarre, at best. DeAndre would sometimes shake Sterling's hand courtside, because Donald Sterling signed the checks and because DeAndre Jordan is always the most gregarious person on the floor right before any NBA basketball game. But Sterling would shake his hand a little too long, as if appraising his six-foot-eleven body.

He knew that each year Sterling would throw a party at

which guests wore all-white and watched as players trudged around, wearing black long-sleeve warmup shirts that read *CLIPPERS* on the chest. Sterling would lurk up and say, "Look at this guy! OK, next."

And DeAndre was aware that Sterling had been sued in 2009 by the former Clippers general manager Elgin Baylor for paying the executive less than white employees—for the owner's "vision of a Southern plantation–type structure" and for racist comments in which Sterling portrayed himself as "giving these poor Black kids an opportunity to make a lot of money." Before Elgin Baylor was the Clippers GM or in the NBA Hall of Fame, he was a star rookie on the Lakers in 1959. During a road trip to West Virginia, he and his fellow Black teammates were denied rooms at the team hotel, despite a benevolent promise from the head of the NBA to end such segregation, and then were refused again at a local restaurant. So Elgin Baylor refused to play or wear a uniform on the bench. When a white teammate encouraged him to play on, he said: "I'm not an animal put in a cage and let out for the show."

In 2014, DeAndre and the Clippers had a real shot at the title—until that Friday night in San Francisco, anyway, when the TMZ link dropped in the players' group chat. The vile something was a phone call recorded by the owner's mistress, who is Black and Latina. Sterling's voice crackled, like some villain from an old-timey radio play:

Yeah, it bothers me a LOT that you want to BROADCAST that you're associating with BLACK people.

DeAndre pulled his phone a little closer, listening on low volume.

I'm just saying, in your lousy FUCKING Instagrams, you don't have to have yourself with—walking with Black people.

Man, DeAndre thought, *he didn't just say this shit.* DeAndre turned up the sound and listened again. Sterling was repudiating, with unvarnished bigotry, his girlfriend's appreciation of Magic Johnson, one of the top Black entrepreneurs in America. It was more than vile.

I'm just saying it's too bad you can't admire him privately, and during your ENTIRE FUCKING LIFE—your whole life— admire him, bring him here, feed him, fuck him, I don't care. You can do anything, but don't put him on an Instagram for the world to have to see so they have to call me. And don't bring him into my games, OK?

DeAndre was mad. At the team breakfast on Saturday morning, Doc Rivers could see it in his face. "What's going on with you, DeAndre? Talk to us."

"I don't want to play," DeAndre said. "I think that's bullshit."

His white teammate, J.J. Redick, signed up: "Yeah, DeAndre, fuck that. I'm not playing either."

More and more players in the room agreed, and several broke down crying. That was when Doc gave a speech: "OK. My name's Glenn Rivers. I'm from Maywood, Illinois, and I'm Black. . . . And if *any* of you think you're more pissed than me, you gotta be fucking kidding." His house and his dog had burned down in 1997, in a suspected racial hate crime; only family photos and his Muhammad Ali memorabilia had made it out. And still the coach was staving off racist management when he could be game-planning for the Warriors. But Doc dreamed of winning an NBA championship, he told the athletes before him, ever since he was a kid, and he never thought about earning that title for Donald Sterling. Did this group of men, living the dream, ever grow up wanting to win it all, for some *owner*?

The players agreed that Doc would shield them from the media so they could do their job. If they didn't want to play, they wouldn't. If they wanted to make some sort of statement, Doc said, please just give him a heads-up, and consider doing it as a team, together.

It continues to be a despicable and particularly American reality that the oppressed so often, and especially with the undue pressure of television and social media, are expected to both withstand and overcome, to survive and speak out at once. Jamal Crawford, then the Clippers' first man off the bench, remembers his mind racing so fast that he could not fall asleep for his regular post-practice nap. "It wasn't like we gotta do something for Twitter," he told me. "It's more like, fuck, we have to do something to let people know we're fucking pissed off, and this is bothering *us*—not even just for the people, like *we* don't stand for this."

DeAndre opened Instagram and posted a black screen with no caption. Famous people had blacked-out their profile photographs before, in solidarity beyond selfies. But this square was an acknowledgment: The racism had made itself so evident and so loud that DeAndre wasn't sure what more to do or say. Fans responded to his post with the fists-up image of John Carlos and Tommie Smith at the 1968 Olympics, and wrote: *Take a stand. Nobody play tomorrow. Clippers or Warriors. Like the bus boycotts & the lunch counter sit ins. Use your influence.* The Reverends Jesse Jackson and Al Sharpton called the Clippers superstar point guard Chris Paul, talking about a rally at the next game. LeBron, who, before The Decision, had considered signing with the Clippers on the condition that Sterling sold the team, said on TV: *There's no room for Donald Sterling in our league.* Even Obama chimed in: *We just have to be clear and steady in denouncing it, teaching our children differently.*

The Clippers practiced that weekend at the University of San Francisco's gym, where the great Bill Russell had starred in college. In 1961, on the day of a Boston Celtics preseason exhibition game in Kentucky, two of Bill Russell's four Black teammates had gone to the team hotel's café for breakfast, where they were told that they would not be served. So the great Bill Russell simply booked five flights out of town. The opposing team's Black players boycotted, too. "We've got to show our disapproval of this kind of treatment or else the status quo will prevail," Mr. Russell said. "I hope we never have to go through this abuse again. But if it happens, we won't hesitate to take the same action again."

With their competitive spirits weighing as heavily as the exigence of history, the 2013–2014 L.A. Clippers seriously considered initiating the first mass boycott of a non-exhibition NBA game. The Warriors stars Andre Iguodala and Draymond Green prepared to unify their entire team in shutting down Game Four of the series by refusing to play, so long as all the Clippers would lead the protest.

DeAndre was still onboard with an official boycott—he refused to represent that *CLIPPERS* name on the chest of those black warmups at Sterling's white party—and considered splintering off to do it without a united front from his teammates. "I wasn't being negative or anything, but I was standing for something bigger than myself," he said.

When the players took a vote, however, they could not come away with a unanimous move to go on strike. Several agreed that the team could be more like Jesse Owens running on, in front of Hitler, than Bill Russell flying straight home from the Jim Crow South. They still had a platform and could still pull off basketball's version of the Black Power salute during the national anthem on the medal stage. Dr. John Carlos, who put that gloved fist in the air only after activists and athletes had failed in their attempt to get all of Team USA to boycott the '68 Olympics, was watching very closely. "I don't think the athletes realized the power and the unity that they had," Dr. Carlos told me. "They had the power at that time to bring ownership to the table and say, 'We have concerns about social issues that confront each and every one of us here, particularly the Black players within the league.' I think they let it slide through their hands. Had they been a little more focused, in terms of unification, it would have been a lot stronger throughout sports."

Thirty minutes before tip-off of Game Four, the players huddled inside the tunnel, that final liminal space between the locker room and the outward-facing world of courtside. "It's just us," passersby could hear them saying. "Only us! We are all we *got.*" The teammates followed each other jogging toward the court. DeAndre jumped up and tapped the top of the entryway. Doc Rivers was so busy trying to keep the owner out of the building that he didn't know which act of defiance the players had decided on. Suddenly, every player on the team gathered around center court, pulled off the top layer of his *CLIPPERS* gear, tossed it down onto the ground and revealed the red warmups issued by the franchise—long-sleeve T-shirts that they'd worn . . . inside out. No more logos on the chest. Just fifteen colleagues going to work for themselves, with a pile of laundry on the floor. "It was," said their superstar Blake Griffin, "a stand for respect—respect for humankind."

And then the silent T-shirt protest was over, and the game continued.

"Obviously, it wasn't enough," DeAndre admitted in 2019. He still didn't regret changing his mind from a solo strike, even though Los Angeles got their asses kicked that afternoon. Jamal Crawford believed in retrospect that a boycott "would have probably been the more lasting thing to do," and many Warriors agreed. If Sterling's ensuing punishment ended up seeming too weak for the players, Jamal told me, "I'm sure we both end up boycotting one of those next games. It became something where the whole league was behind what we wanted to do." Players around the NBA were ready to consider threatening a boycott of the following *season* if Sterling still owned the Clippers franchise by then.

Adam Silver had been NBA commissioner for less than three months. Watching Game Four's pregame protest from the stands, he realized firsthand what NBA players were capable of—that they could shut down sports culture on the spot, if they wanted to. LeBron's Miami Heat performed the same demonstration at center court of their series in comradeship, then continued their march through the playoffs over Brooklyn and into the Finals, where The Big Three lost one last time. Silver appreciated that these players had found a symbol that didn't stop the game but made very clear the new power dynamic: This would not be the dress-coded, express-mail-to-China, top-down sellout NBA of Silver's predecessor. DeAndre and his teammates had turned that inside-out.

Nevertheless, Staples Center staffers were covering up scoreboard ads for sponsors like Kia and State Farm before Game Five because Donald Sterling was still taking their corporate dollars. Clippers staffers didn't want to get paid by him. Organizers made signs for a demonstration outside the arena. Kareem, who had promised himself since he was a teenager to be "Black rage personified, Black power in the flesh" and refused to play for Team USA in those '68 Olympics that ended with fists in the air, gathered for a rally at city hall, alongside Steve Nash, who was by then starring for the Lakers.

But that same day, at the Clippers practice facility, Doc Rivers walked over to his team and gave them the heads-up: The new commish had banned the bastard.

"Damn," DeAndre said. "For how *long*? You know, he *owns* the team."

For life. And he wouldn't, not anymore.

Shanghai

SUCH WAS THE FERVOR for basketball in China that even NBA bench players on tour were used to getting the Beatles treatment at the hotel. When the Nets team bus pulled up from the airport, however, the nervous mini-throng of fans in the garage offered only a brief *Kyrie!* before he got whisked off by security and told a friend it was better that KD had stayed behind in New York. A single old fan of Wilson's let out a shout. As the crowd headed home, Garrett Temple carried his own garment bag, last off the bus and straight through the lobby, into the Ritz-Carlton Shanghai. He would barely leave all week.

Garrett and his girlfriend, Kára, were jet-lagged and hungry, so they headed upstairs for the buffet at the owner's welcome dinner. The orb of Pearl Tower floated close outside the smoggy window, like Epcot Center glued to a smokestack; the mood inside the hotel, too, was at once glitzy and unclear. After a half hour, Garrett got word that Joe Tsai was about to give a speech. He'd learned good things about the Nets' new owner and his wife, Clara, who was an advocate for criminal-justice reform, about which Garrett cared deeply. Garrett, who is Black, appreciated that his new team had just the fourth majority ownership group of color in the NBA. Then he spotted printouts strewn about the restaurant, of an "open letter" that Tsai had posted on Facebook during the team's flight. The middle of this letter read like a propaganda flyer:

> What is the problem with people freely expressing their opinion? This freedom is an inherent American value and the NBA has been very progressive in allowing players and other constituents a platform to speak out on issues.

> The problem is, there are certain topics that are third-rail issues in certain countries, societies and communities. Supporting a separatist movement in a Chinese territory is one of those third-rail issues, not only for the Chinese government, but also for all citizens in China.

Huh. Garrett had played in China while he was at LSU and returned several times, so he understood that Chinese heritage included complexities over the fragmentation of its territory. He'd come into the league undrafted in 2009 with the Rockets, when the Chinese superstar Yao Ming had transformed Houston into one of the most popular sports franchises in the world. And Garrett sat on the executive committee of the increasingly powerful NBA players' union, so he understood, too, that the tweet from the Rockets general manager about the situation in Hong Kong could damage some relationships, maybe even threaten a lucrative TV contract or two.

But Daryl Morey's tweet was in line with the same basic American values that made Garrett's own platform, even at fifteen-thousand-odd Twitter followers and a union vote, strong. There should be no "problem" with that. This perspective from the new boss, though, seemed to contradict those values, straight up. This was a perspective more complex than Garrett had heard before: Nobody in the NBA was "allowing" players or executives to say or do anything. And "separatist"? Huh.

The Brooklyn players broke off from their families into a side room with their head coach, their general manager and the owner. Tsai stood up and introduced himself, since he knew only a few of the guys and only so well. He summarized his letter—there were no questions, not in this forum—and told the team he would do everything he could to mend fences with the state. But that week's game against the Lakers, he warned them, might not happen.

Garrett had been in the league for a decade—had signed nine different ten-day contracts with five different NBA teams, had played in Italy and Memphis and, for four years, in Washington, D.C.—but he'd never seen something like a basketball game get cancelled over politics. He'd even sat in an arena surrounded by protesters, all trying to refocus attention from a game back onto the police killing of an unarmed Black man—Stephon Clark, who was trying to get into his grandmother's place and got shot eight times instead, was 22 years old—but that demonstration hadn't changed much of anything by tip-off, not back then. In a lot of ways, Garrett knew, not a damn thing had ever since. Alas, foreign policy was not his forte. "I don't have as much skin in the game," he said. "It's very different to speak out on something when you're in America." That night, seven thousand miles from home, he would try to fall asleep on the right side of history.

In the morning, Garrett and Kára found their way to a dining hall at the Ritz blocked off for the Nets. Kyrie sat at one table—he liked to be alone with his security guard—and Kenny Atkinson scurried up to another, seeking the latest update from one executive that his team would play . . . only for another executive to tell frustrated players that they probably wouldn't . . . and then that they *would*, just not on Chinese TV.

Kára, who'd been wondering if the Rockets GM would get fired just to make the whole thing go away, found herself sitting at a table with Joe Tsai. He was a sweet little guy, for a tech-industry mergers-and-acquisitions tactician, and joined the Nets for a team photoshoot on the roof. Tsai tried to ignore his phone during a private chat with Kyrie, but the chimes didn't stop: The league desperately needed his government connections in Beijing, and Alibaba had an army of lobbyists preparing for trade talks in Washington on game day.

"He was put in a very difficult, almost impossible situation,"

Tsai's friend Andrew Yang, then a Democratic presidential candidate, told me. "Everyone in the NBA was looking to Joe to figure out what to do, but he has feet planted in both East and the West. It's hard to imagine what he could have said and done that everyone would have been happy about."

As the Nets players prepared to load out for a ribbon-cutting ceremony of new courts at a local elementary school, China's education bureau shut down the event. Tsai had to visit alone, telling the principal her kids could still come watch his team at the stadium in two days. They certainly couldn't watch anywhere else, because the NBA's billion-dollar Chinese partners had just officially and publicly cancelled their streaming broadcasts of the Nets-Lakers game. This was in response to Adam Silver, at the Rockets' preseason game in Tokyo, where the commissioner had backed up Morey's right to freedom of expression, even as James Harden, the Rockets star and global ambassador of Adidas Basketball, offered a "We love China." James had been pulled over in Shanghai that summer for a traffic violation after hosting an Adidas hoops camp full of children wearing elastic versions of his beard—if he lived in certain parts of China, a ban on "abnormally" long beards, created to target ethnic minorities, might relegate him to a prison camp.

Encompassed by confusion, Garrett still managed to learn how to make dumplings on Chinese TV, but then the NBA dinner welcoming the Lakers to Shanghai got cancelled, too. Some players were told it wasn't safe to leave the hotel—better to stay in their bubble.

LeBron and the Lakers got word of the cancellations as they rolled into the Ritz from the airport, after a long-haul flight without WiFi. The Nets and Lakers would be required to answer questions from two hundred assembled journalists after practice in the morning—if there *was* practice—but the players didn't know what to say, and so didn't want to say anything at all, really.

"I could feel the tension, a very weird vibe," Wilson Chandler told me, back in the United States. "You know, *How you feel about this?* and *How you feel about that?* But then when we here, it's like, you don't want us to talk about politics and fucking human rights and Black rights."

Wilson kept thinking how inevitably dumb it would be when the players would have to do the talking, once again, when it was convenient to the basketball business. In the NBA, Wilson said, "You *kind* of have freedom of speech, but you don't have a hundred percent freedom."

4

A CONSPIRACY OF SILENCE

OCTOBER 9, 2019 🔘

Shanghai

THROUGH A WINDOW in the dining hall, the players watched a man on the side of a shopping center across the street, hopping sideways down a Lakers uniform. He peeled and peeled at the thirty-foot-tall wraparound billboard, rappelling lower and lower until he could discard each vertical strip of their likenesses, like wrapping paper, to the sidewalk below. The commissioner had arrived at the hotel for his emergency meeting to save The China Games, but still Kyrie Irving could see the cherry-picker out there hoisting the poster-man back up the building, only to tear down Spencer Dinwiddie and Anthony Davis, and all the NBA's ex-sponsors, from the near side of the wall. Soon they'd be coming around the corner for him and LeBron James, the last symbols standing, on the Super Brand Mall.

As the athletes convened into Grand Ballroom No. 2 of the Ritz, most players on the Nets and Lakers still wanted to play ball the next evening—they just felt too vulnerable and underinformed to become the face of something as political as the protests in Hong Kong. Kyrie didn't merely want to duck the media or skip the game. By the third day of the Shanghai trip, Brooklyn's practice had been moved—the arena hardwood needed to be re-sanded, its advertising stripped from the court—and Kyrie wanted to leave the continent entirely.

Nets and Lakers sat down, row by row, as Adam Silver took the dais. In Japan the day before, the commissioner had made clear that the NBA would not censure its players or executives but also that "there are consequences from freedom of speech"; Chinese state media called him a "honey-mouthed" supporter of "indiscriminate violence," and a U.S. senator told him to call off the games. It was, as Silver had advocated since the Donald Sterling scandal, a player-first business, so he pleaded with the players in the ballroom to unmute themselves to the press. To *use* their platform. Because to stay silent could be perceived as the opposite of "what you guys stand for."

LeBron James raised his hand.

In 2007, when LeBron was 22, a Cavalier named Ira Newble handed a packet of information to each player on the team plane. Ira, a role player, had learned the art of education-by-private-jet as a Spurs rookie from his coach Gregg Popovich, who'd handed him a book by the Black Panther Eldridge Cleaver, right there on the tarmac. For LeBron and his Cleveland teammates, Ira had explainers on a genocide: China was selling arms to the Sudanese, who were killing hundreds of thousands in Darfur and displacing two and a half million more. He asked his fellow players to join a petition to the Chinese government, questioning its legitimacy as host of the 2008 Olympics in Beijing. Everyone on the Cavs roster signed, except for one player who had a China-specific shoe contract, plus one guy on personal leave . . . and LeBron. The young king's $90 million Nike deal required him to make a visit every summer to the People's Republic, where he already had his own museum. LeBron claimed—and this became a pattern—that he did not have enough information to condemn the Chinese. "I knew at that point it was about politics and money," Ira told me. "The letter scared everybody—they took it from signing a letter to a boycott." But nobody boycotted, and, ahead of the Beijing Games, Team USA fell silent.

Ira Newble got traded the next season, then cut, before signing one last NBA contract. Following his cold lesson on the imposed boundaries of athlete activism, he found himself alone in the gym with the Lakers assistant coach Craig Hodges.

"Just be careful, 'cuz you're by yourself," Craig told him. "Understand that if you take this path, it can cost you your career."

Back in '91, before he got blackballed from the NBA, Craig tried to convince his Chicago Bulls teammate Michael Jordan and their megastar opponent Magic Johnson to boycott Game One of the Finals, after the LAPD had beaten Rodney King on videotape. Craig believed a precedent had been set in 1964, when the superstars Elgin Baylor, Oscar Robertson and Jerry West, feeling steamrolled by owners, refused to come out of the locker room at the All-Star Game until the NBA commissioner made good on promises for player pensions, post-game rest and road-trip trainers. Soon enough, they did. Craig wanted MJ and Magic to use their stage, and an American confrontation with its racial divide, to demand Black representation in ownership and upper management. Craig remembers MJ calling him crazy: "Come on, Hodge."

Craig Hodges has been remembered mostly for attending the Bulls' 1991 championship visit to the White House in a dashiki. Without a Twitter account to stand on, he passed a letter to George H.W. Bush, pressing the president to address systemic injustice against Black Americans with reforms for rising incarceration and reparations for slavery. But Craig had no lasting beef with Bush, who appreciated the letter; he was concerned with Michael Jordan playing the corporate game. Craig had been in Michael's ear about ditching Nike to start up a job-creating, Black-owned sneaker company in Chicago. MJ's response: "Who's gonna remember me in ten years?" And Craig had been on the Bulls' team bus ride when, after MJ declined to endorse the Black Democratic challenger to the racist senator Jesse Helms in his home state of North Carolina, Michael Jordan defended himself by saying—quite notoriously—that "Republicans buy sneakers, too."

"He's going to laugh it off as 'Republicans buy gym shoes, and I'm this millionaire,' and everybody on the bus is trying to *get* to that status, so it becomes somewhat jokingly said, but I made the point that it's a lot more serious than that," Craig told me. "The superstars during our era, they weren't liberation-minded. They weren't freedom-fighters on the level of studying it to know that it's a commitment, it's a *passion*. That can be born, bred and trained in you at the same time your sport is— all of us came through the saaaaaame shit, riots, killings—but then when you get on that superstar status, you have allies, you have relationships, you have businesses, you have all of this that now becomes almost a *distraction*. . . . It's a choice, and when you come through the funnel, when you get out of the game, you're gonna be like, *Ohhhh shit*, 'cuz now you done made some unholy choices, for real."

Michael Jordan didn't consider himself an activist, but maybe LeBron would. In 2012, LeBron said, the story of one fan hit a switch. Dwyane Wade's girlfriend, the actor Gabrielle Union, spread the word to D-Wade, LeBron and Chris Bosh about how a Miami Heat fan had grabbed his sweatshirt—a hoodie—to go buy some Skittles and an iced tea, while The Big

Three were warming up for the NBA All-Star Game thirty miles away—about how Trayvon Martin never came home. Dwyane's oldest son had just asked for a hoodie for Christmas. Udonis Haslem, the Heat center who signed on just after The Decision, asked Trayvon Martin's mother if his personal foundation could contribute to legal or funeral costs, and could the Heat use basketball to turn such a tragedy into something positive? "We're here to help," Udonis told her. But then the Heat saw Geraldo Rivera on Fox News Channel, blaming the hoodie as much as the neighborhood watchman who chased down the boy and shot him in the chest, and the team posed for a photograph at brunch in a hotel ballroom, their heads bowed in hoodies. It wasn't all LeBron's idea—player empowerment had brought The Big Three together, and they'd found this new form of empowerment as a team—but LeBron directed the composition of the photograph, and he *did* post the picture that afternoon to *his* personal Twitter account . . . to his four million followers . . . with the hashtag #WeAreTrayvonMartin. Trayvon Martin was 17 years old. "Years from now," the ESPN columnist Jemele Hill wrote in 2012, "we might look back on the Heat's photo as an iconic image, perhaps even as a catalyst toward justice."

Entering his seventeenth season in the league, LeBron was transforming into an emblem of democracy, by 'Gram or by tweet—he was nearing forty-four million Twitter followers—and especially by the public demonstration of his own media platform. Just a week before he landed in China, he'd welcomed the governor of California on his HBO show, *The Shop*, to sign a bill allowing college athletes to profit off their own likeness. Though LeBron also felt a private responsibility to protect his colleagues, he disliked, at the time, that the Twitterati had forced every mega-celebrity to have a public opinion on everything. He did not believe "that every issue should be everybody's problem."

And so, LeBron made clear as soon as he raised his hand and took over commissioner Adam Silver's meeting in Shanghai, this shitshow over the one tweet about dissent in Hong Kong was not his fault, or that of anybody on the Lakers or the Nets. If a player had done what "fucking Daryl" had done, they'd probably be fined, or worse. "This is bullshit!"

From the front of the room, Silver responded that he'd never fined players like LeBron, who had called the president a bum on social media, for criticizing the government—that Morey was fundamentally wielding the same right that LeBron used back home.

But, LeBron reminded him, it was another level of politicking to turn up the volume on Chinese soil, and even Silver hadn't done that yet. "If anybody's gonna speak, Adam, it's you."

The Chinese government had cancelled the commissioner's press conference. There was nothing more for the players or the league to gain, Silver repeated, by him addressing the media.

And there was plenty for the players to lose. LeBron's fortune had shed a few pounds on this trip. Kyle Kuzma, his 24-year-old teammate, said he was in danger of losing lucrative Chinese sponsorship deals. Spencer Dinwiddie got his own sneakers manufactured here, and Spider-Man outside the window was almost done yanking the rest of his face off the side of the mall, as members of both teams sat in Grand Ballroom No. 2, curious if the league might cave to its number one superstar pleading the fifth on their behalf.

Michele Roberts, the executive director of the NBA players' union, contends that ducking the mic in China was not a limitation of the league's progressive credentials so much as a right of capitalism. "If there was any conspiracy of silence," she told me, "it was motivated by guys not wanting to lose any more money."

On behalf of the Los Angeles Lakers, then, and the players of the NBA, and LeBron James, Inc., the king stayed resolute: "We don't need to be talking."

Nets players young and old were impressed, texting friends that LeBron, sensible and self-assured, had done what they felt was necessary—if The China Games were to be played, at least the athletes wouldn't have to be the voices of foreign affairs. *Phew.*

Still, eyes bounced around the ballroom, from the jade ceiling on down, between each row of canvas banquet chairs, unto the silent slump of a superstar: Kyrie.

"Why are we in the middle of this?"

Players in the room understood Kyrie to be suggesting that the situation had escalated into international politics, more the business of Donald Trump and the Chinese government than himself or LeBron James.

"Why are we still playing this game? Why are we still here?"

They *were* in the middle of it, and they were going to play. "He's trying to be a leader, but he's not," a Nets official later complained to me. "He's saying we should go home. What the fuck?"

But Kyrie was speaking up, and not for the last time, on behalf of the athletes' rights. "He had a different view on it," Taurean Prince told me of the meeting. "Ky is a very smart guy. Some people may not like it, some people may think he's hard-headed, but it makes sense, just probably not how you *want* it to make sense."

The commissioner walked out of the ballroom to let the players decide whether they wanted to go on with the game, but by then the Nets and Lakers were already resigned to playing the next day. Nonetheless, Kyrie tried, as players from each team broke into smaller groups on either side of the room, to convince the Nets to participate in one game in Shanghai, then skip the scheduled Lakers rematch two days later in Shenzhen and "get the fuck out of here."

On game day in Shanghai, some fans approaching the stadium did not want to be seen in their LeBron and Kyrie jerseys. When American cameras tried to film them, many covered their faces. Hundreds of Chinese flags were handed out to ticket holders as they made their way from the Metro to the front of the arena. Inside, though, in the hallways and stairways, the NBA die-hards of China redressed themselves in Nets and Lakers merch and pulled out their camera phones for a glimpse of Kyrie Irving's dribble-dazzle warmup show.

Kyrie had been elbowed in the face at practice back in Brooklyn, so he'd been forced to wear a clear plastic shield on the court in Shanghai. Fans thought the face guard gave him a mythical quality—he'd worn one in the past, and played well, despite the eye holes—but Kyrie hated that thing, as well as the easy symbolism that came with it. "Somehow it's caused a craze on Instagram," he said. "It's Masked Man."

On the fourth possession of the China game that everybody and nobody wanted to happen, Kyrie's first game in a black-and-white Brooklyn jersey, he got elbowed in the face again and—*Fuck!*—threw his face mask onto the refurbished hardwood. He made his way back to the locker room for evaluation and stayed there. He'd come all this way for fifty-seven seconds of basketball.

When the second half began, the fans still chanted his name, and neither the broadcasters nor the players said a word more on air or out loud about the delicate business of defiance and democracy. That one tweet was costing the NBA millions by the day, and some Nets executives thought their global superstar could at least show some respect by sitting on the bench for the rest of the game. Kyrie was hurt, yes, but he wasn't emerging from that locker room—not then, not for the rematch two days later, not until his team had gotten the fuck out of China—and no suit nor LeBron could tell him otherwise.

⏮ **DECEMBER 8, 2014**

Brooklyn

LEBRON AND KYRIE HAD been in NYC, new teammates at the launch of Kyrie's first signature shoe with Nike, when the verdict came down: A grand jury cleared a white NYPD cop who'd been caught on video, in broad daylight, choking to death a Black man named Eric Garner, for selling loose cigarettes on the sidewalks of Staten Island. The week before that, a grand jury failed to indict for murder the white police officer who killed a Black man named Michael Brown, for allegedly stealing a box of cigars in Ferguson, Missouri. And two days before that, Tamir Rice was shot twice and killed by a white policeman in Cleveland, for carrying a toy gun in a park five miles from where the Cavaliers played basketball. "It's a sensitive subject right now," LeBron said at Madison Square Garden after the Nike event, before beating the Knicks. "It doesn't matter if you're an athlete or not. If you feel passionate about it, you have the right to speak up on it. . . . If not, don't worry about it."

Tamir Rice was 12 years old. Mike Brown was 18. Eric Garner, at 43, had five children—his youngest daughter was three months, and his oldest son, Eric Jr., was a hooper. If LeBron's post with the hoodie photo after the death of Trayvon Martin was a symbolic catalyst in 2012, there had been little justice to show for it, and no peace, by the autumn of 2014. There was, in fact, a lot to be worried about, and LeBron defaulted to what some activists saw as a careful non-activism defined by thoughts, prayers and a condemnation of violence in the streets, but not yet support of a rapidly emerging civil rights movement that would come to be known commonly as Black Lives Matter.

As demonstrators began filling the streets of New York, LeBron and Kyrie's Cavs were back in town, in Brooklyn, to play the Nets at Barclays Center, and Kyrie knew he wanted to wear a special T-shirt for pregame warmups, as soon as he'd seen the Chicago Bulls star Derrick Rose rocking it two nights earlier. Beyoncé and Jay-Z would be sitting courtside, as would Kate Middleton and Prince William—a royal stage for walking protest signs.

When LeBron had made clear that he, too, wanted a T-shirt, Jay-Z's friends spun up a frenzy of social-justice organizers, screen-printers and security guards to have a fancy-looking version waiting for him. But about an hour and a half before tip-off, the Nets backup point guard Jarrett Jack stepped out the players' entrance to the arena, which was lined with cops, then hand-delivered two cheaper, DIY shirts to the visitors' locker room. He didn't especially care who wore them, but if anyone famous was going to bolster the activists with passive support that night, it should be two megastars whose every layup and layer of clothing had impact.

The message on the black-and-white shirts was simple, with lettering in the same crude font the Cavaliers owner had used to condemn LeBron's free agency with instant animus. Except now the message would speak on behalf of someone who, so senselessly, no longer could:

I
CAN'T
BREATHE

LeBron and Kyrie shared a quiet nod as they changed into Eric Garner's last words.

Upstairs in a Barclays Center private dining room, Adam Silver stepped away from the Russian oligarchs (who still owned the place), the Duchess of Cambridge (who may or may not have been pregnant) and the future king of England (who really wanted to see LeBron), so that he could take a call. The Nets GM was on the line: "Just want to give you a heads-up, the players have *I CAN'T BREATHE* T-shirts, and they're planning on wearing them." None of this had been cleared by the league, which has rules mandating that all players must wear official NBA gear on-court starting at thirty-two minutes before tip-off. One of the Russians asked if management should discourage the Nets players from wearing the shirts, too.

Absolutely not, the commissioner made clear. One high-ranking official recalled that somebody on the business side for Barclays Center had made an offhand suggestion that players wear NYPD hats that night, but the height of white privilege gathered up there in the C-suite was not about to stop two of the most popular Black men in America from helping the social-justice movement go mainstream.

On the floor, LeBron and Kyrie went about their business, stretching, jumping rope, shooting free throws and getting photographed even more than usual in their T-shirts. Courtside, Jay-Z didn't wear one—friends claimed their XL shirts were too big for his six-two frame—but he took a photo with Jarrett Jack and three Nets teammates who did. "Proud of you," he told them. Beyoncé and Jay-Z eventually and awkwardly made their royal way across the court for a photo op with the *royal* royals. During a free throw, a small group of demonstrators stood up behind the Nets bench, their arms interlocked, demanding justice for Eric Garner. But nobody remembered that, or the score, as much as what was printed on LeBron's and Kyrie's chests.

"The T-shirts mattered," DeRay Mckesson, one of the most

prominent early voices of the movement in the streets and online, told me. But DeRay and his fellow young activists were quickly learning that police loved celebrity symbolism, because it rarely transformed into structural change, and that A-list athletes had an undeniable "pick-up-the-phone power" with police chiefs and politicians to pressure them for difficult reforms instead. "When you think about the basketball player," he said, "we see the limits of awareness—it can be like a gateway for people . . . which is dope. We just don't win that way."

The meaningful action that night was outside of Barclays Center, where Eric Garner Jr. let out a deep breath and followed its mist toward Flatbush Avenue. He was confused. Hundreds of people, maybe a thousand, had been lying down on the plaza at the entrance to the stadium, illuminated by the billboard glow. A die-in, they called it. He pulled a little tighter on his New York Giants beanie and stepped onto the sidewalk. He squeezed a jacket over his new sweatshirt from Essex County College— his father had been looking forward to watching him play ball from the stands that fall—and began to cross the street. He watched as the demonstrators stood up, came back to life and started chanting again. They were saying his name.

Eric Jr. loved basketball, ever since his dad gotten him into it at seven years old. He liked to score, but he hadn't come to appreciate the team aspect of the game until his family moved to public housing on Staten Island in junior high and he started hooping for real. Father and son would practice together in the back of their building, but they were able to play one-on-one just twice; Pops, unstoppable down low in the post at three hundred ninety-five pounds, won both times. No favorite team ruled their apartment—"The Knicks," Pops always said, "lose too much"—but they would watch the NBA together, arguing over which individual player was better, LeBron James or Kevin

Durant. Eric Garner was his son's hero, but LeBron and KD were Eric Jr.'s role models.

At 19, Eric Jr. had never been to a protest before. And the police presence that night at Flatbush and Atlantic, organized by the NBA and Barclays Center for the royals, was alarming: The pepper spray was out by tip-off.

"Hey," Eric Jr. asked his new friends. "Am I gonna be OK?"

"Safety-wise? Yeah, bro," said one of the activists, Michael Skolnik. "Emotionally, though: Take your time."

Eric Jr. approached the plaza slowly, struggling to fidget through the crowd and to hold himself together. He was still coping with the grand jury's decision from five days earlier, still grieving. He kept getting pressed up against folks, Black and white and all over, calling for action: *No justice, no peace! No racist police! How do you spell racist? N-Y-P-D! How do you spell murderer? N-Y-P-D!* His asthma was kicking in a little. But he found an opening in the congregation, and he heard some good news: *LeBron got the I CAN'T BREATHE shirt on inside!*

"It touched me, emotionally," Eric Jr., nearly six years later, told me. "I'm not even gonna lie: The things that LeBron do? I be *amazed*, the way he use his platform to go out there. A *lot* of these NBA players use their platform to go out there and protest, and all that."

When a grand jury failed, the following Christmastime, to indict the officers responsible for the death of 12-year-old Tamir Rice in Cleveland, the boy's mother found it "quite sad" that LeBron claimed not to have enough knowledge about her son's situation, as he had previously claimed when the twenty-first-century movement against police killings and systemic racial injustice began. LeBron said he was "not much of a social media guy" and so hadn't heard about the calls for him to boycott: *#NoJusticeNoLeBron*. Tamir's mom, Samaria, did not expect a basketball strike for her son, nor did she think the most famous athlete in the world would take the risk of marching into city hall. "If LeBron were to go and demand justice and do the things that activists do, he would jeopardize his career, his money, everything," she told me. "It's a dangerous game. Shame on him."

Eric Garner Jr., though, was not too worried about LeBron's influence. He'd been more inspired by the people continuing to fight without him, and for him, in the streets. Protest to Eric Jr. meant demonstrating pride on behalf of someone you may not know, so that someone like them won't be wronged again—unity, by way of disruption. He hadn't been recognized in the crowd outside Barclays Center, but he was cool with that. That was the point: to do the right thing, without having to justify it to anyone.

OCTOBER 18, 2019 ▶

Brooklyn

BARCLAYS CENTER HAD NOT exactly been the National Mall of revolution since The Royal Shutdown. An animal-rights group had boycotted the circus. Some WWE fans wanted Donald Trump kicked out of the pro wrestling hall of fame. Police killings kept getting recorded, but the nationwide protest movement after Ferguson had in many ways maneuvered from the streets to social media during the Trump administration, which spawned its own resistance. In July, Eric Garner's mother had returned to Barclays, after the U.S. Justice Department, too, failed to charge her son's chokeholder.

But here came the undercover activists, more than a hundred strong and growing. They huddled outside the McDonald's on Flatbush and Atlantic, changing into their T-shirts, then quickly pulled their jackets on top, into the indistinguishable camouflage of fandom. As the group approached the arena for the Nets' first pre-season game since the China trip, two of the ticket holders stuffed parts of a mascot-size Winnie the Pooh costume under their sweatshirts. More of the activists waited in line for the metal detectors, each holding a smaller piece of a giant banner, and snuck it in, to perform the first mass political demonstration in the stands of a professional basketball game.

An official involved in security preparations for the game said that Joe Tsai was frustrated when he discovered that his arena had a limitation only on the size, not on the content, of a protest sign. The rule at Barclays would be: *Act as if it's a Black Lives Matter protest.* And Brooklyn management told Tsai that it was ready for someone who'd bought a hundred or so tickets: "We can know who the credit card is, and found out that it was somebody that was going to be a protester, through name recognition."

Barclays Center insists that security remained straight-forward and the owner was calm. But when I relayed this sequencing to the man who paid to block out Section 1, the film producer and civil-liberties lobbyist Andrew Duncan, he was not entirely shocked. Activists are frequently surveilled, and he knew the Daryl Morey scandal had only kept escalating: Duncan told me he'd received a call while the Nets were still en route to China—just hours before statements from the NBA and Tsai inflamed the situation—alerting him that the Rockets general manager was worried about losing his job. About ever getting an NBA job again. And about the safety of his family. Under attack, Morey had asked to be connected to several people in Washington who could do something about basketball diplomacy. Once Morey made it clear to them that he was in the middle of a geopolitical "shitstorm," current and former U.S.

government officials and spooks reached out to their networks on Capitol Hill and Foggy Bottom. Word of Morey's concerns got to Senators Marco Rubio and Ben Cardin, a Republican and Democrat, respectively, as well as senior advisors to Secretary of State Mike Pompeo. "Marco never called Adam Silver," a person familiar with the situation told me, "but at some point the NBA is not going to be able to sustain firing Morey if enough people are aware of the issue—and the average American's going to give a shit about this."

The demonstrators inside Barclays would make sure of that, by surprise. They planned to use the readily broadcastable, retweetable platform of an NBA game to say what they felt the league had censured Morey and the players for expressing: *STAND WITH HONG KONG*, read their T-shirts. Under the baseline, steps from the Nets bench and right in front of the cameras, the undercover activists took their seats: Hipsters from Brooklyn and Hong Kong, Tibetan monks, college students, a blind civil rights dissident known as The Barefoot Lawyer—none of them visiting the house of Tsai to cheer for basketball. "We are here," said the former Tiananmen Square protester Chen Pokong, "to pressure the NBA to keep their venues not only for sports." They tucked black surgical masks over their ears, like the demonstrators did in Hong Kong. The Pooh Bear got dressed, in a nod to the meme for navigating around China's internet firewall. The activists waited for timeouts, so as not to annoy the kids watching Kyrie's first home game in Brooklyn, to put an open hand in the air. And in the fourth quarter, they assembled the pieces of the big banner: *MOREY OR MONEY.* Then multiple security guards began snatching at a sign that read, of all the nonviolent things, *FREE TIBET.* Too big, the Barclays staffers concluded, but only after snatching hard enough that one of the activists in the front row almost fell into a railing. Fans, among those who were still around, booed at the muscle. Maybe it was at the Nets, too—they were down almost twenty—but the protesters drowned out the game and held up one final sign: *Tsai & LeBron, Morey Was Right.*

LeBron had made it clear that he was not wading any deeper into this State Department shit. He'd been asked about it for two weeks by then, which was plenty of time to become educated on the issue at hand. Yet when he finally spoke out that week, he said he still didn't have enough information—and believed Morey, who had several business-school friends involved in Hong Kong, was the one who'd been misinformed and uneducated about the ramifications of his tweet in the first place. Conservatives ate this up—*Communists buy sneakers, too!*—and LeBron sought to clarify on Twitter: *I'm not discussing the substance. Others can talk About that.* LeBron's mixed message drove fans to burn his jersey once more, this time in the streets of Hong Kong—and, as players from the Rockets to the Lakers and Nets admitted to me, the imbroglio's pseudo-resolution left LeBron's colleagues unsure if a smoggy chilling effect was settling in, upon the NBA's platform.

After the protesters had filed out of Barclays, the beat reporter from *Newsday* asked Kyrie in the locker room about the T-shirt he was wearing home—*PROTECT KIDS, NOT GUNS*—and suggested that the season ahead might unveil a more political Kyrie. "It's more than just political values," Kyrie said. He thought about the nonstop nature of division outside of basketball's hopey-changey glow—"government all across the world, global crises that have happened all the time"—and he started to confront the presence of an athlete's education in activism.

"The government gets involved, it impacts communities in different ways. The reality is, as individuals, it's our job to stand up for what we believe in. Now, I understand Hong Kong and

China are dealing with their issues, respectively. But there's enough oppression and stuff going on, in America, for me to be involved in the community issues here as well," he said. "Colored people here in America, we're still fighting for *everyday* freedoms. So when I think about Hong Kong and China, the people are in an uproar and, for us as Americans to comment on it, whether it's African Americans or American Indians to comment on that, you're connected nonetheless, especially when it impacts freedoms or world peace. . . . I can understand why protesters come to the game: America was *built* on protesting, built on slavery. But things happen all across the world, and we're just taking notice, and social media puts it *right* in front of everyone's faces."

This was interpreted, at the time, as a dodge from the philosopher king of the NBA, the flat-Earth guy citing his all-seeing, all-knowing Sioux ties and rambling about world peace again. But Kyrie was declaring an identity and an intent, to be involved in what was going on, right then and as ever, in America and with the planet. He was his own brand of revolutionary in evolution, and the good fight was not going to be won with T-shirts or silence. The NBA would need to get loud.

5

THE CIRCUIT BOARD

OCTOBER 23, 2019 ⏭

Brooklyn

KD EMERGED HEAD-DOWN from the aurora borealis smoke and lifted up his drawstring pants, the old habit of a too-thin kid holding his always-oversize shorts with one hand at a time and crossing over a basketball to it with the other, switching his grip without missing a dribble. The Barclays Center public-address announcer had blown his cue and started to introduce the Nets roster before the beat dropped, but now KD was vibing to the boing-da-doing of The Notorious B.I.G.'s "Hypnotize," in front of his new fans. The franchise player picked at some earwax, shoegazed toward center court, then wound over to greet his friends from the other team, out of the spotlight on opening night. The applause was, generously, an excitable smattering. Ticket holders doddered in late, beholden more to the rush-hour subways and byways, the night out surrounded by friends, than to Kevin Durant, who was getting paid more than $450,000 a game not to play.

During this season on the sidelines, KD took to wearing

a black blazer with vintage rock-band shirts underneath, often paired with basic red low-top Nikes. On the left heel: *EASY.* On the right: *MONEY.* @EasyMoneySniper was his account on Instagram, which he'd only been checking twice a day lately, direct-messaging with friends like the mega-rapper Drake, or with a stranger struggling with his mental health, or else with a middle-schooler asking for tips on how she could break down a zone defense. Of course, KD was still sliding into the DMs of the occasional reporter from the NBA media establishment: *You're a clown.*

KD's persona had a stockpile of nicknames on top of Easy Money Sniper. Kyrie called him The Sleeping Monster, and the friends would practice what KD called "shadow moves," one-on-one without a ball, during breaks in the game. Fans liked referring to KD by a downer of a sobriquet, The Slim Reaper, because he was a killer on the court, with a point guard's skills in an elastic six-ten frame and jump shots for days, but he disliked that nickname. The *Silent* Reaper, though? That might stick, he told a friend, returning to the bench and twirling his ski-jump goatee.

He was not contractually obligated to say or do anything until he felt like it, not until his heel was healed, but KD felt like studying, and he felt like giving back. The Silent Reaper would become the world's most expensive, if unofficial, assistant coach.

During each timeout of the season's first game, KD slinked back up and hovered near the coaches' huddle, waiting for his favorite *actual* assistant coach to peel off so that he could drop his guy a hint about how to contain the top scorers on the Minnesota Timberwolves. Then Kenny Atkinson poked his head above the assembled shoulders.

"Hey," Atkinson said, half-fan, half–head coach seeking expertise. "There's Kevin *Durant*! You got anything?"

"Nah," replied the star.

KD nodded at Joe and Clara Tsai courtside, as the owners watched Kyrie shimmy-drive on one defender, lift off to the
hoop in front of another, humpty-dump the outstretched arms
of yet another, then count off his flailing opponents with his
index finger, one, two, three, as they all fell down. The owners
guffawed—they were super-fans in their own right—and they
understood that the basketball hierarchy started and often ended
with the faces of the franchise. "They're literally megastars—
very, very powerful—so you can't treat your players as employees
anymore," Joe Tsai said. "They're your partners in the business."
That partnership was why he wanted to buy an NBA team to
begin with: Each franchise kept its local TV money and ticket
sales—a metropolis like New York helped those—but thirty
teams split billions in national-television rights and marketing
deals, evenly. "League-level wealth," Joe Tsai called it, for the
worst team in the NBA and the Lakers alike. The owners then
split half of everything with the players themselves. "It's kind of
a socialist system," Tsai discovered. Which was easy to say when
you were worth $9.6 billion.

Tsai had been up late pinging his senior staff on DingTalk,
the Alibaba-owned Chinese equivalent of the office-messaging
app Slack, that *Shaq is wrong!* The night before, on *Inside the
NBA*, TNT's preeminent pregame show, Shaquille O'Neal had
held court, saying, "Daryl Morey was right." The next day, Vice
President Mike Pence said that "the NBA is acting like a wholly
owned subsidiary of that authoritarian regime" and that the
league's players "lose their voices when it comes to the freedom
and rights of the people of China." But the NBA and its players were on their way toward losing more than $200 million in
broadcast revenue if Tsai and the league office couldn't get their
games back on Chinese TV—and highlights back on Chinese
phones.

When Adam Silver finalized a nine-year, $24 billion deal with Disney's ESPN and Time Warner's TNT in 2014, it wasn't just for the rights to televise teams playing other teams; future broadcasting fortunes were to be made in the wellspring of highlights of NBA players—a fountain of the fantastic, purchased for the purposes of going viral. Silver wasn't trying to get in bed yet with Netflix, Apple and Amazon; he was interested in how influential users on Instagram and Twitter remixed the content of the game to hip-hop soundtracks and movie references in a constant refresh of the endless scroll. The NBA and its corporate partners *wanted* players like KD posting in the comments section and clapping back at random fans on #NBATwitter, to leverage that irresistible combination of live programming and personality, chasing a generation of cultural consumers who were already running away from institutions toward individuals. The business model was a 24/7 reality show. "ESPN, TNT, they already use all our likeness, and everything we are, in order to build up these characters," Kyrie later said. "The audience at this point for our sport *expects* drama. They *expect* locker room tension. They *expect* teams to break up over time."

Just that week, the debonaire Nets sideline reporter for YES Network, the regional sports channel that paid Joe Tsai's franchise some $40 million a year to broadcast the team's games in the New York market, asked Spencer Dinwiddie what he thought about a brewing rivalry between the Knicks and Nets as a boon for the NBA. "It's good TV," Spencer told him. "It's part of why the Kardashians are famous, right? People *love* that shit, and it's made them billions of dollars. So, NBA, if you're smart, create drama, we all make money."

The superficial trending topics of NBA Twitter on Nets opening night were that Drake had received a championship ring for being a fan of the Toronto Raptors, and that Draymond

Green, the Warriors star forward, who made an easy villain—he'd kicked a guy in the balls during the playoffs, after all—had said it pissed him off that KD never felt like part of the team when he played with Golden State. On any given night, if a fan didn't take the time to sort through their feed, they might not be able to appreciate that there was much basketball being played at all: Kyrie dropped fifty points in the Nets opener, the most ever for an NBA player in his first appearance on a new team, but missed the winning shot in overtime.

After the game, as they were being driven their separate ways, Atkinson called KD. Many of their early conversations were overwhelmed by ass-kissing, while the coach tried to sell the future Hall of Famer on helping him level up the Nets' younger players. But their hoops talk was genuine, and KD expected his underexperienced teammates and coach to develop a championship mentality—the DNA of hard work and perfection, every play, every scouting report, every day. Each jump shot, KD liked to say, had a hundred hours of sweat in it, and the Nets had been out of sync during the first half that night, until Kyrie did his thing and got the joint jumping. The new era opened with an L, but the new Nets would be fun to watch.

"Can you give me some more feedback?" Atkinson asked.

"Coach, don't overreact," KD told him. "It's one game."

⏮ **APRIL 15, 2015**

Oklahoma City

KD HAD ONE FOOT toward the door, toe up on a couch again, watching the Oklahoma City Thunder fail to qualify for the 2015 playoffs without him. After that season's *first* two surgeries on the funky fracture around his right pinky toe, KD and the boys had been trying to enjoy his year off. He was the reigning MVP, a single man who'd just signed a ten-year, $300 million Nike deal and who had only recently taken his first vacation. "The frustrating part about Oklahoma, though," said his roommate Devonte Young, "is that there is *literally* nothing to do. But we made the most of it. We *gonna* do that." It hadn't been all watching ESPN and playing as himself in *NBA2K* on PlayStation with a screw in his foot: KD used to pull up with thirty people to a club, and TMZ caught him dropping a pill bottle full of weed outside another. "But it lingered, from the start of the season all the way 'till the next year," KD told me of his injury. "That's the thing: You can't *move*—you can't, like, do the *normal* shit that you used to do."

Despite the setbacks, he'd attacked his rehab with the precision of a pure hooper, hitting thirty shots in a row while seated on a stool and helping Thunder bench players hone their craft. "The challenge was Kevin's leadership," said Adam Harrington, his former private trainer who became a Thunder coach that season and his favorite assistant coach in Brooklyn. "Because normally Kevin's the best player on the planet, and obviously the best player in the gym, and he would just grab the ball: *Follow me.* So when the air was essentially out of the ball for him, he could learn how his teammates responded. He *had* to communicate with them." The Thunder's front office tried to show off its state-of-the-art facilities and sports science—KD's inaugural window of free agency was a year out—even while teammates and coaches watched their franchise player begin to disconnect. "I'm sure he puts on a good face," said Scott Brooks, his head coach at the time, "but mentally it's hard."

As a personal brand, KD's face had been everywhere. At All-Star Weekend in NYC that winter, he'd been backstage with the Kardashians at Kanye West's Fashion Week concert for Jay-Z's

Roc Nation, on the cover of *GQ* and in a Twitter spat with a 24-year-old middle-school teacher named Andrew Williams, who had all of two hundred followers, all at the same time.

@KDTrey5 when did you become so arrogant and boastful? Andrew asked. *Is being a role model a goal for you?*

@Andrew_W8 my goal is to show these kids that we aren't robots, we have emotions and feelings, KD wrote back. *We teaching them to live in a fantasy world.*

KD had finally moved out of his bachelor pad on the outskirts of OKC, into a townhouse downtown, when KD broke his foot *again* in March. His favorite orthopedist, who happened to work for the Nets, wanted to graft part of KD's own pelvis onto what the ESPN writer Jackie MacMullan called "a bionic foot," which would most certainly shut him down for the summer of 2015. "We didn't know if he was going to be able to play basketball again—it was that serious," his father, Wayne, told me. KD was 26 and scared of his increasingly obvious fragility. At night, he fell asleep wondering, "Am I gonna be alone forever?"

Posted up on the couch, he watched Steph Curry and the Golden State Warriors motor through the playoffs, all pop-a-shot threes and no-look dunkeroos. Their energy reminded KD of the high-octane style from his youth-hoops team back in Prince George's County, Maryland—the PG Jaguars, mythically good on the AAU circuit, accused of running up the score, or else of not winning by enough. *Overrated!* parents would shout from the bleachers. *Run his little ass into the bleachers!* KD's coach, Taras "Stink" Brown, instructed 10-year-old Kevin from the sidelines, when the Jaguars first played against 11-year-old Stephen Curry. Seeking that old feeling of no-doubt domination once again, KD watched the 2015 playoffs continue—*Steph Curry comin' alive! On his way to the MVP!*—and he called up Stink. "I miss being young," KD said.

Stink's traveling team had shown the boys how to travel down to the basketball tournaments in Florida and straight to the top of the diving ladder at the water park and out on the ledge, where Kevin stood, slim and shivering, afraid of heights. "Fear, to Kevin, made him focus," Stink told me, sitting in the same old rec center in Seat Pleasant, Maryland (population: 4,721), where he trained the superstar, eight hours a day and all night, too, with a nap in between, behind a curtain in the corner of the gym.

Yes, even KD played JV his freshman year at National Christian Academy, a humble private school with a team that still plays on a rubber court without a three-point line, still practices without a weight room and shares a cheap ankle brace called The Miracle Boot. And when KD scored twenty-eight points in his first game on varsity, his mother still sat him down in the car and told 15-year-old Kevin: *You didn't do shit. You didn't play well enough.* "It was the same thing with the foot," KD said. "The doubt feeds me."

Kevin Durant has long resisted hype and haters in favor of hard work. But he grew up in an entrenched system of recruiters hunting the next All-Star, feeding information and cold hard cash to the hucksters and bagmen who could turn a teenager into sports-marketing dollars for decades to come. Stink called this The Circuit Board, as families were forced to plug into one socket or the other—Nike or Adidas—at around fourteen years old. "He realized, at that point, there's a business—it *is* a business," Stink said. LeBron had been able to ascend directly from high school to the NBA, but KD's wave of talent was effectively required to perform a one-and-done year of college, beginning in 2006. The league hoped to change the rule back for its rookie class of 2023, leaving KD relegated to the old-school star-searching industry longer than any other NBA All-Star—

the accidental leader of an entire generation of hoopers with enterprises built around them, used for everyone else's influence more than their own, from high school through their first unchoosable job as a professional until free agency, if they even got that far.

The Circuit Board sent KD packing, constantly: If you were NBA-level good and your "amateur" traveling team was funded by a different sneaker company than your high school, you were probably going to a different high school. KD's coach at National Christian told his mom it was that simple: "I'm sponsored by Adidas, he's with Nike. Nike done figured out that he's really good. It's a wrap." Days before his junior year began, KD was shuffled off to Oak Hill Academy, a Nike school in the woods of western Virginia with three ESPN games on its schedule. By 16, he'd already committed to the University of Texas, which wore Nike gear, and joked with friends about pushing a check from Adidas back across the table. Homesick and hoping to develop his game instead of his brand, though, KD returned for his senior year of high school in Maryland, where his development coach at Montrose Christian encouraged him to finish an additional class: calculus. KD didn't need the extra credit—he met all of the NCAA's qualifications to help make millions for a state-university system without getting paid—but to pass the exam would prove that he was more unpredictable than an industry's presumptions, that he could reach that extra, *extra* level now. "These are the rules of the game," the coach told him: "If I'm playing you in a game of chess, and I only know how to play checkers, I'm fucked." Kevin got an 84.

Cooped up in the Dust Bowl all these years later, KD watched the Warriors prevail in the 2015 Western Conference Finals over the Rockets and James Harden, his old teammate whom OKC had failed to re-sign and whose mouth-eating beard had become famous enough to attract a thirteen-year, $200 million deal with Adidas . . . and a Kardashian. But KD needed to unplug, so he took up his friend Drake on an invitation to a concert in Canada. The last time he'd seen Drake perform live, the rapper had joked with the audience about KD joining his beloved Toronto Raptors, and the NBA had fined the team $25,000 for Drake's tampering as a global ambassador of the franchise. But this time, as KD protected his foot from a hideout in the sound booth, he looked around the concert at the Bell Centre in Montreal, at his date, and realized that the fans surrounding him were speaking . . . French? "Man," KD said to himself, "I gotta get out more."

He watched the 2015 Finals, the first of four straight in which the Golden State Warriors faced off against Cleveland. It was hard to doubt the individual skill on the Warriors roster, especially as the former NBA sharpshooter Dell Curry's baby-faced son Stephen blossomed into the *Steph* Curry of backyard dreams, alongside Steph's "splash brother" Klay Thompson and the groin-kicker Draymond Green. But the goosebumps from their harmonic team play transfused through the television screen.

Steve Kerr, who took over as the Golden State head coach that season, traced the Warriors' success to one of his core individual values: joy. "I really wanted our team to exhibit that, and I had the perfect player in Steph to show that joy," Kerr told me. "And it came at a good time, for everybody: People saw the togetherness, they saw the joy, and all the while there was a lot of bad stuff going on. That's kind of what sports and art and literature are for."

There was very little doubt that the Warriors would win the 2015 NBA championship, perhaps several more. The day after they did, a white supremacist shot up an historic Black church in South Carolina, murdering eight Black worshippers and their pastor in Bible study. Obama sang "Amazing Grace" at the pastor's funeral service, on the day that same-sex marriage was legalized by the Supreme Court, and the next morning a Black activist climbed up a flagpole outside the South Carolina statehouse and took back down with her the Confederate flag. Kevin Durant cried. "We have to do better," he told his inner circle, and traveled to San Francisco to surprise a Nike-sponsored youth basketball team for the release of his signature shoe. "As a nation, we need to cry with each other," he said after another episode of gun violence. "As a world, we need to cry with each other. That shows we care."

The persistence of superstardom—in the same feeds as discord, alongside the alerts of alarm—had afforded basketball culture the luxury of presenting a happy distraction. LeBron, D-Wade, Carmelo Anthony and Chris Paul could go on vacation together early that summer and smile so effortlessly for the paparazzi on an inflatable water sled that you'd never know LeBron had jumped off their yacht to save Melo's life—that NBA Twitter would nickname them The Banana Boat Crew. The next day, when Chris heard that DeAndre Jordan had a handshake deal to sign with Dallas, he could 🚁 off the 🍌🏝️ and 🚗 to DeAndre's house. He and his Clippers teammates let Twitter know, with wink-wink vehicle emojis so as not to break any rules the night before free agency started, that the superstar cavalry was ✈️-ing into town to sell the collective promise of a super-team. Blake Griffin, a fledgling stand-up comic in addition to a five-time All-Star, tweeted pictures of a chair blocking a door and a tent in a backyard. These were the same players who had symbolically taken the power back from their former owner and his plantation culture; now they had his replacement, former Microsoft CEO Steve Ballmer—one of the richest people in the world—ready to pull an all-nighter in DeAndre's living room while begging him to re-sign, and they let fans in on the joy. KD would escape to Europe on a tour with Nike, playing one-on-one with kids on refurbished basketball courts and biking around Madrid relatively unnoticed. "When he finally took his head out of his hole," KD's dad said, "what he realized was: 'As much as I thought basketball was life, it's not.'" Chess, not checkers.

In July 2016, KD rented a house in East Hampton for ten days, for $100,000, to welcome recruiters one last time for his first free-agency choice—for The Decision 2.0. The NBA was so popular, its top-tier stars were so marketable, and the influx of cash from the new TV rights deal had sent salaries skyrocketing so high that a max-value player could sign with a super-team that already had a Big Three—a onetime opportunity for the formation of a super-*super*-team. Jay-Z told KD to keep things simple.

"It was impressive just how much *power* he had at that moment," said Sam Permut, one of KD's negotiators in the room for Jay-Z's Roc Nation. "Essentially the entire sports world was waiting: the Spurs, with probably the greatest coach of all time in Gregg Popovich; the Celtics with their whole ownership group plus Tom Brady; this Golden State team that had just come off a grueling Finals loss—they were all showing up at this house in the Hamptons, at the time *Kevin* wanted, to sit where *he* wanted." The Heat and the Clippers came with pitches, too, along with a last-ditch effort from the Thunder. "But he could ask the questions *he* wanted, and everybody was on *his* time," Permut said. "That's a rare thing. There's very few guys in history who've been able to make that decision."

After the Golden State front office delivered a virtual-reality presentation in the mansion, the Warriors superstars chopped it up with KD outside, and they knew he was worried about what the haters might say if he left OKC in the dust. "We can all do our best to take the heat off of you. But the most important thing is that *you* have to not give a fuck," the veteran Andre Iguodala counseled him. "What's more important? For you to enjoy life being where you want to be, but with a bunch of strangers not liking your decision? Or to be where you're not enjoying your life, but with a bunch of strangers approving of you?"

KD had played coy when visiting friends like James Harden that off-season, but he was pretty sure he'd made up his mind, before his Hamptons rental was up. He just wanted to feel better about being on the move again, was all. So he called Steve Nash. They had worked out together in Los Angeles during the off-season as peers, and again once Nash finally succumbed to a bad back and retired after a Hall of Fame career. Yoda, KD called him. Nash found KD to be a curious person, always searching—for what, exactly, he didn't know, but he sensed that his Sky-walker was ready to take the next step, as a man. The Warriors had hired Nash to consult that season, a friendly apprentice to Kerr, and the team had become a selfless constellation of stars, Nash promised KD—with egos, sure, but what culture-shifting personalities didn't deserve those?

If KD could not bring himself to make a power move like this, Nash told him, there might be no stopping the next superstar from joining Golden State the following year instead. And who knew what next year might bring? He would lose an opportunity, Nash said, where he would be "in complete control." KD joked that whenever Nash was in town, Yoda would have to work out with him first. Other than that, he was in. "It's not about championships," KD told Nash. "This is about challenging myself."

BEFORE NETS PRACTICE on Halloween, KD rolled up to ESPN's waterfront studio downtown, frenemy territory, for *First Take*. His promotional guest appearance on the high-rated morning debate show was almost like Donald Trump going on *Fox & Friends*: If the public refused to take him seriously enough on direct-to-consumer social media, he could feed the old-school sports-media apparatus what it craved, which was polarization by any news necessary. "Fake is what runs the world right now," KD had told ESPN a year earlier. "Narratives are what matter. Perception is what matters."

On set, the co-hosts Stephen A. Smith and Max Kellerman were obsessed with a two-word scandalette pulled from an ESPN.com article on the Nets—that Kyrie's "infamous *mood swings*" had "followed him from Cleveland to Boston to Brooklyn"—and attempted to trap KD into reigniting it. "You guys don't like him," KD said, looking down at Kellerman's loafers with a side-eye stare.

Stephen A., who had an exclamation point constantly emerging from his larynx, as if a magician were tugging on an interminable handkerchief of hot takes, had called KD's free-agency decision to join the Warriors *the weakest move I've ever seen from a superstar*. KD had won two titles with Golden State, and the Warriors had been great for ratings. But ratings for NBA games were down through the first week of the 2019–2020 season, and nobody quite understood why. It was an unfortuitous year already: KD was out, and Zion Williamson—the rookie sensation drafted by the New Orleans Pelicans, whose catapulting dunks and Jordanized anticipation had dictated the design of the nationwide primetime schedule—tore his meniscus. The night before KD wobbled on to *First Take*, his former teammate Steph Curry had broken his hand. The Warriors were going to be terrible. Lacking more superstars and super-teams, the NBA and its exclamation economy sounded fainter, a reality show drowned out by reality.

"When the hell are you gonna come back?" Stephen A. asked KD. "Is it *possible* that you gonna come back this year?"

"Not right now," KD said. And he didn't "plan" on returning if the Nets made the playoffs in the spring either. But, he added, "I'm not a doctor."

Before finishing the interview and heading to Brooklyn for rehab at the practice facility, KD made news by admitting that, yeah, Draymond calling him a bitch at the end of a game had "a little bit" to do with his leaving the Warriors. And "a little bit" was enough to crank the cycle of retweets all over again ahead of the Nets game in primetime on ESPN—only this time the replays would have a promotional banner for KD's own show running along the bottom of the screen: *WATCH "THE BOARDROOM" WITH KEVIN DURANT ON ESPN+.*

The Boardroom was a 101 on fame and the business of sports: a streaming TV show and an Instagram account for conversations between ballers, rappers and tech bros. It was created and co-hosted by KD's 41-year-old agent and business partner, Rich Kleiman, a former Roc Nation music manager with a squeaky scalp who had become the superstar's protector, promoter and private-equity partner. Kleiman occasionally went by the nickname Ace, as in the De Niro character in Scorsese's *Casino*, a sports gambler hired by the mob to run a casino, despite not having a license to run much of anything. "People say all this stuff about how he only got all this because of KD, how they do this and that and it's thirsty," said Wilson Chandler, an early Kleiman client at Roc Nation Sports. "But he put in a lot of work behind the scenes."

In 2015, Kleiman and KD drove by the San Francisco office of a food-delivery app called Postmates, and KD got them a meeting; they invested a million bucks at a celebrity-share discount that, by the time Uber bought the app, might turn into $15 million. While KD was on the Warriors, he and Kleiman's company, Thirty Five Ventures, made dozens of investments across Silicon Valley and beyond. "A good chunk of deals by celebrities gets done because so-and-so rich white person in Palo Alto wants to have this person over at dinner or go to their game and be in the lounge," said one founder, who said his startup took last-minute funding from Thirty Five because the venture capitalist leading the investment round asked, "Hey, can I also get my buddy KD into the deal?" Other startups were intrigued by Kleiman's promise of celebrity connections and consulting, only to have few substantive conversations after an initial run of PR. "The danger," said a founder who accepted funding, "is taking advantage of KD to make good deals and build his own portfolio." Another founder, Will Ahmed of the wearable workout-data system WHOOP, said that "KD seemed genuinely interested in the path to building a business" and that Kleiman offered his Rolodex and continued screen time on *The Boardroom*.

As KD's rehab continued ahead of schedule and without setback in Brooklyn, Rich Kleiman became more ubiquitous to New York sports junkies than the most famous athlete in town. "Talk that shit," KD had once told him. As Kleiman preached the future of content produced by athletes and signal-boosted by their social-media followings, he also appeared frequently on the same local talk-radio station that he'd listened to growing up, the FAN. He explained his client's millennial habits to the slightly older white men behind the mics, defending his guy so that KD didn't have to inflame too many Twitter wars of his own. KD was a child of the social generation, Kleiman told the radio hosts, and Twitter was "an epidemic" of information and misinformation—and, in case you missed it, celebrity myth-building by tweet and by 'Gram had a recipe: "All of it is sprinkled in with a little bit of entertainment, and a little bit of manufactured back-and-forth."

A couple of hours after his ESPN interview, KD lurched around Nets HQ, iPhone in hand. His spot in the practice facility's main gym wasn't the courtside glass panorama overlooking the Manhattan skyline from whence he'd just come. He preferred the corner, back by the massage table the Nets had just rolled out for him—the Adapta MT-100, extra long. This is where the recently signed veterans gravitated: KD, DeAndre, Wilson, Garrett and, once he was finished with the three coaches working him out on his individual hoop, Kyrie. Eventually Spencer Dinwiddie walked away from the younger players getting in their development work with The Program and headed back to The Clean Sweep corner, where talk could gravitate to spirituality, policing . . . and Trump. The president had been booed at the World Series the other day—*Lock him up!* chanted the crowd, as Congress moved forward with his impeachment over corrupt diplomacy. The Nets veterans had heard Trump was going to be at Madison Square Garden that weekend, to take in the Ultimate Fighting Championship's mixed-martial-arts fight for the Baddest Motherfucker belt. They laughed, and left KD alone to receive even more attention from Stef Rizzo and the trainers, while he watched YouTube clips of himself on ESPN and kept an eye on Kenny Atkinson.

The head coach had a soft spot for his projects, tracing back to 2012, when he was responsible for the last moment of pure mass joy in New York City basketball: Linsanity. Jeremy Lin was the Knicks' fourth-string point guard out of Harvard, and

Atkinson was a player-development assistant coach pushing for his teacher's pet to get minutes. Over a seven-week stretch, Lin averaged almost eighteen points a night, reminding twenty thousand people at the Garden that anyone can be a star. Now Atkinson believed that Jarrett Allen, his 21-year-old center, had the potential, with the right guidance and enough playing time, to transform into a Kareem-type of player. The analytics said that he could block more shots, create more space on the floor and spring back from the previous game faster than DeAndre Jordan. But, as KD had tweeted at one of his followers a few days earlier, *Who the fuck wants to look at graphs while having a hoop convo?*

As a boss, Atkinson did not perhaps fully appreciate that a modern workplace depended on sustained personal interaction more than the action at a physical office, more on what he called trust decisions than success decisions. If he was a players' coach, he had still never coached a persona before this season. DeAndre sucked it up and brought the joy, faux-combing Jarrett's Afro as the starters entered each game without him—he eventually accessorized his barbershop on the bench with hairspray from an airhorn on the scorer's table—but Atkinson realized in the first week of the regular season that it had been an idiotic move to bench DeAndre for this kid. KD and Kyrie were loading up the roster with veterans who could form a base in Year One, with an eye toward the Finals in 2021, 2022 and 2023—Years Two, Three and Four of their contracts. But deep down, Atkinson didn't think the window began until '22. And honestly, he wasn't sure how long he could put up with these superstars. He worried that he might've lost The Big Two-and-a-Half already.

Trust was a long process, Atkinson knew, and he did not live in fear of losing his job, despite NBA head coaches having established, as of 2019, a higher churn rate than any of the

American sports leagues—if not any high-paying public profession this side of the West Wing. He was nervous, to be sure— "Kenny's crazy," DeAndre said, "in a good way"—but he'd been led to believe that his merit would be judged by the action on the floor, that season. He walked up to a whiteboard with a fill-in-the-blank—*NETS IDENTITY . . . ?*—and he started bending toward Kyrie's desire to create his own game-on-the-line shots, without any play designed by coaches. Atkinson sometimes worried that he was too harsh on the non-superstars—to drill his "no-three D" into their heads, he planned to hold up a laminated cue card on the sideline the next night when James Harden dribbled past him, as if flashing play calls from twenty yards away on a college-football field—but Kyrie liked that the coach got on the team for small details like that. "I could connect with this man," Kyrie told himself.

Toward the end of a short practice, Atkinson started gravitating over to The Clean Sweep corner, once he noticed KD could shoot an actual basketball again—one shot, two shots, three shots, crossover, four. He walked softly as Stef took photos of the most valuable tendon with her iPhone, the paparazzi of footwork. The head coach knew he was bad at explaining directly to the max guys why the Nets enforced the NASA rigamarole, and the postgame phone calls had fallen off. "Sometimes," he said, "you want to put that Maserati in a glass case." But he wanted to tell his franchise player that the system was in service to the talent, to protect Kevin Durant from his own yearning.

Atkinson walked over more purposefully, once KD hit his fifteenth jumper in a row, and the coach rocked up onto his tippy-toes: "He can do *that* now?"

6

RISE OF THE UNDERDOG DISRUPTORS

WHEN SPENCER DINWIDDIE first announced plans to IPO his contract, Brooklyn's sixth man thought he'd outsmarted the NBA. Generations earlier, in another hemisphere of entertainment, David Bowie—who was, as provocateurs go, way more famous than a backup point guard—had forfeited his album royalties in favor of up-front Bowie Bonds. Such was a rock star's self-confidence, and Bowie's foresight that streaming would upend the music economy, that the starman sold himself to the world. Now Spencer had invented a digitized investment vehicle for his own performance on the Nets and on his NBA platform. His megawattage teammate KD could parlay talent and a Nike deal into Silicon Valley seed funding for a personal brand, but Spencer Dinwiddie *was* the startup. The League was merely a stockbroker.

"What they gonna do, try and *stop* me?" Spencer asked at a charity gala before the season. "Do they *really* wanna do that?

Because wouldn't that be bad PR for them to do that? I would think. Because then I would start to look kinda like Kaepernick. That probably wouldn't be a good thing. Probably the *last* thing that we would want. Don't turn Spencer Dinwiddie into Colin Kaepernick. That's *not* a good idea, folks."

Spencer was not the quarterback who'd been blackballed—whiteballed—by the NFL when he stood up—and knelt down—in the name of racial justice. Not nearly. But the NBA still seemed to view its entrepreneur-in-residence as a punk and a threat. On that November morning, hours after Spencer had led the Nets in scoring again, he was publicly accused of "gambling on NBA-related matters" by white-shoe lawyers for The League. *All* of his ideas, they suggested, were breaking the rules.

Spencer's latest big idea, Fan Shares, had nothing to do with sports betting. After improving even faster than the Nets expected when they plucked him from obscurity, he was in Year One of a three-year, $34 million contract extension. The third year was a so-called player option—he could opt in for the 2021–2022 season if he wanted to stay in Brooklyn, or bail out into free agency if he was worth more money by then. In the meantime, Spencer wanted to sell against his own revenue-generating potential during Year One—by way of a security backed up in the booming block-chain market—then pay back investors with the dividends from Year Three.

Most investors could agree that Fan Shares would've been a good bet: Spencer could average twenty-five points a game if he tried, and he was carrying the Nets while Kyrie rested a bum shoulder. Nobody playing this well would ever opt in for Year Three when he could hang over the Nets a threat of leaving in the middle of a potential dynasty, in order to swap out his contract for a deal worth maybe $18 million a year or more, anywhere he pleased. And the more engaged his following became, the more valuable he was to the franchise and his co-op of fandom from the future. "Our power source *is* the fans," Spencer explained to me. "It's very much like Superman and the sun— the business would die if there were no fans—and so the closer we get to *them*, the better it is for *us*. Obviously the NBA doesn't necessarily like that, because they want control, and they want to keep their finger on the button at all times."

Lawyers for the NBA, in their first round of negotiations over whether Fan Shares violated the collective-bargaining agreement with the players' union, had ranted about how Spencer was just another 26-year-old hooper getting used for his millions by a snake-oil third party. They told him to back down. But Spencer was not another backup point guard. He had fought The League before, for the right to design sneakers, and won. Then there was that time when Barclays Center consulted him about a fan giveaway of bobblehead dolls with his face on the body of Marvel's Iron Man, and Spencer had spec'd-out how to engineer a fully functional Tony Stark suit. He was also trying to get a passport from Nigeria so that he could play on its national team at the 2020 Summer Olympics, and he was already involved in the emerging bazaar for virtual trading cards and speculative rights to player highlight clips. In a sponsored Instagram post for Don Julio, Spencer joked that he'd inspired Dos Equis' ad campaign about . . . the most interesting man in the world.

For his next meeting with The League, he called in the union, plus two firms' worth of his own suits, and made his case: Non-superstar players had considered themselves employees for too long. The NBA was not the product, and the corporation was not the asset; the players were.

At Nets HQ the morning after a loss, by twenty-nine points to Indiana, the head coach was hoarse from a marathon film session. Kyrie was over in The Clean Sweep corner in flip-flops, preparing to miss his third game in a row. Caris LeVert, the team's third-leading scorer, was injured, too, recovering from thumb surgery by teaching himself how to play video games one-handed. Spencer Dinwiddie, being Spencer Dinwiddie, was out here in the practice gym talking with tabloid reporters about bond-yield curves and quantitative easing. *I can never fully grasp what it is that Spencer Dinwiddie is trying to do with Bitcoin & cryptocurrency*, one NBA writer would admit on Twitter, *but I can't knock that hustle. Get your (version of) money, man.*

After this latest round of legaling, The League had looked at Fan Shares and determined that Spencer could be *suspended* if he went through with "gambling" on the option year of his deal. He found this ironic, given that the NBA was jumping in bed with Vegas to profit off his likeness across a country that had increasingly legalized *actual* sports gambling. Fans had been betting on Spencer's performance, and "owning" him in fantasy sports leagues, for years. But he was not about to let these NBA regulators bench him, in the midst of a scoring outbreak that could help redefine his career, just because they continued to misunderstand his genius.

Spencer was convinced that a certain kind of rule-breaker with a platform was supposed to stretch limitations, an act of resistance from one generation, for the next. "There's always gotta be somebody that's willing to get in trouble," he said, "to make something happen."

◀◀ JULY 7, 2016

Chicago

SPENCER KNEW HE WANTED to disrupt the sports industrial complex, its oppression and regression, as soon as he'd finished his second year with the Detroit Pistons, struggling to be seen and heard. The head coach, Stan Van Gundy, was tough on up-and-coming players, and small mistakes meant no playing time. That made 23-year-old Spencer play scared. Scared to drive, despite rarely losing one-on-one. Scared to shoot, despite shouting out *Steph Curry!* when he chucked up thirty-two-footers in practice. Scared to commit to the G League, a junior-varsity NBA in which prospects could get more playing time and be called up to a big-league roster at a moment's notice—a constant tryout, which Spencer saw as an underpaid demotion rather than an educational tool. He recalled Van Gundy telling him in a post-season exit interview that the coach thought Spencer was the team's best guard but would still never play—that Spencer was destined to play overseas instead. He winced whenever he re-membered a Pistons assistant coach saying, *You're smart enough to go to Harvard. Why are you even PLAYING in the NBA?*

Harvard had been Spencer's safety school. He dominated the gym there on his recruiting visit when he was 16, and his fourteen hundred out of sixteen hundred on his SATs was al-most enough to get him in without the basketball. But Spencer wanted to make it to the NBA in two years, so he went to the University of Colorado for bigger-time college hoops, only to burst open his left knee. Nonetheless, he entered the draft ear-lier than he had to, falling to the second round on account of his ACL. After the depressing tirades from Detroit's coaches, Spen-cer sensed his moment to resist: He'd forced a trade to Chicago in June 2016 and bought a new house as an investment . . . only to get cut by the Bulls a month later.

Like a good sports fan and the publicly insecure millen-nial that he was, Spencer still LOL'd through his teeth as he live-tweeted the success of franchise players during 2016's free-agency window, while he lived on a nothing contract of his own.

He tweeted about KD signing with the Warriors on Independence Day. He saw the Nets reuniting Jeremy Lin with a first-time head coach named Kenny Atkinson. He wondered if he might have to pretty much end his basketball career by taking a paycheck to play in Europe, like the curmudgeon coach had predicted. "But there's something to be said for people who are confident, even when it doesn't look like they should be confident," said his close friend in Chicago, the WNBA star Imani McGee-Stafford. "He's always bet on himself."

Spencer excelled in the G League, and scouts from The Program in Brooklyn took notice. The intelligence gathered by the Nets front office had come in positive: He was very smart, and he was very big for a point guard. "If you look at the great ones," said one of the head coach's lieutenants, "they tend to look like Spencer Dinwiddie." But he was "too outspoken" in the locker room, and "unsure" of himself on the court, scouts and skeptical assistants reported. Did he really "want" to be a great one? As a developmental coach with the Atlanta Hawks the previous season, it had been Kenny Atkinson's job to scout Detroit's games, even when they were all but over. He watched Spencer get a few minutes in garbage time and asked himself, "Why isn't this guy playing?" Brooklyn's rookie head coach went with his gut to sign Spencer to fill an empty spot on the Nets roster, encouraging his new backup point guard to move fast and break things.

"Stop *worrying* about mistakes," Atkinson told him. "Just go out there and *make* mistakes."

"That's music to my ears," Spencer said.

Spencer showed out during his first year in Brooklyn, starting eighteen games and displaying promise as an occasionally explosive scorer. Still, he couldn't get signed by Nike or Adidas.

He'd always been a sneakerhead, and he knew endorsements

were how the real money could get made, even if you weren't in the class of NBA players with a signature shoe named after them. But there was a reason that the corporate brand logos were getting smaller on sportswear: Every no-name "creator" with an Instagram account could be their *own* personal brand; to Spencer's generation of insurgent influence, a swoosh was an accessory, not a badge. And so, in the spring of 2018, between trolling his colleagues on Twitter and listening to podcasts about block-chain technology during treatment at Nets HQ, Spencer sketched the silhouette of a high-performance basketball sneaker. He wanted to become the only player in the NBA to self-endorse, and self-fund, his *own* signature shoe—and he wanted to wear it by the beginning of the next season.

His footwear collaborators emphasized his design rather than simply letting him choose the color of the tongue and take credit for the rest. He learned about glue-stitching and how to produce a more comfortable sole, then watched the K8IROS 8.1 Perception come to life at warp speed inside a Chinese factory that July. "If my name was James Harden," he said at the time, "this would be the biggest story in the NBA."

The League had long been receptive to a little innovation; its non-superstar middle class could always paddle another rising boat in the NBA's vast salt lake of cash. But the hoops-culture disruptors started to go rogue in the late 2010s, and their presence was difficult to ignore upon the arrival of LaVar Ball's Big Baller Brand. The bombastic basketball dad had burst onto the national scene during a Twitter war with @realDonaldTrump in 2017, when the president took credit for freeing his son from a Chinese shoplifting charge while UCLA's basketball team played abroad. (Alibaba was sponsoring the game, and Joe Tsai ultimately lent a bigger diplomatic hand than Trump's little ones.) Ball had two more sons—one in the NBA, the other in high school—and both already had their own signature shoes from the Black-owned family business. Except the sneakers retailed for $495. Orders went unfulfilled. The oldest Ball brother, Lonzo, injured his ankles while playing in his BBBs. NBA Twitter thought Big Baller Brand was an opportunistic farce. But the youngest son, LaMelo, planned to play professionally in Lithuania and Australia for a year or two, to sell his own likeness and his own shoes and maybe even buy a part of his own team, before returning to the The League, which would desperately need to market him as one of its own, as a potential number one pick in the 2020 NBA Draft. "People don't understand the movement," LaVar told ESPN's Ramona Shelburne. "This is a power play to show everybody, 'Yo, we don't need you to make this shit.'"

This was the landscape in which Spencer Dinwiddie tried not only to rush one signature shoe to market in time for October's tip-off, but to get *eighty-two* different versions approved by the NBA, one for each game of the 2018–2019 season. He wanted to wear custom, graffiti-style designs devoted to his inspirations: Beyoncé and Drake, *The Fresh Prince of Bel-Air* and *Do the Right Thing*, Oprah and *Iron Man*. Spencer considered this idea, if he could pull it off, to be a breakthrough in branding and fashion—a blank-canvas tour of his brain, on TV and all over his Instagram feed. To which The League told him no—he could be profiting off the iconography of his influences. "The NBA didn't want him to wear the shoes," said Michelle Obeso-Theus, the celebrity manager who negotiated for Spencer's sneaker independence over the course of that summer and went on to operate Kyrie's personal brand. "Some people felt because LaVar Ball had pushed Big Baller Brand, and now Spencer was doing this, that there was gonna be a rebellion against a lot of players signing with these bigger companies, the Nikes and

Adidas, which pay the NBA—that they were gonna mess up their revenue stream."

While he awaited The League's sneaker decision, Spencer finally made it to his safety school. He'd been invited to attend the September 2018 edition of "Crossover into Business" at Harvard Business School, a sports-marketing seminar turned celebrity summer camp, where the students were football players and footballers, boxers and ballerinas and ballers galore. At the welcome dinner on campus, all the talk was about Colin Kaepernick's reemergence from the shadows to narrate a Nike commercial that was going viral: Kap had been unable to find work in the NFL since the 2016 season, when the San Francisco 49ers quarterback peacefully protested systemic injustice during the "The Star-Spangled Banner"—a song with an oft-forgotten verse about the perpetuation of slavery, written by a slave owner. After some Nike executives questioned whether to continue their sponsorship of Kap because he . . . wasn't playing on an NFL team, he recorded the voice-over for Nike's 2018 marketing campaign in a trailer in downtown Los Angeles, a siren song for the rise of the underdog disruptors: *What non-believers fail to understand is that calling a dream crazy is not an insult—it's a compliment.* The commercial featured a female football player, a one-handed linebacker and a refugee: *Don't believe you have to be like ANYbody . . . to be SOMEbody.* On-set and on the fly, Kap helped rewrite and approve Nike's ad copy, a cameo by LeBron James included: *Don't become the best basketball player on the planet. Be bigger than basketball.*

"Damn," the famous Harvard attendees said, watching the clip again at dinner. "And Nike's stock is booming!" Perhaps they could glean some more insight into Kap's impact from the seminar's A-list student-athlete, Boston local and resident Nike expert, Kyrie Irving . . . if Kyrie ever showed up. In the morning, the seminarians joined a classroom full of Harvard grad students for a case study on Jay-Z. Lunch came and went . . . still no Kyrie. Alas, the professor continued to outline the afternoon case study, about how a superstar accumulates wealth and power faster than the average athlete and so can take creative risks earlier in their still-finite playing career. Twenty-three-year-old LeBron, she explained, had considered offers from three NBA video-game franchises, deciding on a revenue-sharing deal with Microsoft because he could create and own the game. Ten years later, the lesser stars took notes.

"Superstars," the professor had insisted, "often emerge as the biggest winners."

Kyrie, as if on cue, hustled into the classroom and made sure the professor got a pair of his signature shoes.

"We're doing a case study on LeBron," classmates remember the teacher telling him with a smile. "Hope that's OK, Kyrie. If not, you can step out, because you're late."

Settling down with his study group, Kyrie dug into Harvard's financials on the LeBron gaming deal and rediscovered just how much better his ex-teammate was at leveraging likeness than Kyrie had ever been. Kyrie had been on the "cover" of *NBA2K* the summer before, but they had to redo it, with a Celtics jersey swapped in, when he demanded a trade from Cleveland. For the upcoming cover, LeBron didn't have to wear a Cavs uniform; *KING*, it read next to his head, with a Basquiat crown on top. Even back in 2008, the case study reported, 2K Games offered LeBron as much as $4.1 million all-in with sales incentives, for three days of work plus a few interviews.

"Hold up, this is what Bron got? I gotta call my agent!"

Kyrie and Spencer grew closer that day. If they had as much time to learn about investing as they'd dedicated to hooping, Kyrie acknowledged, he'd be a very different person. Spencer offered to be as much a consultant as a friend, likening himself to the quantum physicist Dr. Werner Karl Heisenberg, who'd kept secrets from the Germans to prevent them from building the A-bomb. "If you see something before it's coming, whether only one person hears it or many people hear it," Spencer said, "if you're the spark that changes the mind that *actually* changes the world, then you owe it to the world, to the people, to do that."

Spencer formed connections at Harvard that would help the expansion of his project for signature shoes, all eighty-two of which were finally getting approved by The League. Throughout his third year with the Nets, then, he planned to wear tributes on his feet to Black history: When Spencer played against OKC, he would be a squeaking reminder of the Tulsa massacre on Black Wall Street by a white mob, so frequently written out of textbooks. When he hooped in Chicago, he'd shout out Obama on his feet. In Memphis, Dr. King. What was the NBA going to do: Say no to Frederick Douglass and Rosa Parks?

He began the 2018–2019 season wearing shoes for true revolutionaries—for Jesse Owens and Muhammad Ali (a butterfly and a bee on the toe), for the NBA's original national-anthem protester, Mahmoud Abdul-Rauf, and the NFL's notorious outcast Colin Kaepernick. *WITH KAP* read straps over Spencer's shoelaces. A *Sports Illustrated* reporter asked if he was concerned about drawing extra attention due to the controversy surrounding Kap's defiance of racism and police brutality during the anthem. "I'm not afraid of it," Spencer said, "because this is exactly what I wanted."

NOVEMBER 21, 2019 ▸❙

Brooklyn

PLAYERS FROM ACROSS THE NBA, the NFL and Major League Baseball were asking Spencer how they could take back the power of their own contracts, to own a bit more of themselves one bitcoin at a time. But he encouraged his fellow insurgents to hold off before joining the Fan Shares revolution; he didn't want them attaching their names just yet, in case the approval process with the suits kept going sideways. "Some people," Spencer said, "are going to have carte blanche—like a LeBron or a KD—where they're just gonna be like, 'We don't care if our names are on it.' Where it's gonna be OK. And some people are going to be, you know, the minimum-contract guy or the Spencer from four years ago where they say, *Oh, you want to side with THAT side? We'll get you outta the league.*"

In one corner of the Nets practice gym, Spencer sat down on the makeshift set of *The Boardroom.* KD rehabbed over by the Clean Sweep corner, off camera from his own show in a body-tracking vest, resistance bands strapped around his thighs. Rich Kleiman threw up a few buckets and schmoozed with the GM and the head coach by the skyline windowsill. Spencer told the episode's host, the retired player and ESPN analyst Jay Williams, that he remained frustrated with The League for vehemently rejecting his free ideas to turn what fans called "real fantasy sports" into what he thought could become many more billions of dollars for billionaire owners.

"Is it a power play?" asked Jay-Will.

"Yes, for sure, it's all about power," Spencer said, "because they came up with the hard stance: *Spencer's gambling. We'll terminate him if he does this.*"

He'd come to realize that The League was no incubator of progress without profit, and now it was the NBA that had gotten afraid of *him*—afraid that he would set a precedent for players to truly appreciate their intellectual property. And his visibility was increasing as the de facto best basketball player in New York City, if for no other reason than half of Brooklyn's starting lineup was injured and the New York Knicks continued to be a laughingstock. Spencer dropped thirty at the Garden a couple nights later, in front of the Knicks superfan Spike Lee, who wore a No. 7 *KAEPERNICK* hoodie and hat.

"Utilizing his platform to create change, working with the league to get them to look at contracts differently moving forward, that's the kind of thinking that we need," Jay-Will told me later. "Just because they may be the third option on their team does not make them a B-lister in the game of life. Trust me, they're on the A-team."

Spencer sent his lawyers to convince The League that he wasn't technically "gambling" or IPO-ing anything with Fan Shares. He had even bigger ideas—a long con for building his personal platform instead of finagling it through his teammate's show on ESPN—and he was preparing to present them to a council of Google and IBM, not the NBA. Maybe it was better to hold off a few months, the agitator conceded, than rushing "to launch it, stick the middle finger to them, and then have them take extreme action to prove a point. 'Cuz I'm not LeBron—nah, they'd have found a way to get my ass outta there." Maybe he could launch Fan Shares at 2020 All-Star Weekend in Chicago, the city where he'd almost packed it in for the Euro leagues. He was certainly playing like an All-Star, and he hit another game-winner in Cleveland, as the Nets kept winning without Kyrie. In and out of Brooklyn's Death Row group chat with that sore shoulder, Kyrie told his teammates, *Keep this boat afloat as long as we can. When I'm back, we make a push for the playoffs.*

That week, the Nets group chat had bubbled up news of a feud between Colin Kaepernick and Jay-Z when, much to everyone's surprise, including No. 7 himself, Kap was presented with a tryout—after two and a half years of silence, misunderstanding and the white supremacy of the National Football League's management on full ignorant display. Roc Nation and Jay-Z had gotten in bed with the NFL, trading the Hova reputation of Black excellence for a stake in the Super Bowl halftime show and the league's new social-justice initiative. That initiative had involved a coalition of woke players, whom Kap felt were selling out the cause for oversize checks and public-service announcements. But Jay-Z never gave Kap the heads-up before partnering with the NFL, and when they did talk, it didn't go well. Now, Jay-Z was apparently "helping" Kap get back in the league. But first, Kap would have to sign on to the NFL's rules for a rushed staging of his return to the field. "Something didn't smell right," his agent said, and the "tryout" ended in a mess of rescheduling, tight spirals and, to nobody's surprise, zero callbacks for Kap.

The Nets debated over text: Was it Kap's fault for refusing to cooperate with the NFL's demands, when he could have swallowed his pride for one last chance at playing? Teammates argued and emoji'd that it was a sham tryout to begin with, an excuse to keep whiteballing a real one. Why had Jay-Z inserted himself behind the scenes, even if he didn't want to take any credit or stamp a J-Hova seal of approval on the tryout, when Kap was clearly—given the NFL's cruel intentions—never going to get another QB job? All the more reason, another Net thought, that the NFL should have to pay Kap reparations beyond his settlement in a collusion lawsuit. KD was pro-Hov—he predicted Jay-Z's partnership could do no wrong—but Brooklyn could agree: Hova's power play was not on point, and nobody remembers easy-money progress.

As part of the NFL deal, Jay-Z's Roc Nation produced a handful of PSAs featuring the families of victims of police violence. The mother of Tamir Rice, the 12-year-old boy killed for carrying a toy gun at a playground, said she was offered $5,000 to appear in a PSA and in a luxury box with Jay-Z and Beyoncé at the Super Bowl. She asked for $50,000 for her son's foundation instead, and was told that wasn't how Roc did its business of doing good. When Roc Nation philanthropists reached out for another initiative, Tamir's mom ghosted Jay-Z's team. "He always been a sell-out," Samaria Rice said of Jay-Z. "He ain't doing nothing for no community. I don't care if he come from the projects—entertainers and actors and athletes can be opportunists."

Jay-Z had worked with Michael Rubin, a part-owner of both the NBA's Philadelphia 76ers and the NHL's New Jersey Devils, to free the rapper Meek Mill from a four-year sentence for a lingering probation violation. Meek was a huge Sixers fan and had taken Rubin's helicopter straight from prison to their 2018 playoff game. In an absurd intersection of sports culture and the inherent absurdity of influencing, Rubin had even been meeting at his apartment with Kap and Meek a month later, when the Sixers superstar Joel Embiid interrupted on FaceTime to let him know that their general manager reportedly had a role in the running of secret Twitter accounts that talked shit about his own team's players. Meek and Rubin, who made his fortune in sports-merchandise licensing, subsequently teamed up with Jay-Z and Clara Wu Tsai, the Nets co-owner, on an organization to influence prison reform. "But when people were trying to say Jay sold out with the NFL, it was the dumbest comment," Rubin told me. "I know the way Jay thinks, which is, 'Hey, I want to effect positive change, and if I can have a front seat, then I can get the NFL to do things to make a difference.'"

There was a difference between the NFL and the NBA, of course: Pro football empowered the owners and had more history with the Defense Department than with activism. But there was a difference, too, between a fading class of what Dr. Ameer "Left" Loggins called The Hovites—a generation of athletes who were led to believe, as the Hova lyric goes, *I'm not a busi-nessman / I'm a business, man*—and the too-rare athlete who was willing to lay his personal brand on the line for bold ideas and real action in the face of oppression. "And the Jay-Z who was the hired gun to appropriate gentrified Brooklyn on behalf of the NBA," Left said, "is the same Jay-Z who became a hitman to eliminate Colin Kaepernick from the NFL."

Left was a sociologist who'd befriended Kap and taught him in his class at Berkeley, on Black representation in pop culture, weeks before Kap's public awakening as an activist. He'd grown up on the same AAU circuit as LeBron, he'd taught the Boston Celtics forward Jaylen Brown at Cal, too, and he counseled basketball players searching for more real talk than they were finding in The Woke NBA. "LeBron is the face of the league, and how he moves, so, too, does the rest of the league," Left told me one morning in the last days of the decade. "You follow leads, and LeBron—he's not a player in the league, really. He's a corporation that can hoop hella good."

Jay-Z and LeBron had built up their empires of cultural capital in the 2000s and 2010s, but, Professor Left continued, "They might end up being *ex*-revolutionaries." The difficult task ahead would be letting go of reverence for the Hovites and listening to the Jaylen Browns and Spencer Dinwiddies of the world, somewhere in what Left called "the residue of that ex-hustle."

Spencer thought paradigms could be changing—that the superstructure might not need the superstars as much as the serial button-pushers. "If you look at any great regime, anywhere throughout history, if you're talking about a dynasty," he said, "the more they crave power or hold on to power and try not to let it slip through their grasp, like, that's when they start to *lose* it. They feel like they're too big to fail, and they start to lose some of their power because they're trying to hold on to it with an iron grip. The more they embrace innovation and let thinkers grow *with* them and give ideas, the more likely they are endeared to the same people that they want to have *control* over."

Just after Colin Kaepernick's initial protest, the ESPN columnist Howard Bryant suggested to Carmelo Anthony that the four hundred and fifty players in the NBA especially had so much cultural capital that they could collapse the entire system of ownership. "We're powerful enough to, if we wanted to, create our own league," Melo responded. "Because at the end of the day, the athletes are the league. Without the athletes, there's no league. Without us, there's no them."

There could be a way, Left concluded, for the non-LeBron rebels of the NBA—the post-Hovites and the would-be Kaptivists—to leverage their allegedly progressive league and their supremely visible platforms into actionable change: "Many of the athletes should use Colin as their shield in some ways to be like, 'Hey, look, I know you're going to try to tell me that this doesn't work, but it worked for him every fucking time. I'm not gonna lose my market, because my demo isn't Trump-supporting old white men. It's kids that fucking hate this idiot. So if anything, you're strengthening my demo, and you're taking my thing and giving it global legs that it didn't have, because the world can see, too.'

"You know what it would take?" Left suggested. "To be like, 'That Colin thing worked. OK, Kyrie, what do *you* think about doing it?'"

7

IRL

Brooklyn

THE NETS HAD NOT YET tipped off against the Celtics, and already the fans in Boston were calling out to Kyrie through the televisions of his Brooklyn penthouse, as he iced his bursting shoulder a hundred and ninety miles away: *Ky-rie SUCKS! Ky-rie SUCKS!* ESPN cut to bannisters around TD Garden, with *COWARD* stamped in red across his face. Beneath one: a crude Photoshop job of Kyrie's empty eyes trapped inside a lion mask from *The Wizard of Oz*. Voices beamed out of the pregame show: *Kyrie CHOSE to leave Boston. . . . The most hateable man in basketball . . . Kyrie looked at the schedule before the season started and planned this whole injury thing because he didn't want to go back to Boston. . . . Kobe would've played tonight. . . .*

It was enough to wake Kyrie's four-year-old daughter upstairs, enough to make the flat-screen in his downstairs den almost impossible to look at. Enough already.

Kyrie *did* chose to leave behind the Boston Celtics, even

though he told their crowd at a fan appreciation night in 2018 that he wanted to re-sign long-term. But his grandfather had died three weeks after that pronouncement. "A lot of basketball, and the joy I had from it, was sucked away from me," he admitted. "I didn't take the necessary steps to get counseling or get therapy." Kyrie distanced himself from teammates in Boston for days at a time, calling out underexperienced rising stars before checking out by early 2019. "Everybody has their ways of dealing with things," Marcus Smart, Kyrie's friend on the Celtics, told me. Another close friend, his Duke teammate Tyler Thornton, said Kyrie was just keeping it 100 percent with a needed emotional availability. "Black men don't talk about crying and being sad," he said.

Now Kyrie was in hiding, between appointments with a shoulder specialist in Phoenix and celebrity dial-a-surgeons whom the Nets generally advised against. The muscles that helped him glide so beautifully, contorting an average of twenty-eight points a night during Brooklyn's first eleven games, felt increasingly weak. He had lost weight over the last two weeks and had missed six games so far, five of which the Nets had won.

The franchise's in-house partners at the Hospital for Special Surgery were at the forefront of orthopedics, and the Nets team doctors preferred innovative plasma treatments to cortisone shots, which only prolonged the pain. But Kyrie didn't always believe team doctors—he'd felt put at risk by the Cavaliers and their partners from the renowned Cleveland Clinic in 2015—and he was considering cortisone to stave off what he thought might be inevitable: that the 2019–2020 season, at least on the court in Brooklyn, would be his year on hold, something borrowed and something blue. He'd ordered a package of "cell food" from a Honduran herbalist online, and iced some more. Kenny

Atkinson wondered if he should have skipped a Nets game to fly private with Kyrie to a second or third opinion somewhere on the other side of the country. He wasn't entirely sure where his best active player had been. But the head coach worried that the team, which knew Kyrie maintained one of the most expensive private medical staffs in the NBA, had lost what little faith Kyrie had in Brooklyn's elite performance group, and might soon lose its last official superstar standing, to season-ending surgery.

The Nets lost in Boston without him, and Kyrie fell into himself once again. But he remained as determined to confront his internal struggle as he was committed to preventing the next generation from having to endure such surround-sound hate.

Kyrie used Instagram during the season primarily as a voyeur, his infrequent posts reserved for promoting Nike sneakers to his fourteen million followers. But when the Boston fans triggered his depression, he began typing and typing until, an hour after the game, without any photograph attached, he hit share on an Instagram Stories manifesto:

It happens all the time and Tonight just shows how Sports/Entertainment will always be ignorant and obtrusive. It's one big SHOW that means Very VERY little in the real world that most people live in because there are Actually things that matter going on within it. Like figuring out a life that means more to you than A damn Ball going into a hoop . . . or even dealing with becoming the leader of your family after someone's passing and not knowing how to deal with Life after it happens. Butttt, This Game of Sports entertainment matters more than someone's mental health and well being right? . . . Think again, It's a GAME. . . . I'll always be the one that takes the stand and speaks on the truth every time though. . . .

Don't fall for the Game that's played in front of you as Entertainment, it'll never be as serious dealing with *LIFE.*

The Post About *LIFE* is how players, coaches and officials around the NBA referred to Kyrie's reckoning-by-ransom-note. Dozens of them completely agreed with his sentiment, and many reached out to thank him for writing down what the average professional athlete could neither entirely comprehend, nor risk, nor fully bring themselves to say on such a large platform. Some simply felt bad for Kyrie. "Superstars are the loneliest people," said Keyon Dooling, a former Celtics point guard who counseled NBA teams about mental health and texted frequently with A-listers and benchwarmers alike. "You always have to keep a certain standard of how you carry yourself in influence and power. That can force you into isolation from role players who spend way more time together, in locker rooms and on planes, talking and eating and playing video games."

While NBA Twitter and ESPN dined on Kyrie's late-night Instagram chum, KD got his back—*seek help*, he tweeted at a blogger. But KD tried to be as honest with fans and content creators on social media as he was obsessed with their criticism of him and his friends and colleagues all over it. *Is it possible*, he tweeted at another blogger later in the season, *to be happy at all times?*

KD himself had gotten shit, almost immediately after joining the Warriors, for never putting down his phone in the locker room—for caring so much that fans perceived him as elite, approachable and ever-loyal. Upon his return to OKC as an opponent in 2017, KD's Golden State teammate Andre Iguodala found it ironic that the crowd in Oklahoma was the only one in the NBA that prayed together before "The Star-Spangled Banner," then screamed *Fuck you!* at KD for two and a half hours straight. Nearly three years later, Andre told me he remained concerned about white entitlement in the stands, about "a slave mentality that still holds true to this day."

"You've got fantasy leagues, and then you've got NBA Twitter, which is great branding for the league," he explained. "You want guys to interact with the fans, and they want to see you up close and personal. You want to build that relationship, but what are the side effects of it? The side effect is the wellness of the players—their *mental* wellness. We never addressed that part. That actually *is* player empowerment."

NBA All-Stars like Kyrie's old Cleveland teammate Kevin Love played what leading psychologists maintain was a symbolic but legitimate role in breaking down stigmas around anxiety and depression, simply by posting to his followers about mental health all the time, as male vulnerability became marketable for megastars like Steph Curry and even LeBron. But they still had to persevere IRL—in real life—through the pressure they claimed to defeat.

A few weeks after The Post About *LIFE*, the veteran Washington Wizards guard Isaiah Thomas split a pair of free throws at Philadelphia's Wells Fargo Center, thus negating a free Wendy's giveaway to every fan in attendance. As he jogged back down the court, Isaiah explained, a Sixers fan thrusted his middle fingers and screamed *Fuck you, bitch! Fuck you, bitch! Fuck you, bitch!* Isaiah calmly approached the young man and his friend, a few rows deep into the rowdy crowd, during the ensuing timeout.

"Don't be disrespectful," Isaiah told the fan.

"OK, I'm sorry," the young man responded. "I just wanted a Frosty."

For this act of decency, Isaiah Thomas was ejected and suspended without pay by the NBA. With his seven-year-old son standing at his locker, he recalled how dozens of colleagues completely agreed with his actions, too. "I know I broke rules," Isaiah told me, "but it was something I felt, as a man, was morally right for me to do." This was a far cry from a 2004 incident known as The Malice at the Palace, when NBA players had fought in the stands with fans who'd been throwing beer at them. Isaiah simply did not want his son growing up in a world in which drunk white men might disrespect his father with the b-word, and he respected Kyrie's Post About *LIFE* because fans "forget we're real human beings—that gets pushed to the side," he said. "That's just the toughest part of this business: All they care about is you putting the ball in the basket, you winning games, when people go through real-life stuff that could be dragging them down."

Kyrie's post was ubiquitous, but nowhere was its meaning as understood and its author as protected as on the Nets' Death Row team group chat, where, after the Celtics game, a text from Kyrie blooped in: He appreciated his Brooklyn teammates for having to put up with the Boston fans' bullshit, and he was self-aware enough to apologize for the lingering distraction. "If he was just sitting at home and watching the games on TV, *that shit* is frustrating," DeAndre Jordan told me, pausing to look at his friend Kyrie's empty locker. "We just want him to be . . . healthy." He paused again, pointing to his brain: "But also healthy up here, too."

Kyrie was in and out of the gym at Brooklyn HQ. The rookie Nic Claxton was feeling depressed about a hamstring injury when Kyrie, rehabbing alongside him at Brooklyn HQ, recommended that Nic read Paulo Coelho's *The Alchemist*, as Kobe had to Kyrie. The allegory, about a boy searching for treasure in the desert, had helped Kyrie detach from Fandom. "Basketball—this life—it's an illusion," he said, "based upon what you've accomplished or how successful you are or how people perceive you. In actuality, it really doesn't mean anything." Hoops no longer got Kyrie up in the morning. Meditation did. Reading did. His family did. This much he passed on to The Young Alchemist on the bike in the practice facility.

"They'll kick you when you're down, but this is just another part of your journey," Nic recalled Kyrie telling him. "It's kind of a circus sometimes, and you just gotta keep sane."

When Kyrie returned home to his penthouse, overlooking downtown Manhattan and the Brooklyn Bridge, he changed out of his work clothes and iced some more. Always with the ice. He was engaged to a professional YouTube influencer who went by the name Golden, but she lived in California. Teammates rarely visited. Except for the nanny helping with four-year-old Azurie upstairs and the chef dropping off a vegan feast, or his childhood friend turned business partner turned Nets ball-boy turned SUV driver, Kyrie was, once again, alone. Over six seasons in Cleveland, he'd hurt a lot of things, including his left shoulder in 2013; all that had been manageable. But now his shooting shoulder was swollen from the inside. He looked out at the city and wondered when he might play again, when he might turn the corner.

"Where," Kyrie asked himself, "*is* the corner?"

<< **MAY 8, 2015**

Chicago

"THERE ARE NO SECRETS," Kyrie said, ice packs on his knees. He'd tried to act as a decoy for the Cavaliers, even as he half-limped around Game Three of the 2015 Eastern Conference Semifinals in plain sight—with the soreness he hadn't felt since a humid Jersey day in middle school, when Kyrie skateboarded over a rock, onto another rock, leaving a crack in his left kneecap. The long-ago skater injury, he'd told friends since, could become "a ticking time bomb."

It was Kyrie's first time in the playoffs, but he felt increasing pain in his knees and feet. LeBron, people around the alpha's entourage noticed, thought his 23-year-old teammate should be playing through it. *Soft*, one reporter recalled them saying. *Pussy*, another claimed he overheard. *He's fakin'*, went the whispers, according to a Cavs coach. LeBron's physical conditioning and cognitive focus were peerless, and at the end of a practice in the run-up to the playoffs, he'd pushed exhausted teammates to add an extra twelve minutes onto their exercise-bike climbing workout: *This is the fourth quarter! You wanna tap out?!*

While word surfaced that he'd been playing hurt, Kyrie had just learned that his ex-girlfriend was pregnant—probably with his child, though he would ask for a paternity test—and reached out to friends to mentally prepare.

His first call on this night was with his hero, Kobe Bryant. Ever since returning by chopper from their boozy dinner four months earlier in California, Kyrie found Kobe's wisdom and leadership style easier on the mind than LeBron's domineering big-brotherness: *Warriors, boy—that team over there, they some bad boys*, Kobe had told Kyrie over another vodka at Javier's Restaurant in Orange County. Kyrie responded that he could beat the Warriors, and Kobe pushed him some more, preaching potential strength, not immediate inadequacy. *Nobody hates the good ones*, Kobe would say. *They hate the great ones.* When I reminded Kyrie of this particular Mambaism and asked what he'd learned from Kobe as a father and a man, he immediately returned to 2015. "I don't think I was probably ready to be a mentee at that point," he said. "But in some ancient text, they say, 'When the student is ready, the teacher will appear.'"

Over the course of their half-hour call during the playoffs, Kobe advised Kyrie to find holes in the Chicago Bulls defense with efficiency, to become tactically dominant, as Kobe had been when he sprained his ankle in the 2000 Finals, then came back to slice apart the Indiana Pacers in overtime all by himself, Shaq be damned. The life advice for Kyrie was there, too: how to be yourself, not the influencer you were expected to be, so that you could be happier—and a better girl-dad. Noise was the enemy.

"Block it out, mentally, psychologically," Kobe told Kyrie. "Don't worry about the injury. Worry about the game."

Kyrie played forty minutes in the next game, which ended on a play that was designed for him . . . only for LeBron to improvise the moment for himself. As the Cavs arrived in Atlanta for the Eastern Conference Finals, Kyrie developed an extreme cautiousness. "Ky was more worried than the doctors led him to believe at the time, and his panic caused panic around the whole organization," a former Cavs staffer involved in Kyrie's rehabilitation planning told me. "It was hectic." Cleveland's GM arranged for Kyrie and the team doctor to fly to the celebrity orthopedist Dr. James Andrews for a second opinion, from Atlanta to Florida and back, on the day of Game Two. Rest, the surgeon recommended. Kyrie tried alternative therapies, ice, measured workouts, everything, to rehab in time for the Warriors, tickety-tock and fuck that damn rock.

After Game One of the 2015 NBA Finals against Golden State, Kyrie's father, Drederick, rumbled into the Cavaliers locker room. He made clear that he felt like his son, writhing in an atrophied swell after knocking his kneecap against another one, had been forced to put his career in danger. "You got him hurt!" people in the locker room remember Dred suggesting, before he clapped thunder into the door of the trainer's office behind him.

Kyrie was done, rendered immobile at a temporary pad in Miami after the Warriors went on to win the title. But he grew up a little that off-season, as his friend Kevin Durant did in OKC during his own injured summer of 2015: "One thing I learned about leadership," Kyrie said on the road to recovery, "is it's very, very, very, *very* lonely. Very, very lonely." He went clubbing on crutches and willed himself in and out of his Lamborghini by himself, rejecting assistance. Slowly, though, Kyrie began opening up to the world around him, to "stop being so fuckin' stubborn and just ask for help when you need it," he said. "Instead of thinking that the world is always against you, and it's just you, I had to let go of that arrogance of just being so independent all the time. There are people to help."

He started reading Indian philosophy and meditating daily—a revolution, he believed, in his mind, and what he hoped would be the end of his self-isolation. He became maniacal in conditioning and protecting his body. He went vegan. He began paying for his private medical staff. He hired a conditioning coach to move in with him in Cleveland. *PEAKS AND VALLEYS*, he wrote in gold marker on his bedroom wall. *FEAR IS NOT REAL.*

Kyrie's daughter was born on November 23, 2015. He ramped up conditioning in December and, by early January, was almost back in proper game shape. The Cavs were on the road in Dallas, waiting for every player on the roster to finish practicing so they could all go shower at the team hotel, when they saw LeBron and Kyrie at it again: a contest, over and over, from the top of the arc, from the right wing—that was Kyrie's spot—and over again, for an extra hour. LeBron found Kyrie to be a pretty good student, albeit a "little hardheaded at times." And while Kyrie still resented that infantilization, the message was clear that LeBron would turn outward, even as Kyrie was facing off inward against himself: "I will never leave the court without him," LeBron told the beat writer Jason Lloyd of the *Akron Beacon Journal*. "Late in games, the ball is going to be in our hands. We've got to be able to trust each other, and our teammates have to be able to trust us. If they see us working like they always do, it gives them more trust in us. And then we have to come through for them." The next night, with sixteen seconds remaining in overtime, LeBron controlled the ball in isolation . . . only to improvise and give up a wide-open jumper, in favor of passing off to the boy wonder. Kyrie caught and released a three, a deep three, from near the top of the arc. Tickety-tock, bang.

The game flowed faster for the Cavaliers in 2016. They fired head coach David Blatt, who had never played in the NBA, in favor of Tyronn Lue, who had. The Cavs won in bursts, and they won by a lot. They even beat KD's Thunder by twenty-three without Kyrie, who'd been freaked out by the bedbugs in his room at an allegedly haunted hotel in OKC, which caused him to miss almost the entire game. They won when Kyrie was struggling after a very public breakup with his pop-star girl-friend Kehlani, who then attempted suicide. (On Instagram, he called out his fans for disrupting her concerts over accusa-tions of her cheating on him: *When it starts affecting real life progress, the shit has to stop. I am responsible as a leader to guide the young males who follow me in a positive way.*) All the wiser, Kyrie outplayed Kobe when he matched up against his retiring hero in his final games, and he texted Kobe that he would attempt to carry on his legacy. Kyrie had found the corner again. The student was ready.

In Game Seven of the 2016 NBA Finals against Golden State, the score was tied, there were sixty-eight seconds on the clock, and Kyrie knew the play had been designed for him. He'd been listening all week over the phone to Kobe encouraging him to stay aggressive, to shoot 'till his arms fell off, to remember the legacy of Muhammad Ali, who'd just passed away. Kobe loved the rope-a-dope of manipulating an opponent's strength to use it against him, which the Cavs had just done, in coming back from a three-games-to-one deficit in the series. With fifty-six seconds left, Kyrie arrived at his spot and stared down Steph Curry. Teammates cleared away. After all that rehabilitation of his loneliness, Kyrie still felt like he had to isolate, to lock in. He hesitated right and stepped back deeper, alone enough, to shoot the shot—*The* Shot—and *BANG!*: A champion emerged.

In the locker room, a ski-goggle'd affair that burned his eyes with bubbly, Kyrie and a coach dialed up Kobe on FaceTime. Kobe hated FaceTime calls, but he and his daughter Gigi picked up right away from their couch in Newport Beach. In between laughter and congratulations, the teacher told the student to en-joy the moment, for having stepped right into it—for rope-a-doping the Warriors and his haters at once.

"You have it in you, bro," Kobe said. "I told you all along: It was *in* you."

But Kyrie felt angry and defensive already, wondering when the non-believers would begin to question The Shot and how he might soon return to another moment like this. In a time of celebration, he asked his dad, "The war is over? There's no more games?"

Meanwhile, inside the Warriors locker room, Draymond Green was already hitting up the game's biggest free-agent-to-be, who was preparing his courtship in the Hamptons. *We need you*, he texted KD. *Make it happen.*

KOBE HATED GOING to NBA games. Too much attention. Too many people. Too many selfies. "To make the trip," he said, "that means I'm missing an opportunity to spend another night with my kids, when I know how fast it goes." He was 41, and he'd hardly watched pro basketball in the two and a half seasons since he'd retired—until Gigi, the second oldest of his four daughters, became a legitimate pro prospect herself, at 13 years old. Now they were watching NBA League Pass together every night. Those Batphone text messages to rookies, the pro camp back at The Sports Academy in August, all that elder shit—Kobe didn't necessarily do all that, except when he was doing it for his guys Kyrie and Kawhi and maybe Russ Westbrook, because he wanted to. He did that because the legends who'd come before him had passed down heirlooms for safekeeping: the blue-chip investments, the public deference of the talented, the all-timer's tricks of dirty play. That was a call of duty. But this, with Gigi, this was love *and* basketball. This was seeing sport through her eyes.

So they went to a game at Staples Center before Thanksgiving—Kobe's first time back since they retired both of his jerseys, 8 and 24, a couple seasons earlier—because the Lakers were playing the Hawks, and Gigi loved Atlanta's deep-range shooter Trae Young, the way he could chuck threes with the flair of Steph, at 21 years old. She and Trae even shared their trainer with Kyrie. And tonight, the Nets were playing Atlanta, in Brooklyn. *C'mon, Dad!*

"Alright, fuck it," Kobe told the trainer. "Let's just go to another fucking NBA game. Gigi wants to go."

He talked his wife out of some extra Christmas plans in the

city and watched Gigi hoop at the office of the players' union in Midtown with another top girls' basketball phenom. By late afternoon, Kobe and Gigi were working out again, in the private underground practice gym at Barclays Center. On their way upstairs to the game, the Bryants greeted some of the Nets' developmental projects heading in for extra work. The players marveled at, though were not in the least shocked by, Kobe grinding through drills in a pinstripe designer tracksuit and low-tops.

Fifteen minutes before tip-off, Spencer spotted Kobe courtside. They'd talked and texted a few times, but hadn't been able to schedule a workout together. All of a sudden, Spencer thought, this was The Mamba in *person*, man! *Finally!* Spencer had a damn *poster* of Kobe on his *wall* growing up, and to that day he had an autographed No. 24 jersey in his room.

"You're playing like an All-Star," Kobe told him. "Keep it up."

"Shit, man, I'm *tryin'*," Spencer said.

"Nah, you ain't tryin' it. You doin' it."

Kobe and Gigi settled down next to Clara Wu Tsai and her son in the owners' seats next to the Brooklyn bench. Atkinson was coaching so hard that he didn't notice Kobe directly behind him. Spencer noticed: He was never shook by opposing fans or by guarding LeBron, but Kobe's presence made Spencer, not two minutes into the first quarter, straight-up clank a twenty-five-footer off the backboard.

The Barclays Center crowd had been pretty dead that Saturday evening, until they put The Mamba on the big screen. Kyrie geeked out, stretching his achy shoulder out of his corduroy blazer and craning his neck for a look at highlights from what became known as the "Mamba Out" game, when Kobe dropped sixty on Utah in his career finale. The Barclays cameraman stepped closer toward Seats No. 7 and 8, and the scoreboard operator beamed Kobe and his daughter up into the Jumbotron. Kobe offered the tacit selfie grin of a purist who'd rather be in an empty gym, but Gigi smiled, her cheeks so wide they made her eyes close. The crowd smiled a little wider, too.

There was another burst of cheer in the second quarter, when Kobe stood up to greet Vince Carter. At 42, his contemporary—no longer living the dunktacular legend of Vinsanity from his heyday on the Nets and Raptors—was on a final season's lap around the league with the Hawks, and the OGs locked fists.

"How you holdin' up in retirement?" Vince laughed.

"I'm happier than I've ever been, man," Kobe said. "Happier than ever."

In the third quarter, with the Nets down thirteen to the worst team in the conference, Atkinson got called for a technical foul. He and Kobe, who was rooting for the Nets, had been shocked by the referees all game long. Expletives had been used. But during this break in the action, a camera scanning courtside spotted Kobe, pleasantly inhabited by an almost unfamous happiness, teaching his daughter about the game. Kobe loved the rhythmic nature of this sport, how sometimes you could hear the ball before you saw it. After he tore his Achilles tendon in 2013, he would listen to Beethoven's Ninth Symphony and marvel at how the maestro had composed it while legally deaf—and then, because he was Kobe Bryant, he learned how to play the piano by ear. Watching the silent cutaway at Barclays, as the girl-dad leaned in and conducted his hands toward the court, nobody could quite tell what Kobe was explaining to Gigi. The clip was only nine seconds long, but pretending to read this maestro's lips became the rare unmean internet meme, a blank caption in which any fan could imagine the lesson of their dreams. Within two weeks, the father-daughter moment would be watched more than sixty-eight million times from one tweet alone.

But Kobe wasn't thinking about his virality. At the final buzzer, he stood up onto the court, in his blue beanie and scarf, and bear-hugged Trae Young, who reminded Kobe what a fan he was—what a fan he was of his *daughter*—then dapped-up Vince Carter again, too. "Let's talk more before end of season," Kobe offered the OG, "but let's continue to teach our daughters. We'll talk more."

In the postgame courtside congregation, Kyrie waited his turn; he'd had plenty of time with the professor. Besides, Kobe wanted to speak with Kyrie *and* Spencer, together. Spencer was sweaty—he'd relaxed enough in front of his idol to score thirty-nine points and keep the Nets in playoff position, after dropping forty-one the game before that—and he was satisfied.

"Man, you know why you didn't get forty?" Kobe asked. "'Cuz you were *thinkin'* about forty. You gotta go out there and think about *sixty*. And then you just fall right *into* fifty. 'Cuz you coulda *easily* had fifty tonight."

The three of them shared a good, strong laugh, and Spencer hugged the poster on his wall. "You're an All-Star in my book," Kobe reiterated. Kyrie said he would catch Kobe later and pranced back to the locker room with his arm around his teammate. "There we go," Spencer said, smiling at him as he turned back for one last glance at the legend. "There! We! *Go!*"

Kobe and Gigi were ready to pull out of the VIP garage at Barclays Center when a New Jersey boys' high-school basketball team shouted: "Yo! It's St. Pat's!" Kobe stepped out of the Suburban and turned back around. He knew Kyrie's alma mater. He used to play against them in his Philly days and talk trash in Italian.

Kyrie had helped to reopen St. Pat's—as The Patrick School—and taken one player in particular under his wing. But Kobe immediately recognized the junior forward Jonathan

Kuminga as one of the top prospects in the nation. Jon, who'd moved from the Democratic Republic of Congo to West Virginia at 13, to Long Island and The Patrick School in Jersey over the past year, knew he was good, but Kyrie had taught him to stay humble.

Kobe and Jon shook hands and stood in the middle of a team photo, inside of which two selfies were being taken. Kobe, of course, was more interested in a matchup that the Patrick School boys were hyping: their rivalry game against Roselle Catholic, which was going down here at Barclays—at Kyrie's own tournament—in less than forty-eight hours.

"What's your game plan?" Kobe asked the team.

All the kids answered all over one another.

"Feel good about it?"

"*Yeah!*"

"Then go out and do it."

Kobe's car drove out of the garage, the boys loaded onto their bus, and Kyrie emerged from the locker room toward his bulletproof Escalade. He had not expected to see his guests, happy to pay their way and receive no thanks whatsoever.

"Y'all good?" Kyrie asked the boys.

"Uh, *yeah*, we met *Kobe!*"

He had missed his mentor by seconds—one limo-size elevator door had closed as another was opening—but Kyrie was more interested in the game plan, too.

"You guys are good? Cool. OK, now what we doing against Roselle?"

After midnight, Jon Kuminga direct-messaged Kobe on Instagram.

Appreciate it today for the pic big bro it means a lot to me and my teammates 🖤 ✊🏿

Kobe wrote back: *My man!! Go get em!!!*

TWO DAYS LATER, Kyrie was running late to his own party, as high schoolers awaited his grand arrival at the same Barclays Center garage. He had missed another practice, too—with good reason: He'd decided to get a cortisone shot after all, and he barely made it upstairs to the gym at Nets HQ in time to join his teammates for the final huddle before Christmas. *Us versus everybody else— Death Row on three!* His teammates gathered their Secret Santa gifts from one another, but Kyrie, still two weeks away from his return to gameplay, grabbed all the expensive juices and vegan snacks from the team chefs that he could find, plus all the jerseys and kicks and merch he could stuff in the Tesla and the Escalade, then sped off.

On the way to Barclays, he gave it all away to people on the streets of Brooklyn. He stopped outside the arena—*KYRIE INVITATIONAL,* the entranceway's neon overhang glared, as the all-seeing eye looked down from a Nike mural on the corner—and asked his entourage to buy some food at Chick-fil-A, then gave that away, too.

There was a deliberate secrecy to the benevolent side of "the most hateable man in basketball." He could not—would not— take credit for his random acts of Kyness: The funeral costs of a Patrick School player who collapsed and died in the middle of practice in 2016. The medical fees Kyrie volunteered to cover the following year, when a tumor nearly blinded another middle-schooler at his alma mater, whom he'd still never met, even as the boy surmounted his stunted growth from the illness to become a heavily recruited prospect. The Patrick School families received a monthly tuition notice in the mail—either it was a bill for $3,100, or it was a receipt marked as *KYRIE DONATION.* It frustrated the do-gooders at Roc Nation and the Nets that he refused to do most of this for the 'Gram, especially when they saw that LeBron was making an entire streaming documentary series about his own state-of-the-art school, conjoining the clout of @KingJames with humanitarianism under "a house of brands." Kyrie's business managers believed that all the scrutiny he'd endured had led Kyrie to form a shell around himself, as a direct response to the "social media monster" that had hyped and then vilified him for more than a decade.

Kyrie outlined to me his grand intentions: "I'm kind of in that role of family stuff, school stuff, youth outreach, changing some social issues"—he felt strongly about the environment, Black-owned businesses, women's equality in the C-suite and in the C-suites of sports—"and making a social impact around here other than just playing for the Nets." His priority remained a championship, and he was attempting to cast off his haters into "a *fictional* world." But he tried re-determining his purpose, pushing it forward behind closed doors to the next generation of entertainers. "Don't get tied up in conforming," he would advise them, "to worrying about high-school *drama* and fitting in and *Instagram* and, you know, trying to be a digital identity of a person."

The Patrick School Celtics rolled back into Barclays, right where they'd met Kobe, looking like an NBA team as they followed their benefactor through the tunnel. Kyrie offered them words of encouragement, especially to the handful of prospects on this Celtics team who had a shot at making the NBA. Kyrie knew that there had been fewer than five thousand NBA players *ever*—that only three of every ten thousand American boys had a shot at the NBA, and just two of every ten thousand girls made the WNBA. Nonetheless, he would tell them, "I want all of you guys to try and take my spot from me."

Seventeen-year-old Jon Kuminga actually could. He had the University of Kentucky coach John Calipari and the pop stars from Migos up in his ears and his phone, as the Kentucky fan Drake had tried to recruit the sensational teenage Kyrie. But if Jon attended enough classes in the next several months, he could qualify to go straight to the G League: The NBA had opened a year-long gateway in its minor leagues—spearheaded by Kyrie's godfather—for America's top high-school prospects to skip the NCAA's for-profit prison and make $125,000 on a for-profit NBA super-team full of prodigies instead. Kyrie would pull Jon aside. "Keep your circle small," he told him before a practice that Kyrie helped lead during shoulder recovery.

For every Jon Kuminga to be shepherded by the caretakers of superstardom, there was a high schooler like Dejake. Dejake knew classes at the Patrick School were "a walk in the park," so he spent his nights as the basketball team's manager, keeping the stat sheet for the Celtics with his right hand while monitoring the team's mentions on the 'Gram with his left. Dejake's dream was to make it to the NBA, as part of his friend's entourage. "I told Jon I would stay with him," Dejake said on his way across Jersey to yet another tournament at another armpit arena. "And when he gets an offer, maybe they could get me a scholarship, too."

Watching Jon Kuminga at that tournament, nobody felt the 'Gramxiety more than LeBron James Jr. He was a backup point guard for California's Sierra Canyon Trailblazers, a team that co-starred Dwyane Wade's son and had a more obsessive national following than the Brooklyn Nets. LeBron's oldest son, even sitting in the bleachers as he awaited his school's game, felt the shifting glare of five thousand eyes in the gym—*Bronny! Bronny!*—and so rubbed his own. He was tired, sure—the power had been out in the Sierra Canyon hotel during study hall after a cross-country flight—but he was slightly embarrassed, stealing attention as heir to the throne at such an accelerated ferociousness of fame, when Jon's game was still on. LeBron bit his nails; Bronny massaged his wrists into his eyebrows. He peeled his vision back open and flicked through the direct-messages from his four-point-five million followers on Instagram, hiding alone within his headphones while mouthing Kanye: *They mad they ain't famous / They mad they're still nameless.* Superstars were still the loneliest people in a gym, even at 15 years old.

During the Kyrie Invitational at Barclays, though, the host felt better than he had in a good long while, and not only because of the cortisone. Kyrie filed from the garage to his courtside seat with his former St. Pat's teammates to catch the fourth quarter of a game between two girls' basketball powerhouses. The crowd of mini-Kyries and their parents hovered closer to him and his family in the front row, drawing their Sharpies. A friend pointed out Kyrie's private trainer from high school, Sandy Pyonin, who was difficult to miss with his creamsicle mop, like Donald Trump with a Jheri curl. Pyonin was an OG's OG, not one for social media, but he'd heard Kyrie was upset—that the haters had been bothering him, and he'd written some sort of screed on the internet.

"Kyrie, why do you listen to all these people who make something out of this and that?" he asked. "You're too tough for all of that. You're mentally tough. You're a good person. Just look: You've got *all* of . . . *this.*"

Welcoming the selfie swarm, Kyrie was, like KD, beginning to see what life could be like without being expected to master and maintain the game of basketball, all day and all night and as soon as tomorrow arrived. I suggested to him that spending extended time throughout his shoulder recovery with his many extended families in New Jersey—and downtime actually *living* in Brooklyn—was a silver lining to missing twenty-six straight games at the beginning of a dynasty of his creation. "My life now, coming back home, has been a tale of kinda *inheriting* everything that I failed"—he corrected himself—"missed in the last eight years of not being home." This meant more hours with his daughter instead of the weekly sacrifices of living in a hotel room on the road. It meant taking more meetings with potential partners in philanthropy, in clean energy and an emerging, player-first media collective. But Kyrie felt liberated, because here at the Kyrie Invitational, among his family and the followers in the crowd, he was no longer alone, and he didn't want to be.

He began posing for yet another picture, straightening his black T-shirt. It featured photos and mottos from Angela Davis, as well as the Black Panther Party leaders Fred Hampton, Huey P. Newton and Bobby Seale—activists of a moment that seemed longer ago then, at Christmastime of 2019, than it would be henceforth. Across the top was a quote from Hampton: *YOU CAN KILL THE REVOLUTIONARY, BUT YOU CAN'T KILL THE REVOLUTION.*

"When I was out, and people were still saying things about me, it's inevitable. They crucified Martin Luther King for speaking about peace and social integration. You can go back to historical leaders and great people in society that do great things, and they're still going to talk shit about 'em," Kyrie said. "This basketball stuff is a *GAME* at the end of the day. It's dramatized. It's entertainment for people and fans. I'm a human being."

8

ACTIVISTS WEAR SNEAKERS, TOO

JANUARY 12, 2020 ⏩

Brooklyn

GARRETT TEMPLE ROCKED a full suit to every game and, on occasion, carried a paperback under one arm. He'd been struck recently by the film version of *Just Mercy*, the true story of a young lawyer who took up the case of an innocent man on death row, and he brought the memoir with him everywhere. "Temple/Jordan 2020!" DeAndre Jordan would joke when Garrett flashed the book. Lacking consistent leadership and having grown sick of the nickname Temp, his Nets teammates had, by this midwaypoint of the season, settled on referring to their evolving conscience as, simply, The President.

It was difficult to miss his suit jacket in the locker room that afternoon, what with the neon-yellow portraits of The Notorious B.I.G. stitched in the lining. As Garrett sought a place to lay down his statement look, though, he couldn't help but stare at an unannounced T-shirt, draped atop the back of his leather chair and those of his fourteen teammates. Beneath the Nets logo, extra-bold letters on the white T-shirt announced: *NO PLACE FOR HATE.*

The Barclays brass had created the shirts hastily, in partnership with the Anti-Defamation League, in response to a wave of anti-Semitic violence in New York, including a mass stabbing at a Hasidic rabbi's house two weeks earlier, during Hanukkah, perpetrated by a mentally unstable Black man who wrote about "Nazi culture" in his diary. Management had cleared the ADL's slogan with the NBA, and Nike sent over some clean shirts, and the @BrooklynNets social-media captions were prepared just so. Franchise executives thought the pregame moment could be an echo of the *I CAN'T BREATHE* effect from five seasons earlier, a message of solidarity for a new year. Except they forgot to ask the players.

Garrett considered the merits of instant activism as suggested by this T-shirt. He recalled not caring too much if his teammates spoke out on foreign policy three months earlier in China. But he frequently wrestled with the expectations placed upon the twenty-first-century Black athlete in America: You could acknowledge the obviousness of inequality—systemic racism, generational gaps in education and wealth, criminal injustice, so much injustice—by performing the act of retweet, by doing the work in the community and with the checkbook, or you could risk financial vulnerability to put yourself on the line for public protest. Figuring out how to finesse the in-between, Garrett thought, was the art of celebrity politicking, which was often spirited in intent and limited in results.

Garrett's father, Collis, had visited Barclays Center that week, decked cap-to-cankle in LSU gear in anticipation of the 2020 college-football championship game. Walking him to the arena's garage, Kenny Atkinson tried explaining to Collis why

Garrett, as a veteran role player, fit in with the Nets' system. He did so much of what management needed, the head coach said, that Garrett had started his last twenty-five games at shooting guard: "Mr. Temple, I think we're gonna have a chance to do some truly great things because he *gets* it—he's a kind of character person who we want."

Collis Temple had been schooling Garrett on character since his son was seven years old, sitting on the family couch in Baton Rouge, Louisiana, watching *Roots* on VHS. He taught Garrett about his grandma, who learned biology from George Washington Carver. About his grandpa, who had joined Thurgood Marshall's class-action suit against racist admissions policies; the state had paid for him to go anywhere *but* Louisiana State for his master's degree. About how, fifteen years later, the governor sat on 16-year-old Collis' couch, apologizing to the family and insisting, again and again, that the times were changing—that the time was right for a Temple to bring about racial progress at LSU. Garrett's dad had considered the state's deal to be essentially reparations in the form of a small forward's scholarship, but Grandpa exhorted him to attend. Collis would be the first Black player on the Louisiana State basketball team. This was 1969.

His first weekend at LSU, three discos—The Cotton Club, The Keg and Common Ground—had already barred Collis from entry when a cook at Pastime, a Baton Rouge po' boy joint that feeds co-eds to this day, told him: "We don't serve niggers here." Collis was not discouraged—"and I don't *eat* no niggers" was his response—nor was he going to stand by: Later that semester, he cut off a litany of N-bombs outside the student union from a raving classmate, the white supremacist David Duke. But Collis understood and was reminded again, during his sophomore year playing under Press Maravich—father of Pistol Pete, the leading scorer in college-basketball history—that he alone, as the governor had suggested to his family, could not make the perniciousness disappear. "These damn jumpin' jungle bunnies are better than us," Coach Maravich concluded at practice one afternoon, in his scouting report of the University of Houston's all-Black starting five. "Oh, not you, Collis—you're a credit to your race."

When he became a father, Collis took Garrett and his brother to a near-empty gym, the Maravich Assembly Center, to witness a wave of generational talent and certain future influence: Shaquille O'Neal and Chris Jackson—the first-team All-American scorer who would change his name to Mahmoud Abdul-Rauf—were LSU's KD and Steph of the late '80s. As Garrett proved to be a talented player for LSU, Collis sat him down for hours at a time, encouraging Garrett to achieve as much as he could in basketball, so that he could reach the most people, without compromising his values or selling out what he believed in. There had always been role models who blazed the trail, and Collis Temple was one of those. "But nobody walks in the shoes of another man," Garrett's father taught him. "Do what your conscience will allow you to do." He told his son that Muhammad Ali was a role model—to Shaq and Kobe, even to the former Republican Charles Barkley—not because he was The Greatest but because he had given up the damn *title* to demonstrate against the war in Vietnam, because he knew he *wanted* to do that . . . and because he actually did. Rarely, but every so often when the times beckoned for one, Collis believed that Americans could witness a hero who *was* the trail.

Garrett had hooped ceremoniously alongside Barack Obama on the White House lawn, once he finally settled down with the Washington Wizards from 2012 to 2016. But he felt that his platform as an individual was only so high, that his capital only had so much pull. He'd made donations in Louisiana and investments in Brooklyn—Jay-Z, at Kyrie's welcome-to-Brooklyn party with Roc Nation in July, advised him and Kára to buy a place in Red Hook—except Garrett had earned less money in his first ten seasons than his friend Kyrie Irving was going to make that season. "The person that's on a ten-day contract cannot say what LeBron James will say on a lot of—on certain—issues and still be in the NBA," he said. "You do activism when you can focus on that. But at the end of the day, more times than not, your family comes first."

As warmups for Kyrie's first game in fifty-seven days began, Brooklyn's four European players put on the *NO PLACE FOR HATE* T-shirt and took the floor at Barclays Center. So did Joe Harris, who'd taken to flexing his biceps after big three-pointers—his teammates thought it was pretty much the whitest thing he'd ever done. Twenty-four-year-old Theo Pinson wore the shirt, but none of the team's other Black players did. Not Kyrie, who had stood so proudly with *I CAN'T BREATHE* on his chest here in 2014. Nor Wilson Chandler, who told me: "We're getting sidetracked with symbols. That's not a victory for us."

Garrett looked at the sloganized shirt still hanging on the back of his chair and—no shade to the nonprofit organization combating anti-Semitism from which his employer co-opted the slogan, because the streak of New York hate crimes was terrible, obviously—but, well, he was getting a kind of All Lives Matter vibe. "There are a lot of things that have been happening over the course of this entire country's history, honestly, but specifically over the last five to ten years that have been put in the forefront, with social media, with African Americans—police brutality—and there were no shirts specifically for that," Garrett said to me by his locker after the game.

Kyrie, having transferred his locker from the corner of the

room closer to the veterans, nodded: "That's what's up." Kyrie was making a surprise run for office to join Garrett as a vice president on the executive committee of the National Basketball Players Association, pledging to devote more time to social issues and to find his place outside of basketball. The players' union had come a long way since the Hall of Famer Oscar Robertson settled a class-action lawsuit in 1976 on its behalf, to kick-start the right to free agency in earnest. And its modern leaders, since Chris Paul was elected union president in 2013, had seemed to effort for dollars and labor rights as much as they counseled members on how best to speak out as citizens, peacemakers and, increasingly, participants in the new American culture wars. Michele Roberts, the group's executive director and player consigliere, was a 63-year-old former star litigator in Washington who played her hand like a Congressional majority whip. While intrigued by Kyrie's curiosity and clout as a new VP, Roberts believed the persistence of a leader like Garrett could be more infectious than Kyrie or even LeBron, because "he had to prove it in ways that LeBron didn't."

Garrett, as the unofficial president of the Brooklyn Nets, understood full well already that hatred and oppression had been on instant replay for four hundred years and counting, not to mention the dog whistle in the White House these past three. "The world is very crazy," Garrett continued. At this rate, and if basketball players were still expected to be walking protest signs instead of future politicians—role players and not role models— then, well, "you might be wearing different shirts literally every game."

⏮ **JULY 5, 2016**

Sacramento

"**WOW,**" **GARRETT SAID** to himself. *"Again?"* The phone alert delivered another of the grim videos he'd sadly come to expect in his feed. "Who got killed this time?" But Garrett remembered Alton Sterling, the guy who was always selling CDs and DVDs outside the Triple S back home in Baton Rouge. Which is what Alton Sterling was allegedly doing on this Tuesday in the summer of 2016, when two police officers thought he was pulling a gun on them. They were wrong. One cop put a gun to the man's head, ordered his partner to tase him, then shot him in his back and his chest, six times. It was Alton Sterling, a 37-year-old Black father of five, who'd gotten killed by the white cops this time, on five different cameras.

Twenty hours later, outside the Twin Cities, 32-year-old Philando Castile was driving past the Minnesota state fair grounds when an officer pulled him over for a broken taillight. Within six seconds of Philando informing the cop he had a licensed firearm, seven shots began ringing into his Oldsmobile. "They killed my boyfriend," Diamond Reynolds cried. "He was reaching for his wallet." She began to live-stream on Facebook, Philando bleeding to death beside her. In the background, her four-year-old daughter wailed.

The streets, too, wailed. Alton Sterling and Philando Castile became the five hundred sixty-eighth and five hundred seventy-second people killed by American law enforcement in that election year; nearly half of the people killed would be people of color. Less than twenty-four hours after Philando's death, a protest in Dallas began and then ended in bloodshed, when a Black military veteran targeted white police officers, killing five of them.

Garrett signed his free-agent deal with the Kings in Sacramento, then decided to turn off the news alerts on his iPhone. This was not an act of ignorance or denial. He was a religious man who preferred to power forward, rather than to dwell on the injustice of the past. He texted local cops—Black cops and white cops, down in Baton Rouge—about what the hell to do with this storm of violence.

Word flowed back to him that his basketball community was fed up, too. That Carmelo Anthony, who had marched in Baltimore after police severed 25-year-old Freddie Gray's spinal cord in the back of a van one year earlier, was calling on athletes to lead a reckoning for change, in a late-night Instagram caption he posted with a photo of Muhammad Ali, Jim Brown and Lew Alcindor, the student who would become Kareem. It was a lasting image, from the 1967 Ali Summit, in which four superstar athletes in suits symbolized resistance . . . even if Melo, in 2016, couldn't figure out how to include Bill Russell within the square photographic confines of social media, and so cut him off. Many sports fans forgot that the photo op had been staged after a room full of athletes tried to convince the champ to take a deal to get back in the ring, instead of continuing to conscientiously object to the war in Vietnam. This cross-sport celebrity kumbaya lasted all of fifteen minutes; the champ, putting his foot down along with his fists, would keep on dissenting. "I'm not worried about Muhammad Ali," Mr. Russell said at the time. "He is better equipped than anyone I know to withstand the trials in store for him. What I'm worried about is the rest of us." But the image inspired Melo, who believed we were living in "the new '60s"— hatred and oppression's cruel and ceaseless sequel, rebooted with new superstars of the resistance taking the stage.

Garrett appreciated that the best team in the WNBA, the Minnesota Lynx, had risked fines that weekend to warm up in customized T-shirts blaring that *CHANGE STARTS WITH US*, even if four off-duty cops working security at their game had up and walked out of the arena. "It's just like in politics, and in *life*: Black women lead so many things and they get taken for granted," he said. Then Garrett heard that Melo, LeBron, Chris Paul and Dwyane Wade—The Banana Boat Crew, who could express such joy, and were unfortunately yet inevitably expected to help overcome such sorrow—had opened up ESPN's annual ESPY Awards onstage in tuxedos, speaking solemnly about the endless gun violence, the shoot-to-kill mentality, the urgency for action. By the time Garrett caught their speech on YouTube, he found the both-sidesism very vague. Chris had made sure to pronounce that his uncle was a cop, that today's athletes were following in the footsteps of Jackie Robinson and Ali and Billie Jean King. But LeBron, confusingly, said this call to leadership was *not* about a tradition of activism? "It's not," LeBron said, "about being a role model."

There had been enough talk about talk, Garrett decided. Messages and movements were already drowning in hashtaggery: Black Lives Matter. Blue Lives Matter. All Lives Matter. Make America Great Again. There were town halls to be organized by the very players who made it their mission to speak up, Garrett himself included. It was time to head home and directly engage white officers about everyday patterns of subconscious bias without too much kumbaya. Before Garrett could manage to leave for the airport, though, texts streamed in, yet again: Three cops had been killed by a mentally unstable Black man in Baton Rouge. Garrett turned his notifications back on. Within another week, Donald Trump accepted the Republican nomination, claiming Obama had "used the pulpit of the presidency to divide us by race and color, has made America a more dangerous environment than frankly I have ever seen." Garrett was house-hunting back in Sacramento, not a month later, when the floods arrived down South—near-biblical, the preachers said—and Baton Rouge was literally underwater. He invited flood victims to stay at his house, and he tweeted as honestly as he could about a nation split in half. It was the least he could do. "He tried to settle things down, but he was on high alert," Garrett's dad said. "When it hits you right in your face, it's hard to deny."

That Sunday afternoon, after Garrett left church, Colin Kaepernick decided not to stand at attention for the national anthem. "I respected the hell out of him," Garrett told me. "I wasn't surprised, either—especially because of who was just about to be elected president—that he was surrounded by hate."

JANUARY 17, 2020 ⏩

Brooklyn

GARRETT HAD INVITED KD to tag along to the movies, but the rehab group kept the franchise player locked at Nets HQ, and Garrett couldn't wait around: He had to get to the theater to meet three dozen Brooklyn teenagers for his after-school activity. It was the Friday of a long weekend to celebrate the birthday of Dr. Martin Luther King Jr., and the students had still gathered on time to see *Just Mercy*. The WNBA superstar Maya Moore was preparing to skip her second straight season to free a man from prison, but Garrett was going to start with schooling these kids on a movie about criminal-justice reform and progress from there.

When the lights came up, Garrett asked questions and guided students from the film's plotlines toward solutions about voting rights, from villainous judges and poverty toward public policy and generational wealth. The students sat up in their seats. The energy of the shared space felt like the Nets' fourth-quarter run three nights earlier against the Jazz, except the man at the front of the theater sounded like a community organizer, and nobody heard the word *basketball* once. Within ten minutes, one teenager stopped talking about the gaze of white cops in Brooklyn and started considering the value of a law degree. "You don't just have to be a lawyer to make change," Garrett told him. "*You* can be a detective." That being said, Garrett revealed to the students that this movie had inspired him to pick back up the idea of going to law school himself when he was done playing in the NBA. One of the teachers in the back of the theater whispered to another: "Politician right here."

Talking politics back at his Jay-Z-approved townhouse that night, Garrett said he wanted to run back the same conversation with white students, with white cops. Even a bench guy getting more minutes than usual, he reminded me, could wield a pick-up-the-phone power with institutions that needed re-thinking. And superstars like his new friend Kevin Durant, he said, were just as entitled to do as they pleased. Garrett wasn't quite sure who Kevin Durant was, though, off the court. Despite KD having contributed matching donations to one of Colin Kaepernick's many drives for policing and criminal-justice reform, he was not a politics guy. What Garrett was sure about was that KD was a disgusted citizen who'd spoken out in August 2017, five days after a deadly white-supremacist rally that Trump said was organized by "very fine people." The new president, KD said, was driving racial tension. "I feel ever since he's got into office, or since he ran for the presidency, our country has been so divided, and it's not a coincidence," he told ESPN's Chris Haynes. "Until we get him out of here, we won't see any progress." When Haynes asked, for good measure, if he would visit the White House for the traditional championship photo op, KD added, "Nah, I won't do that. I don't respect who's in office right now."

None of the Warriors did. And one weekend that September of 2017, the outspoken team had been used as a weapon of division. Trump went off on Kap at a rally—"Get that son of a bitch off the field, *you're fired!*"—then "disinvited" the Warriors from the White House the next morning on Twitter. *U bum*, LeBron tweeted back. *@StephenCurry30 already said he ain't going! So therefore ain't no invite. Going to White House was a great honor until you showed up!* It is one of the most popular tweets, ever. That Sunday, more than a year since Kap had first knelt during the national anthem, more than two hundred NFL players, coaches and owners took a knee on the field or locked their arms in solidarity—and in a mass, if vague, act of defiance against the president. There were two weeks until the 2017 NBA preseason began with a Warriors game, and the NBA players had yet to make a unified, politicized act like this, ever, other than the jingoism of standing for the anthem in the first place.

As soon as Trump had gone after the Warriors, Adam Silver expressed concern that basketball players would kneel—that it would affect the bottom line. Multiple officials and players described to me a chilling effect from the commissioner's office on down that pressured rank-and-file players and prevented them from expanding Kap's protest movement—or at least his protest symbol—to the NBA. "The owners and the GMs and the coaches, everybody was so conscious of that," said the Nets forward Timothé Luwawu-Cabarrot, who was with Philadelphia at the time. "They were like, *Don't do anything. Don't take a knee.* So we're all about locking arms, or hugging each other, or some shit like that."

Many teams conducted advanced, player-only discussions about bent knees and raised fists, and multiple NBA players approached Kap about unapologetic demands for change. But their message to him that season was largely one of guilt and big facts:

They didn't have LeBron money, and they couldn't risk following Kap's lead. Zach LaVine, the Bulls star, admitted that he "didn't want to force anyone to do anything that they weren't ready to do" and eventually decided that locking arms as a team was enough to say that enough was enough. "You gotta leave it up to the higher dogs, like LeBron and the Steph Currys and Kevin Durants," said his teammate Kris Dunn, who had played for Minnesota during the 2016 Philando Castile shooting and helped lead the 2017 locker-room debate in Chicago. "If they come up with a solution, then we follow in line."

The Warriors held a small meeting with players, Steve Kerr and their team president. The word from management was clear to athletes old and young: *Whatever you want to do, do it as a team, and stick with it—even if it's kneeling all season long.* The word from some veterans was clearer: "All the gestures have been done, and all the conversations have started," Draymond Green said. The Golden State vet David West had, for years, stood two feet behind his teammates on the anthem line in silent protest of racial oppression and police brutality, and he found the demonstration painfully isolating. Protest was not a team thing, he told his teammates, and he was not KD, but he didn't fault superstars either, for sitting out on kneeling down. "It's not the role of athletes," David told me. "These individual gestures and individual acts don't do very much to disrupt structural inequalities—and an athlete's voice being the voice of a movement is gonna be just that: a voice—a *face*, a social statement. Change your clothes all you want."

Colin Kaepernick, friends recalled, did not expect the NBA stars to risk business deals and blackballing just to follow his demonstration. "It's all good," he told a confidant. "I'm not doing it for them. I'm doing it for somebody who doesn't have a platform."

The Warriors didn't kneel. None of the basketball players did.

Sitting in his bedroom on Dr. King's weekend in 2020, Garrett decided activism was a long walk upon which some potential freedom-fighters might veer off the road. "People expect that everybody that's a great player should be a great leader and that a great leader should speak and talk all the time, be very vocal about this and that. They put players in boxes when sometimes you're just a . . ." Garrett trailed off. He concluded that his friend KD did not have to be an activist if he didn't want to be and could influence with his excellence. "He really is the epitome of a person that just wants to *chill* and play basketball. He's on his phone, *chills*, plays basketball, that's it. He's going to do stuff to help people because he definitely knows where he came from. But he's not doing it for the spotlight."

Indeed, KD had connected in Silicon Valley with investors in a nonprofit founded by the billionaire philanthropist Laurene Powell Jobs that focused on pathways to college for low-income students. He cut a $10 million check for them to expand in Maryland. Ownership from the Warriors and the Washington Wizards finalized a deal with Powell Jobs: Instead of the Warriors visiting the White House upon their return to D.C. after KD's first championship, his personal brand could announce The Durant Center, and the team could visit the Smithsonian's new museum dedicated to African American history with the kids from his old rec center. "That's *perfect*," the Wizards owner Ted Leonsis remembered the billionaires saying. Kevin Durant approved this message, and he was so moved by the Smithsonian museum that he vowed to return.

For 2020, KD put his father, Wayne Pratt, in charge of a new youth-basketball tournament down in Washington—the Kevin Durant MLK Classic—with the requirement that all the hoopers visit the Smithsonian's National Museum of African American History & Culture. At the museum that Sunday, KD's dad walked among the teenage prospects, through the exhibit on sports in Black history. He looked down at a photograph of LeBron (not Kyrie) in the *I CAN'T BREATHE* shirt, he gazed up at Bill Russell's jersey (Kevin's was nowhere to be found), and he hurried down the hall toward Michael Jordan on a Wheaties box. Wayne was obsessed with Michael Jordan, and the "Republicans buy sneakers, too" excuse had made him teach Kevin, from a young age, to stick to sports. "You're an athlete; you're trying to get to a certain level," he told his son. "Don't have discussions about political stuff—until you're at that top one-percent."

Wayne stopped at the museum exhibit of Emmett Till's open casket, the photograph of which he and Wanda hadn't let Kevin see as a child. Kevin Durant's father wasn't around to give The Talk about the threat of police to Black boys, and he remembers using basketball to shield his son: Around Kevin's college decision, a racist letter arrived in the mail with a death threat of what might happen if he chose to play at the University of North Carolina instead of Texas—*We're going to hang you from a tree*—but the Durants never showed it to him. A noose had been found at the museum in 2017, on the same day that LeBron said at a press conference how much he appreciated the bold funeral plans of Emmett Till's mother: "Hate in America, especially for African Americans, is living every day. It is hidden most days. It is alive every single day." This was right before Game One of the NBA Finals, and right after LeBron learned the N-word had been spray-painted across the front gate of his home.

The teenage hoopers of the Kevin Durant MLK Classic gathered outside the museum for a photo with Wayne as he looked down the National Mall, past a flag-football game and toward Congress. He'd served as a U.S. Capitol Police officer until Kevin's MVP season; Trump's impeachment trial in the Senate would begin in earnest down there at the Capitol—that epicenter of democracy—in a couple of days. The boys were excited to see KD, on Martin Luther King Day, and his father was looking forward to seeing his son.

KD, free to travel as he pleased all season long, did not show.

JANUARY 20, 2020 ⏩

Philadelphia

THE NBA REQUIRED its employees to stand "in a dignified posture" for "The Star-Spangled Banner"—no hands in pockets, no talking, no special T-shirts, no gum. Not a single player had made an effort with the union to change the rule since Kap drew so much attention to its racist roots and to the persistence of systemic racism in America and American sport. But only two of the Nets put their hands to their hearts during the pregame ceremony. Several prayed. By *o'er the land of the free*, one player from each end of the Brooklyn flank swerved behind the lineup, like planes dog-fighting midair.

Wilson Chandler respected his family in the military. But he stood there during the national anthem with his hands behind his back, wearing an NBA-issued MLK shirt on Dr. King's holiday in Philadelphia, and remembered the song's missing verse about slave ownership. He thought about the carceral attack from Washington on Black America during his childhood, how "tough-on-crime" bills had helped send his father and his uncles to prison. And he had nightmares about his sophomore year in high school in Benton Harbor, Michigan, when a white cop had chased Terrance Shurn, who was Black, off his motorcycle and into a wall. Terrance Shurn was 28 years old. Days later, Wilson had walked into a riot, flanked by the National Guard.

"When I look at the American flag, it is not as racially symbolic as the Confederate flag, but a lot of stuff has *happened* under the American flag," Wilson said. "So I feel like, what's the difference between the Confederate and the American flag? Slavery was legal, but that's the only difference."

Wilson had been reading *The Assassination of Fred Hampton*, about how the Chicago police and federal law enforcement conspired to kill the Black Panther hero. Then he read two histories of the socialist activist Eugene Debs, concurrently, and the prison letters of the self-taught revolutionary George Jackson, too. Wilson was more curious about radical thought than mainstream Black history for the same reason he liked Tupac more than Jay-Z and The Hovites. "Jay-Z," he said, "is what you wanna be as a business guy: He's influential; he's Jay-Z. But Tupac is like that '70s, like Black Panthers, Fred Hampton—the way *they* speak to you is, like, they're not talking *over* you, they talking *at* you. They talking *with* you."

This from a guy who dropped out of DePaul in the middle of class, drove home right there and then to enter the NBA Draft early; who hadn't known whether Beethoven was a man or a band, but who'd recently taken his friend from the West Side of Chicago, whose son had just been killed in a drive-by, to the symphony; who saw contemporary art shows weekly, on the road with the Nets. Wilson's education in activism had begun when he returned from China to Obama's America at 25, talking with his Denver Nuggets teammate Andre Iguodala on the team plane about what power meant to an athlete with a platform—about what a "platform" even was.

Wilson enjoyed speaking his mind on Twitter, which he likened to flirting with women over text as opposed to masking his shyness in person. Watching a 2020 Democratic presidential primary debate alone in his hotel room at the Four Seasons in Philadelphia, he was the only active NBA player tweeting, to his 150,000-plus followers, about politics: *Love how they always apologize when they want those black votes.* He tweeted his frustration at the governor of Michigan and urged clemency for a man who had been locked up for twenty-four of potentially sixty years in prison after selling three pounds of weed to a police informant. Wilson considered really going after the governor on prison reform, on the legacy of The War on Drugs. He thought "I'm not educated enough" was an excuse from players more scared of losing an endorsement deal than he was, and Wilson told me that he still felt the NBA was too conveniently woke: "They seen all the backlash the NFL got, so they're like, 'Well, we can't be the NFL, but we can't also go *all* the way over to this side either. We've gotta be a *little* bit more progressive, make it *seem* like we have total freedom of speech. But don't kneel! That's in your contract that you can't, so don't kneel! But you can have freedom of speech.'"

Wilson and Garrett raised their eyebrows at their conjoining lockers one night, when a video of Jay-Z and Beyoncé went viral—the power couple was sitting down for the national anthem at the Super Bowl, and the internet wondered if it was a sly stand-in for a kneel.

"He got what he wanted," Wilson said of Jay-Z. "He got a partnership with the NFL. What the fuck he gonna kneel for?"

The internet had placed great expectations upon the A-list; Jay-Z, who was ostensibly in charge of the Super Bowl performances, said he'd been peering toward the field over concerns about the singer's microphone. "I think it's just because it was them," Garrett concluded of the social-media speculation, as followers hoped for a leader and the haters kept hunting.

"I'm gonna start taking a knee at the anthem myself, actually," Wilson said. "Yeah, I'm gonna start next game."

Garrett looked at his teammate, spellbound, because Garrett never thought he would kneel himself, and because this would be a very big deal, the first NBA player to demonstrate as Kap had, even though an entire WNBA team, the Indiana Fever, had knelt more than three years earlier. But Wilson, as serious in his swiftly activating approach as he was realistic about the execution of celebrity dissent, was joking—sometimes he worried that the best he could do was tweet. "Politics is a touchy subject," he said. Like Colin Kaepernick, he didn't vote in the primaries.

Garrett and Wilson had made plans to watch a debate together on a road trip a few days later, but Wilson, awaiting the birth of his son, had to take a sudden leave of absence. From home in Michigan, Wilson watched the former New York mayor Mike Bloomberg say of teenagers that marijuana may be "damaging their brains," and texted: *Clown!* Switching back and forth between the debate and ESPN at the Four Seasons in Washington, Garrett was just glad to see the Democratic Socialist senator Bernie Sanders talking about judicial reform and legalized weed in the same sentence. But, he told me, pulling on the vest of another three-piece suit after the next night's loss to the Wizards, "I'm not sure Bernie is electable."

As the Nets left Washington for Atlanta, Garrett's father drove through the night to see him play against the Hawks, seven and a half hours from Baton Rouge, and flopped on the couch at the team hotel. "Wake your ass up, son," Collis said. "Time to talk." And they talked for hours. About the charter school the family owned in Louisiana. About the Nets' losing streak. About America. Collis saw his son evolving from a religious idealist into a Democratic pragmatist, and he knew by then that Garrett would have a major impact on this Brooklyn team—on the development of Kevin Durant and Kyrie Irving, of Wilson Chandler, as men. When you're losing, whether you're a family, or a team, or a country, that's when a leader comes in, Collis told Garrett. The permanently unfinished work of the fed-up and the sensible need not be fulfilled by athletes, of course, but athletes were, due to their accomplished wealth and aging bodies, provided second and even third careers. Garrett didn't have to pull a Kap if he looked up to Obama instead. "Colin Kaepernick decided to take a knee," Collis said, "and he did that because he knew he *had* to do it. Because it was *in* him." Everybody, he reminded Garrett, must walk in their own sneakers.

The Nets lost by twenty-three in Atlanta—"a wake-up call," Garrett said in the locker room—but Collis couldn't wait around afterward: There was more history in the making to attend to, at their alma mater in Baton Rouge, so Garrett's dad hit the road back down I-85.

LSU was finally retiring the jersey of Mahmoud Abdul-Rauf, the shooter Collis used to take little Garrett and his brother to see. "He was Trae Young and Steph Curry before Trae Young and Steph Curry," said the commentator on ESPN before the halftime ceremony. "If he was coming up in the game right now, he'd have a million Instagram followers."

Now that social media ruled the conversation, Mahmoud did not believe that athletes should make a difference in silence. "When you see something that's wrong and unjust," he told me, "there should be some type of expectation toward doing something. Now, I'm not saying everybody has to be a Kaepernick, or Muhammad Ali, but at least do something visible."

Mahmoud's protest of "The Star-Spangled Banner," like Kap's, was supposed to be invisible. Sometimes he tied his shoe during the anthem, which, since he suffers from Tourette's syndrome, could take a minute or two. Sometimes he stretched, or else stayed behind in the Denver Nuggets locker room for a few minutes longer. For nearly a year, nobody noticed—there *was* no social media—until a local reporter did, in March 1996. Then Mahmoud called the anthem "a symbol of oppression and tyranny," setting off a full-blown scandal. The commissioner at the time, David Stern, told him to remain in the locker room or come out and stand, or else face suspension. Mahmoud said no. He eventually made a deal to stand and pray, but Mahmoud knew that a setup was in motion, by the same system of oppression he'd been peacefully protesting. He got traded, his minutes disappeared, he kept resisting and researching—covered up the swooshes on his sneakers, visited Section Eight housing on road trips—but he was out of the NBA within twenty-five months of being seen and heard. By the time he made one last run at his first career, in 2001, somebody burned down his house.

Kap hadn't known much about Mahmoud when he began such a similar protest in 2016, and no NBA players had reached out to Mahmoud either, back when hoopers considered kneeling in 2017. "It was definitely disappointing to see them not take a knee, but even more disappointing," Mahmoud said, "was, look, man: *Protest the game.* Hit 'em in the pocket, right? Some people say this is too radical. Well, what's happening to people of color—what's happening to Black people—is *super*-radical, is super-oppressive and unjust." Mahmoud saw the same structure in place that had blackballed Curt Flood in baseball, and Craig Hodges and himself in the NBA, and, for going on three years now, Colin Kaepernick in the NFL. He thought that hoopers—if they really wanted to be activists rather than spokesmen for the cause, wanted to fight the good fight instead of preaching it— could *boycott* basketball until something changed. But, like any successful rebellion, they would need a plan, in this case to ease the economic burden of protesting without playing, and so likely without paychecks. Perhaps, Mahmoud thought, they could call it The Revolutionary Fund.

Up in Section 218 of the Pete Maravich Assembly Center, a true revolutionary was smiling as wide as when he'd first met the man of the hour. At six-foot-four in a green army-style jacket, plus eight inches for the 'fro, easy, he was tough to miss, Colin Kaepernick was. But he was quiet, and he'd slid into his seat after the anthem—he'd been too busy catching up with Mahmoud in the green room to make LSU's game on time. At center court, in a red windowpane sportcoat, Mahmoud hugged his former coach—the one who gave him a copy of Malcolm X's autobiography—and shed a tear into the old man's sweater. "I knew he was gonna start crying," Kap told a friend sitting next to him. "But you know what? He still look *good*! He didn't have that *ugly* cry!"

After the halftime ceremony, Kap began making his way toward the exit. One friend had been worried about accompanying him in such a potentially hostile environment. Since his blackballing, he'd been seen in public at only a single pro game—a basketball game, rooting for the Warriors in the 2019 playoffs "because they've always supported me." Steph Curry had introduced his baby son to Kap, saying he should remember the name Kaepernick: "If you don't know who this is, you'll read about him in the history books." But that was at a game in *Portland*, and this was still Louisiana, where legislators had threatened to cut LSU funding in 2017 if there was any kneeling from the football team, which had just visited Trump at the White House. An older gentleman—an older white gentleman, round as a basketball—approached Kap in the aisle and shook his hand. "I just want to tell you, I was in the service—I was in government—and what you're doing means so much to me." The act of taking one knee had, in fact, been suggested to Kap by a white guy who'd played on the Seattle Seahawks and served as a Green Beret—kneeling is a military sign of respect for a fallen brother. This LSU fan had fought to defend the very principle Colin Kaepernick was expressing: freedom. Who couldn't root for that?

Back in the arena's makeshift greenroom, Collis Temple looked out at the scene. He saw one man rightfully celebrated—No. 35 was in the rafters at last. And he walked up to another man, whose livelihood had been assassinated by the sports business—No. 7 was still unemployed by football, though he was so clearly alive with activism. Collis could appreciate, with the distance of time, that even a trailblazer like himself had not been willing to call out a racist restaurant worker to his face, nor a racist coach, back in the height of the civil rights movement. He had not risked his career for his principles. "I wouldn't have put it all on the line," he said. "I probably would have preferred to earn money."

But occasionally, Collis thought, along come the bravest of Americans, who tell it like it is when the game is rigged and the nation is on a losing streak—and who actually do something about what is wrong. These American heroes *are* the trail, along the barbed pathway to progress. "Just you being here," Collis told Kap, "that's a huge deal." He thought of Muhammad Ali, holding up the torch in his fist for Team USA at the opening ceremony of the Olympics in '96—of how the champ's conscientious objection had finally been accepted as a principle of the United States of America. "All these years later, everybody was like, 'Well, maybe he was right after all.'" He looked at Colin Kaepernick on the sidelines at the basketball game, and he hoped the trail might henceforth be the way.

9

KEEPER OF THE SOUL

LEBRON JAMES REMOVED HIS JEWELS, emptied his floral brown jacket for the metal detector and strutted through the Barclays Center tunnel. Photographers and camera operators backpedaled onto each other's toes, defenseless to his championship acceleration. This was the primetime crew, and in the beam of their lights, stardust collided: The L.A. Lakers were in town. LeBron walked in tune to his headphones made by Beats, a company from which he'd made $50 million when it sold to Apple. He walked down the red carpet, which was black, and stomped over the logo of its Nets corporate sponsor, a sneaker app named *GOAT*. This acronym translated, for sports fans across the globe, to Greatest of All Time.

There could never be a single greatest basketball player, or else the debate would die out. Even Michael Jordan, during a rare public speaking appearance that very afternoon in Paris, said that LeBron James was "*one* of the best players in the world," reminding the record-counters that the two 23's had played in different eras, with evolving rules and atmospheres. LeBron, though, was a constant ballast; having absorbed all challengers with an exuberant gravitas and adapted to a more generous style, he'd redefined himself as one of the best passers in the NBA—a point guard, actually. Kevin Durant, occasionally sick of his own talent, had a player-of-the-year trophy on the floor of his closet, propping up a stockpile of his fashion-designer housemate's latest streetwear collection. As these two towering figures and their fellow superstars of the 2010's aged into their thirties, they were hyper-conscious of both their place in the pantheon and how the next wave of complete players might render them slightly more forgettable, sandcastle memories washed back into a legendary sea.

NBA players especially enjoyed quibbling over their own GOAT lists: MJ, LeBron and Kareem were in the top five, for sure. Bill Russell had to rank over Wilt Chamberlain, for more reasons than one. KD, at 31, was already in the mix. Magic and Bird. Shaq, too. And, of course, Kobe Bryant, the singular bridge from one generation of greatness to the next, who was in the process of being elected to the Naismith Memorial Basketball Hall of Fame's Class of 2020.

Here in the tunnel, LeBron led his team from the bus to the visitors' locker room, through a corridor decorated by Brooklyn's general manager with large framed photographs to lure (the Nets' state-of-the-art practice facility), to re-celebrate (Jay-Z in the black-and-white jersey) and to intimidate (that time Jarrett Allen blocked LeBron). No such feeble distraction, however, nor any damn list, could deter King James from his business of champions. Not this year. The Lakers hadn't made the playoffs during his first season in L.A., but they sat atop the powerful Western Conference now, largely thanks to the production of 26-year-old Anthony Davis, for whom LeBron and his associates had traded most of the franchise's young core of talent, and who was playing better than the 35-year-old GOAT directing The Lake Show. Where LeBron had sensed an irrevocable misalignment with Kyrie's ornery reflex to his wisdom, he saw AD relishing in a dominant partnership. "It's just unfair," AD told me soon thereafter, while playing a game of *NBA2K* on PlayStation as the new-look Lakers.

LeBron was about to pass Kobe for third place on the all-time scoring list, but none of the hyperbole around his thirty-three-thousand-and-somethingth point fazed LeBron. That meant it didn't faze his team, which, aside from its two franchise players in the underground hallway, was an amalgamation of deferential veterans with lots of playoff experience, welcomed like new brothers-in-law setting out for a family vacation. "When we go on the road," LeBron said, "it's just *us*."

Two minutes after LeBron had made his black-carpet entrance, Kyrie sashayed past the *GOAT* logo alone toward the home-team locker room, locked-in with his head turned away from the cameras. He snapped, at no one in particular: "What are you guys, paparazzi?"

Swaggy though he'd been during the first three games of his return from the sore shoulder, Kyrie had peeled back the curtain, with an Illuminati eye toward the off-season and 2021. "I mean, it's transparent, it's out there," he told reporters, even though it wasn't. "It's glaring, in terms of the *pieces* that we need in order to be at that next level." He went on to rattle off the Nets' many injuries, to compliment the "complementary young guys" developed by Kenny Atkinson and The Program. He hinted at rosters now and rosters to come. "Collectively, I feel like we have great pieces," he said, "but it's pretty glaring we need one more piece or two more pieces that will complement myself, KD, DJ, GT, Spence, Caris, and we'll see how that evolves."

Pieces.

There had been speculation in the press, since Kyrie and KD arrived in Brooklyn, that the franchise might maneuver to add another player of their elite caliber who could propel the Nets into the Lakers stratosphere. Bradley Beal from Washington, perhaps. The car-jumper Blake Griffin. Maybe one of their former teammates like Kevin Love or even, if Houston continued to crumble, The Beard himself—James Harden, who'd taken to wearing a headband over corn rows as an accessory to his facial hair, had just scored his twenty thousandth career point. *The Nets*, surmised the ESPN insider Zach Lowe, *are gonna be the team that most faces the question: "Do we want to cash some of that depth in for A Third Star, or are we gonna ride with that depth?"*

But "pieces"? NBA Twitter loved that one: *Kyrie really playing GM through the media?* Charles Barkley shouted on TNT, too: *That ain't yo job!* And on ESPN, the pundits Michael Wilbon and Tony Kornheiser went hoarse: *Why is he judge and jury?! He's a fabulous player to watch, except he can't lead a group of Cub Scouts! That's why teammates are happy when he's not there!*

In the lead-up to the primetime Lakers game, after his word-salad transparency forced him to apologize to his coach and to Jarrett Allen and Joe Harris, assuring them that he did not mean to throw them under the team bus by leaving them off his list, Kyrie explained to me why he felt so misunderstood by people who yammer on television for a living. "It's not like I'm an asshole yelling at everybody in the frigging locker room all the time," he said, although by several accounts he was, some of the time.

He admired the legacy of The Decision upon control: Superstars could commandeer the front office to install their coaches and former colleagues of choice, because superstars could deliver the championships. That much he'd learned from LeBron James in Cleveland, enough to walk into the owner's office and demand out. Was that the city Kyrie really wanted to champion, if it wasn't his roster to manipulate and his culture to dictate?

"I'm going to continue to push," Kyrie went on. "I'm going to continue to demand greatness out of myself and demand greatness out of my teammates, and we go from there. If it's harsh as a leader or too much for anybody, if you're not in our locker room, stay the fuck out. It's as simple as that."

Since the cortisone shot powered him back to the court a month earlier, Kyrie had been over-indexing on basketball over life, watching game tape with his trainer and his daughter, before putting her to bed at night. Why yell at Joe Harris on the free-throw line in front of the cameras, the trainer asked Kyrie, when you could school him at halftime, or hold him accountable for his shot selection in the film room the next day? Kyrie continued to become self-aware enough to realize that he could lead with softer power, that Joe Harris was not the problem— that maybe Kyrie was. When Kyrie literally pushed the 20-year-old Dzanan Musa into position with a healthy twelve-foot shove earlier in the season, Kyrie took the heat and the GIFs, while Musa remarked, "He's one of the best players in the world. You *got* to have an ego, you *got* to." As KD put it: "He's not a dick in the locker room. He's a *solid*-ass teammate. He's not doing too much. He's doing just enough."

It's as simple as this: Somebody's gotta be the asshole. Kyrie learned that from Kobe Bryant.

The student had followed all the Mambaisms since he and his assistant coach in Cleveland, Phil Handy, sat down to that dinner with Kobe in 2015 and they'd taken Kobe's helicopter back to the team hotel. "Don't be afraid to be who you are," Handy remembered Kobe telling Kyrie. "You don't have to blend *in*—you can stand *out*." After Kobe lost to LeBron and Kyrie's

Cavaliers one last time on their title run in 2016, The Black Mamba offered this assessment: "Every team should have that lightning rod, because the happy-go-lucky stuff doesn't work." The locker-room asshole had to be good at driving "inner conflict," to make a dynastic team stronger. Kobe had, for example, once told his teammates at practice, "You motherfuckers are soft like Charmin in this motherfucker!" LeBron couldn't create this sort of tension on the Cavs if they were to be champions, Kobe assessed back in 2016, because LeBron was too good at uniting people. "But you have to have somebody else that's going to create that tension, and"—Kobe gulped, into a smile—"maybe it's Kyrie."

Handy, who'd coached Kobe, LeBron and Kyrie and was back on the Lakers bench, seeking his fifth consecutive Finals appearance and his second straight title, was a kind of Jedi of the post-MJ era of GOATs. He thought The Mamba Proverb of Necessary Conflict remained strong in the still-young man who could inherit Kobe's lightning rod. "There were a lot of things that Kyrie took from Kobe, and there's a lot of things he took from LeBron, and meshed those things together," Handy said. "But people don't really understand what it takes to win a championship in this league."

Weaving between LeBron and Kyrie on the court as the ex-teammates avoided pregame eye contact with each other at Barclays, the coach appreciated that LeBron had needed a down year to build back the Lakers into this contender, and that LeBron was now trolling haters online who'd labeled him an aging #WashedKing. Coach Handy knew that Kyrie, who'd missed nearly 25 percent of his teams' regular-season games in a nine-year career, only got happier when he entered important games, like this one, healthy in mind, body and soul. The coach listened to a full arena begin to uncork a new rivalry—

Whhhhhhhhhoooaaaaaa—as LeBron backed down Kyrie's bad shoulder on the wing, for their first confrontation in Brooklyn. He saw the arrogance on display as Kyrie, imposing himself between LeBron and the referee when a call went Brooklyn's way, let out a spit-spraying *Yeah! Yeeeeah!* The coach witnessed the Lakers run away with the game when LeBron scored four times in just over a hundred seconds, including a turnaround jumper over Kyrie, complete with a staredown of Kyrie's friends in the front row. The competitiveness had spilled all over the crowd like the baby powder LeBron clapped into the air at the scorer's table before every game—he hadn't been able to find any that night, after a part-time equipment staffer for Brooklyn, kid-brother franchise that it remained, conveniently left his bottle of talcum in the tunnel.

After the game, LeBron walked over to Bill Clinton, who'd been sitting courtside with Joe Tsai. This was an extra, *extra* echelon of GOAT status, because there was family, and there were championships, and then there was building a legacy bigger than one's own ambitions, up in the rarified air of executive power. "If you do anything," the former president implored King James, "go make a difference." LeBron lingered in the locker room with his longtime business partners until close to midnight, making decisions and deals.

LeBron eclipsed Kobe's scoring record two nights later. The number didn't matter to him, he said. But to be linked with the GOATs, however it happened—to live in infamy—was deeply meaningful, and it made LeBron remember when he'd traveled to a summer basketball camp on the circuit, way back in 2001. He was 16, a rising junior in high school; Kobe was 22, already the reigning back-to-back champ, on his way to a three-peat. "Don't rely on basketball for your happiness, because it's not gonna happen," Kobe told the students. "You make sure you balance your life out, you have something there for yourself in life, so when the game is over, you know exactly what you want to do."

KYRIE IRVING'S ALTER EGO, the septuagenarian shit-talker Uncle Drew, was not meant to last in Hollywood. Pepsi had financed the script for a film version of its viral ad campaign, and *Uncle Drew* the movie had gotten made. But Kyrie was annoyed by the filming and had walked off set in August 2017 to process the news that his trade demand from Cleveland had been fulfilled in Boston. (He and Kobe had discussed where a deal to someplace far-flung, like Phoenix, might have left his priorities.) He was exhausted again this subsequent summer from performing in the movie's ceaseless marketing campaign, as he recovered from another knee surgery—the screws placed in his leg during the 2015 playoffs had become infected at the bone, ending his first season with the Celtics before the 2018 playoffs began.

Then, four days after he walked the red carpet with his family at the New York City premiere of *Uncle Drew*, LeBron upended the culture at the start of 2018 free agency, announcing that he was taking his talents to the Los Angeles Lakers. The mega-brand of LeBron & Co. could become as gigantic as the sign in the hills, an unchaseable GOATness.

Kyrie planned a boys' trip to Vegas with his friend Kevin Durant and their respective entourages. A good time was had by all. Maybe too good of a time. But having each won championships, Kyrie and KD shared a curiosity for, as they called it, life on the mountaintop: "That steady climb, it starts in the summertime and goes throughout the season," Kyrie explained on the podcast of the Boston super-fan Bill Simmons. "Once you get on top of Mount Everest and you're standing there, you're enamored with your personality. Like, people are just *loving* it: Finals MVP, NBA champion. And after that, it's like: *So what's next?*" He'd yet to answer his own question.

To recalibrate during the injured off-season, Kyrie waved off some of his usual promotional schedule and flew to Seattle. His friend Jamal Crawford—an ageless Uncle Drew type himself, having helped lead the Clippers through the Donald Sterling scandal while maintaining a Kyrie-level crossover at 38 years young, and an even better Rolodex—set up a series of stealth five-on-five games for him, alongside rising NBA stars borrowed from his pro-amateur tournament. Kyrie had been in town for two weeks, grinding hard with both eyes focused on the mountaintop, toward a championship with the Boston Celtics. He was warming up for another pickup run at Seattle Pacific University, shooting spot to spot in the trance of his pregame routine, when he thought he saw a GOAT, as if from the corner of a third eye, cane-stepping his way to the bleachers in a Celtics hat.

He did a double take. "Whoa. Wh—" Was that Bill Russell? "Wow."

That it was. They'd gotten to know each other when Mr. Russell made a cameo in an Uncle Drew ad: "I remember at my best, there'd be nights when the whole world would slow down and get very quiet," the legend saged, "like nothing existed outside of this game." Before the cameras rolled, Kyrie had peppered Mr. Russell with questions on-set in the kitchen of a small Cleveland home—this was in the middle of Kyrie's championship season, and he was in full elderly makeup, looking a bit like the gentleman before him. They'd made each other laugh in that funhouse mirror, but Kyrie had to run after an hour, and he left Mr. Russell on the porch, talking to crew members about his favorite players from the emerging generation.

At 84, Mr. Russell kept a low but spry fan's profile in the Seattle area to accompany his *very* active Twitter feed, trolling @realDonaldTrump with an unabashed liberalism honed through his living history. That week when he showed up at the secret pickup games, he'd amplified a viral video of the congressman Beto O'Rourke telling voters that he could "think of nothing more American" than athletes kneeling for the national anthem in peaceful protest, in the heritage of John Lewis on the bridge in Selma and the Freedom Riders on the buses in 1961, and of Medgar Evers, whose assassination led Mr. Russell to run basketball clinics in Mississippi in '64. He was living a fuller and rollicking life, as ever, in his experiences beyond those quiet nights at the empty-seeming arena.

Mr. Russell watched Kyrie's comeback runs for two hours— all five periods, first to a hundred and twenty-five wins—and then Kyrie and his pickup mates from across the NBA pulled up chairs to gather 'round the Hall of Famer by the stands. Mr. Russell came back for the next day's mythology lesson, and he came back a couple more times after that, too. Some days he would talk for five minutes; some days he would drop knowledge for an hour. Mostly the athletes cherished Mr. Russell's stories connecting the civil rights movement to their current overlapping era of two Americas, its celebrity leaders more in-the-making than back in his day.

"You guys have a voice and a platform," Mr. Russell told them. "It's your responsibility to use it."

The storytelling went both ways, as players shook their heads at the vestiges of Mr. Russell's fight. "This generation, especially," Jamal Crawford told me, "they've *heard* the stories, and they have the energy where, like, *enough is enough,* and they're not standing for it. And with that, in turn, they're waking up older generations."

Dr. Martin Luther King Jr. had invited Mr. Russell to join him onstage at the March on Washington in 1963, but Mr. Russell didn't want to helicopter into that movement, so he respectfully declined and chose to sit front-row instead. It was a time when Mr. Russell felt very lonely playing a child's game, because he wanted to help change the world instead. Malcolm X opened young Bill's eyes more than Dr. King, who continued to give him pause because "the white people in Boston liked him, and so I knew something must be wrong. To me, Boston itself was a flea market of racism."

Kyrie was crafting a portion of his history with the Celtics— Mr. Russell had a shamrocked title ring for all but one year in the '60s—and found it interesting that the franchise enshrined its legends in the rafters with numbers only, no names allowed. The banners looked like bingo cards. In 1972, Mr. Russell had tried to get out of the retirement of No. 6 at the Boston Garden; his number should be able to go about as it pleased, he figured, and being made "immortal" by Boston fans did not make him any happier. "I thought of myself as playing for the Celtics, not for Boston," Mr. Russell declared. "The fans could do and think whatever they wanted. If they liked what they saw, fine; if not, the hell with it." Kobe, who had remained close with Mr. Russell since he reached out to him for advice in 2000, had been so happy that Kyrie landed with an historic franchise, but the student wasn't so sure. "It was like this power shift going on in Boston," as the Celtics' young stars shined in 2018 without him, said Kyrie's close friend Brett Carroll, who stayed with him in Seattle that summer. "And then he also realized, 'Wait a minute: I'm trying to champion Boston, but now that I'm looking at the history of Boston, is this a city that I *want* to champion? In terms of their racial history and stuff like that . . . is Boston the type of place I want to represent?'"

In the Seattle gym's bleachers, Mr. Russell spoke with Kyrie about the Celtics heritage, but Kyrie had to leave, to say goodbye to Grandpa George, a local Lutheran minister, and to Grandma Norma, a health-care worker. They'd spent the summer telling Kyrie and his sister how they'd adopted their mother just after birth—from the Standing Rock Sioux reservation in the Dakotas—and raised her in the suburbs of Washington State to become a politically outspoken student-athlete in Boston, where Kyrie's parents had met. Kyrie was born in Australia—his dad had tried to make it as a pro hooper there—but the Irvings moved back to the States and separated. Shortly thereafter, four-year-old Kyrie's mother fell ill with sepsis, a sudden inflammatory condition, and survived only two days in the hospital. Elizabeth Irving was 29 years old. Before he could climb again in 2018, Kyrie felt a need to be grounded. So he channeled his mom through Grandpa George, who had developed a passion for Indigenous ministries, immigrant outreach and evangelical missions. "Government-sponsored greed" had led to genocide, George preached, but people of good will, living or dead, could keep hope alive—young Elizabeth included. "She's with him now," Kyrie said.

The vision quest continued, as Kyrie lifted off in a private jet through Washington's wildfire skies and landed in Bismarck, North Dakota. From the tarmac, gazing far along the plains toward Standing Rock, he and his friends wondered if they could bottle the air and sell it. Kyrie's heritage and headiness were combusting in the sagey breeze: He hated Twitter and was about to quit it, but he was there because of a political tweet. To his three million followers, he had posted his support for the ongoing demonstrations of the proposed eleven-hundred-mile Keystone Pipeline near tribal land—less than an acre of which, unbeknownst to

Kyrie, belonged to him. A biological sister of Kyrie's mom, Kelly Brinkley, had been signing Kyrie and his sister's land grants for years, but she didn't make much of it until she looked up at a restaurant one evening in 2011 and saw that he was expected to be picked first, out of Duke University, in the NBA Draft. Still, she told me, "I didn't want to intrude on their lives." Nobody else in the tribe seemed to know of Kyrie's Indigenous ties until his 2016 pro-protest tweet led to a follow-up question during an interview about Kobe's mentorship on ESPN, when he let slip that he was "actually Sioux Indian." Elders watched the ensuing viral clip at tribal council, and Kyrie's family tree was unearthed. Meanwhile, Kyrie had gotten the emblem of the Standing Rock Sioux tattooed on the back of his neck and on the tongue of his signature shoe. Another secret was out.

Days after sitting with Mr. Russell and Grandpa George in the gyms and tony outskirts of Seattle, drums thumped and the sacred circle enclosed around Kyrie, a cluster of two thousand people strong, as he put *family* business first. The elders of the tribe placed a feather in his hair and, to conclude the Lakota naming ceremony, bestowed his tribal name: *Hela*, also known as Little Mountain.

Onstage, he was introduced to an eight-year-old boy named Kyrie Irving—the child's father had been a hooper and, when he couldn't think of a first name for his son, had spotted highlights of a kid from Jersey who he thought "played like a Native: effort-less moves that you've never seen before, fast-paced, more free." The guest of honor called out to the boy on the other side of the stage like fans did for him: *Ky-RIEEEEEEEE!* Backstage, he met his mom's sister, Kelly; she, too, had named her oldest daughter Kyrie, a year before the superstar was born. "It's pro-nounced *Keer-ee-ay*," she said. Kyrie Irving—the famous one—laughed at all of this . . . "home loving," he called it. He looked at Grandpa George, who'd given him the name. He learned that his mother's mother was a hooper on the reservation, and a high-school coach, too. He'd never felt closer to his elders, or to a permanent team. "I'm with you guys forever," he told the tribe. "I hope you don't mind that." Little Mountain wished Kobe a happy birthday, then flew back to Seattle to bid farewell for the summer to Grandpa George.

Two months later, Kyrie's grandfather died suddenly, at 77. From that moment, he later told his friend Kevin Durant, "life became way more important than basketball. Anything I was doing in basketball, I didn't really care." He tried to stop internalizing the media's misperception of his ego. He no longer felt beholden to his promise of a long-term deal in Boston. Uncle Drew was long gone from his brand and his grand plan, and Grandpa George was looking down upon him. Kyrie, aging fast but on the mend, felt a clearing air. He skipped a game to attend his grandfather's memorial, and he started climbing the path home, toward Brooklyn.

JANUARY 26, 2020 📷

Manhattan

THE GREAT ONES are never late to work, they say. Michael, LeBron, Kobe, whoever's got next—first ones in, last ones out. Kyrie, for cosmic reasons he still could not possibly understand but also because he was scheduled to play the Knicks and his shoulder still hurt, arrived extra early to Madison Square Garden on the last Sunday in January. His game-day routine, three and a half hours before tip-off, was a roundball ballet: Kyrie rested his iPhone below the hoop, adjusted his wireless earphones, turned on his playlist and rehearsed his spinning and fading and pogo-sticking swirls, adapted from Michael and Kobe and choreographed on his own, three shots at a time, all over the court without saying a word, save for flowing the occasional Kendrick Lamar lyric, out loud, when he made several in a row: *How they look at me reflect on myself, my family, my city / What they say 'bout me reveal if my reputation would miss me.*

A couple of the Nets' benchwarmers stood by on the sideline, watching and waiting to get their extra work in, but most of Kyrie's teammates were waking from their naps or pulling up to the Garden in an Uber when the texts began streaming in from all over, with equal measures of disbelief and fear, and into the team group chat: *Y'all see about Kobe?*

Almost all of the players in the visitors' locker room thought such a horror as this must have been fake news. Some more of that TMZ paparazzi bullshit. Text messages kept arriving—soft buzzes and faint alarm bells, ringing with the impossible. A helicopter crash? Up in the Calabasas hills, in Cali? Heavy fog? "What the *fuck*?!" No way. But it was true, and Gigi had been in the air, too, next to seven more souls onboard the chopper, on their way to play in her basketball tournament, with the girls of Team Mamba, at Kobe's gym. Everyone, everywhere, was so very confused. "What the *fuck*?" Kobe Bryant was 41 years old.

A whimpering hush fell over the locker room as Kyrie sank into the arms of the third-string point guard Theo Pinson, and wept, then gathered his things to head home. DeAndre Jordan placed a towel over his head. Wilson Chandler stared at the wall. Garrett Temple carried an engagement ring in his pocket. For an hour and a half, the only regular sound in the room was that of overgrown men crying. "Kobe was right there with us," Kenny Atkinson reminded them, "just a few weeks ago." Not a single member of the Nets wanted to play against the Knicks that day. Kyrie told his coach that he would not. He could not.

Arriving home to his penthouse in Dumbo, Kyrie sat on the couch with his personal chef, Corey Bryant, who had no relation but helped his boss smile through the shock. Kyrie remembered the summer of 2012, when he was on USA Basketball's next-generation team, as one of the young studs in a Vegas gym for the implicit purpose of warming up the GOATs for the Olympics. He was only 20, but he'd gone coast-to-coast in a scrimmage, crossing up Kobe behind the back, then crossing over KD on the hesitation, then spinning past James Harden in the front court, then crossing over Kobe—who'd been chasing him down the floor—*again*, behind the back and through the legs, before dishing off in front of Carmelo Anthony. "Kobe couldn't stop me, Kev couldn't stop me, nobody could stop me," he said on the couch, quivering. "It was magical." The chef asked about Kyrie's challenge that week before the Olympics, to a game of one-on-one with the 33-year-old GOAT. Kyrie had rehearsed his pitch in the mirror, and though his heart was pounding, he was confident in his craft. "Son, are you crazy?" Kobe asked. "Are you *crazy?*" They compromised on playing for $50,000 for charity, sometime down the line, and Kobe told Kyrie to go watch some game tape in the meantime. The GOAT was only entertaining the conversation because Kyrie was so talented. But he also sensed a glint of himself, in that the kid possessed the balls to ask. They never had, Kyrie realized at his kitchen counter in Brooklyn, gotten to play that game.

While the Nets and Knicks trudged onto the court at MSG, Kyrie watched highlights of Kobe's eighty-one-point classic from 2006 on his flat-screen instead. He was following the Sioux mourning ritual to *walk on*, laying down your craft for a while, so that you can lead the way; tradition assigns a Keeper of the Soul, who vows to live in harmony among the living for one calendar year, until the soul of the dead can be released to a heavenly spirit named *Wakan Tanka.* "When a party of warriors go on a hunt," the Sioux holy man Black Elk preaches in *The Sacred Pipe*, "he should sit alone on a hill and with his pipe he should send his voice to the powers above for the good of the hunt and for the good of all the people." Kyrie was a loner, but the last thing this Keeper of the Soul needed was to be alone. He'd been depressed for a year, since losing what could feel like his mother and grandfather together. He thought about opening night at Barclays, when he'd dropped fifty on the anniversary of Grandpa George's death, but only because KD, DJ, GT, Spence, Caris . . . even the young guys— they'd all gotten Kyrie's back to cheer him up that evening. He needed a team.

The next day, Kyrie invited his Nets teammates to a rooftop seance at their spot, The Secret Side Bar at Downtown Brooklyn's Tillary Hotel. Kyrie rolled up in a vintage Lakers jersey—*BRYANT 8*—and somebody rolled a little sacred pipe of their own. Almost all of the Nets had lost someone close in the past few years: KD's adopted brother, in a parking-lot assassination; Spencer's high-school teammate, shot when he entered the wrong apartment; DeAndre's friend he talked to during the national anthem, in a car accident; for Taurean's grandmother, it was breast cancer. And all of them had a connection to Kobe: In Maryland, 17-year-old KD had woken up his dad at midnight to watch The Black Mamba drop eighty-one on the West Coast; in Bosnia, seven-year-old Dzanan Musa stayed up with his father even later—both hoopers were transfixed by how one man could so effortlessly conduct the crowd and the game in unison. "He knows nobody can guard him," KD said, "*and* he's smiling while he's doin' it."

Kyrie made a toast to Kobe and Gigi, offering his reminder that time was not promised. The Nets celebrated Garrett, who had still popped the question on the night of the tragedy, after running in place for the required game at the Garden; he and Kára agreed to love with urgency—they thought Kobe and his wife, Vanessa, would appreciate that—and to begin trying to have a child. Spencer had an idea to effectively retire Kobe's jersey, by switching the number on his back from No. 8, even though it was against league policy; players around the NBA would soon follow. But some of Kyrie's friends legitimately wondered, especially at a time when he'd been trying to connect more with his daughter, whether he would ever play again. Whether he would retire. They texted him their condolences, and he texted back: *Journey doesn't stop here for us, we keep this shit going just like Kobe wanted us to! We got shit to tackle, I want to leave this game with nothing left! We in this together. We are all hurting but we are all family! That's what he did, he connected us all to be family.*

JANUARY 29, 2020 ▶️

Brooklyn

A MOMENT OF SILENCE was in order, and teams across the NBA, returning to play with a shiver and a sigh, bowed their heads before the national anthem, mourning for an American icon. Barclays Center, though, had been remixed into Chinese: red-and-yellow scoreboards, red-and-yellow spotlights, Lion Dancers in the hallways, Fan Dancers on the hardwood—details up and down the arena seemed plastered with everything but the five stars of a foreign flag, to celebrate a previously scheduled Lunar New Year theme night that Joe Tsai wanted to get just right. Players muttered about the awkwardness of the evening from under their franchise-issued red-and-yellow warmups, with *BRYANT* on the back and *NETS* on the front . . . in Mandarin. It would come to be one of Kyrie's favorite shirts, but even he was tapping his sneakers in impatient sorrow.

As an ambassador from the Chinese consulate began to steal the pregame stage at center court, Brooklynites eye-rolled through his two-minute oratory and paused their Instagram broadcasts.

"Enough about the Corona thing," a fan said, and headed for the beer line.

The ambassador continued, introducing thousands of Americans to something so profoundly obscure and jingoized as to seem nonexistent. "This new year has extraordinary circumstances," he said. "Right now, at this moment, many people are bravely fighting the coronavirus. I hope you could join them and support them in this fight. Because we are a global community and a shared future."

Finally came the spotlight's ember of Lakers purple and gold, and with it The Mamba on the big screen: Kobe D-ing up MJ. Kobe buzzer-beating D-Wade. Kobe celebrating with Shaq. And, in the final highlight of his public life, Kobe the father teaching his daughter Gigi, courtside, as they cheered on the Brooklyn Nets. Flowers rested upon Seats No. 7 and No. 8, helping to fill an emptiness in the spirit of the game. A young woman started playing "The Star-Spangled Banner" on the violin—in her Kobe jersey—and Kyrie shed a tear.

There was no easy path to follow toward Kobe's place on the mountaintop of basketball greatness. He had spoken to LeBron on the morning of the crash, congratulated the veteran for passing him in the history books, for continuing to push the game forward. As for KD, he had yet to prove that he could return from a torn Achilles in his prime—even The Black Mamba had never been the same after he'd ruptured his in 2013. But Kobe's gift to his immediate successors, KD tried explaining to me with a tearless stoicism, was to help them sense his multilay-ered renaissance—his symphony—for themselves, as for others: "The lessons that Kobe learned through a game and how he was so eager to give it off to the younger players—not just myself and guys that were No. 1 options on their team, but even role-playing guys," he remembered. "A lot of people said they didn't know him, and I'm like, 'You've seen Kobe in every situation, from rapping, to winning championships, to having kids, to get-ting married, to getting injured on the floor, to crying on TV.'"

Kyrie was not a GOAT, on the court. Not quite. I asked him how he'd been able to transcend what he looked at as just a game—entertainment—to overcome all the loss and hate of the past year and a half, and how Kobe had taught him to spread love to his own daughter, as well as to fans who looked up to Kyrie the way he looked up to his hero, for greatness beyond basket-ball. Kobe had offered him clues, he said, to chasing something bigger than himself. "When you're trying to leave a legacy or leave something of a mark on a game, they're gonna come with a lot of sacrifices, it's gonna come with a lotta heat, it's gonna come with a lot of love, it's gonna come with a lot of *balance* that you must create in your life. And he left a lot of teachings—a lotta breadcrumbs, I call 'em—and I just followed all of them. I just followed every single one."

Upon all the public displays of admiration, a great fathom-less something else encroached. Something more grave, some-how. At a reception upstairs amidst the Barclays Center tribute to Kobe, Adam Silver ran into Dr. David Ho, the pioneering AIDS researcher who had advised the NBA in 1991, when Magic Johnson's revelation upon testing HIV positive helped to normalize that virus. The NBA's relationship with China was still fraught, but the league had more than two hundred em-ployees in Shanghai and Beijing, where the authorities, bracing for an outbreak, cracked down into lockdown: Canonizing Kobe footage had been the first American basketball on Chinese state television since the Morey tweet, and it served as a heartwarming binge-watch for hundreds of millions forced to stay home over the national holidays by a new and deadly virus. The NBA commissioner wanted to know what would come next, half a world away over there, then next after that. Adam Silver wanted the facts, but he wasn't too worried about this thing's impact on the NBA bottom line.

This 2019-nCoV thing presented many unknowns, Dr. Ho warned. It was a bad sign that Chinatown over in Manhattan was so empty, he said. The American entertainment industry might want to prepare for mass testing and for harsh implementations upon mass gatherings, just in case. The White House had launched its own task force for the novel coronavirus that morning; there were five confirmed cases of the respiratory illness in the United States, and Trump told workers at a manufacturing plant "it's going to have a very good ending for us—that I can assure you." The dwindling crowd at Brooklyn's Chinese Heritage Night amped up once more, as Kyrie exited the game—he had mustered twenty points—and Adam Silver, suddenly shook, could only applaud anxiously, after Little Mountain pointed a finger up to the big Black Mamba in the Jumbotron.

Two nights later, Kyrie got to the arena even earlier than usual again. He was always relatively quiet before any game, but a little more so this time. "I'm just locked in," he told DeAndre on the bench as the Barclays public-address announcer began to introduce the starting lineup. "Locked in."

Kyrie could hear, softly, the voice of his mentor, reminding him to keep his right elbow tucked toward the rim for every shot—it was the same breadcrumb Kobe had left him before Kyrie hit the game-winner in Game Seven. And he could hear, loudly, a crowd of 17,732 united in a fragile embrace: The Nets general manager passed around Modelo tall boys to the fans, who chanted *M-V-P*; Kyrie raised the roof and pointed toward the sky again with one hand, thumping his chest with the other. The Keeper of the Soul had summoned enough greatness to score fifty-four points, even as the cortisone was wearing off and a place among the immortals seemed far, far away. He hugged his coach, and the rapper Common, and Clara Wu Tsai, who were sitting next to Kobe and Gigi's empty seats. He hugged his dad, and his stepmom, and anyone close he could find.

The Nets had a record of 21–26, but if the playoffs started that night, they would make it. They had another game, in Washington, D.C., in less than twenty-four hours. Security said to hurry; the bus was packing up, with wives and girlfriends and children waiting for them in the tunnel. So Kyrie spoke quickly and unphilosophically through his postgame media appearance while his teammates cleared out, and he made time for the foreign reporter seeking a message for Kyrie's friends in China: "My condolences going out to everyone dealing with the virus, Kobe, just everyday life—dealing with life."

Through the sliding wooden door off the locker room, LeBron James appeared on both flat-screens inside the Nets players' lounge, grabbing a microphone at Staples Center. Garrett Temple nibbled on crudité from the salad bar. Jarrett Allen stood in silence. Spencer Dinwiddie heard the eulogistic boom of King James and swam his way inside to watch the Lakers' tribute to their lost GOAT. "Oh, shit, I gotta see this!" The State of the Union address was not for three more days—a vote in the Senate all but acquitted Trump of the impeachment charges brought against him—but to the culture, before the state of the world collapsed, this might as well be it.

"Now I got something written down," LeBron began. "You know they asked me to kinda stay on course, or whatever the case may be. But Laker Nation, man, I would be selling y'all short if I read off this shit, so I'mma go straight from the heart." He did, because he had a big one, even if his love was expected to be a performance.

"So in the words of Kobe Bryant, *Mamba Out*," LeBron said on the televisions. "But in the words of *us*, not forgotten." He literally dropped the mic at center court.

The bus engine started up again, the players hugged their sons and daughters tight, and the Brooklyn Nets headed onward to Washington, quietly through a heavying winter's night, alone together.

10

DISINFECTED

FEBRUARY 5, 2020 📷

Brooklyn

IT HAD BEEN a *week*. As if the Kobe grief weren't enough, Kenny Atkinson had suddenly dropped Spencer from the starting lineup after Kyrie's surging return, only for Kyrie to get hurt *again* with a tweaked knee and a worsening shoulder. Unfortunately for Spencer, this had all gone down at the end of voting for the All-Star Game, and so Spencer, despite averaging twenty-four points per game as Brooklyn's incidental superstar during Kyrie's twenty-six-game absence, got snubbed. But he was resigned to life as an underdog, and he saw the All-Star team as a popularity contest among the elite of The League. Being an All-Star in Kobe's book was all the validation he needed. "You don't win things like that," Spencer said, "when you're me."

On the eve of the NBA's midseason trade deadline, Spencer walked into work at Barclays Center and found it difficult to avoid the breaking news on ESPN: The Lakers had called the Nets to inquire about his availability in a deal, as Brooklyn sought to acquire the proper pieces alongside KD, Kyrie and DeAndre. He was not surprised, and had in fact begun pitching himself to investors interested in his block-chain idea not as a gamble but as a commodity, the value of which had never been higher than this season. League lawyers and regulators, however, had only approved Spencer's Fan Shares platform on the condition that he delay it for a year, when he would have the option to play somewhere he felt wanted. Until then, Brooklyn's sixth man remained a flexible asset for a front office to wager with. The general manager, Sean Marks, had sat down with Spencer to reassure him that the Nets were a family, with a franchise culture and a team system that could make anyone a star. But, Spencer told me, "superstars *are* the culture—superstars *are* the system." In the pecking order of the NBA, he felt as expendable as ever.

"For all the stuff we talk about—player empowerment, where we get mad at players for making decisions that they feel are the best for them, or best for their families," he said that night, "these teams are gonna do what they do. I very well might not be here tomorrow."

It was a relief, then, that the Golden State Warriors were visiting: Confronted by serious injuries after five straight Finals appearances, the Warriors had the worst record in the NBA. Plus, everybody got to chat with the champs in Brooklyn, and Spencer always enjoyed chopping it up with his old friend from the University of Colorado, the Warriors backup shooting guard Alec Burks. As Spencer watched the ESPN report about his own market value, however, Alec was informed that the Warriors were about to trade him, too. In the visitors' locker room, Spencer's friend stared at a plate of fruit on the floor, as if recalling a nightmare about pineapples—it was the second time Alec had been shown the door in here in the past fifteen months. Draymond Green, the lone healthy All-Star left on the once-loaded Golden State roster, walked out of his pregame shower and asked what was up. The Warriors were busy shedding more than a third of their roster, that's what—and only the superstars were safe.

A glimmer of joy had returned to the NBA, though, as Steph Curry began tuning up his beloved pregame shooting display; while supporting actors processed their potential next destination, Steph flung effortless three-pointers from the Nets' center-court logo, and fifty-one New York supporters dangled over the railing back to the locker room, screeching for an autograph. His broken hand would be healed by early March, but that didn't stop pundits and fans from insisting that Steve Kerr shut down the golden boy and "tank" for the rest of the season—that Golden State should lose on purpose to secure high draft picks, as Philadelphia had attempted and Brooklyn had refused to do in the mid-2010s. Kerr was aghast at the mere suggestion that Steph might not return: "If the point is because he might get hurt," the coach would say, "then what's the point of ever playing anything? I guess the argument would be, *Well, we're not going to the playoffs*. Are we not trying to entertain our fans? We're selling tickets to all these people who love basketball, and Steph Curry is one of the most amazing, graceful, exciting basketball players on Earth."

The joy principle remained strong with Golden State, even in the bitterest of winters, just as it had in January 2017, when Kerr invited KD out for a drink at Wood Tavern in Oakland. It was that first season of the super-*super*-team, and the Warriors were rolling. But they had a difficult and dramatic stretch ahead, against LeBron's Cavs and KD's former teammates Russ Westbrook and James Harden, who'd begun referring to himself in the third person as The Beard. Nothing had been made easier by KD and Draymond going off during practice—or KD monitoring a pseudonymous "burner" account, tweeting at haters about himself in the third person. When KD arrived at the restaurant, his coach was already sitting at a table in the back, under an oversize mirror that stared back at the star.

Kerr began the lesson: "You know what I respect about Le-Bron? I respect that after he got to Miami, he got sick of the narratives. Sick of the haters. All the talk. So you know what he did?"

"What's that?" KD asked.

Kerr paused for impact. "LeBron just said, *Fuck it.* And then he was great again. Same with Michael. With Kobe. All the greats. First they had to say, *Fuck it.* And then they were on that next level. So you know what you have to do?"

"What's that, Coach?" KD asked.

"Go out and be you. You gotta just say, *Fuck it*, like LeBron did."

KD, looking up at the mirror behind his coach, understood this to be solid advice. He just wasn't sure he bought it. He'd grown wary of the LeBron comparisons, but he'd always been a Jordan guy—KD still frequently watched MJ highlights on YouTube—and it gave Kerr street-cred with his new superstar that he'd played next to the GOAT. Kerr remembered reading negative stories in *The Chicago Tribune*, back in '93, that he might get cut from the Bulls, then playing horribly in practice. He didn't own a portable phone, and nobody was throwing shade by way of the beeper. But the media was consuming him. "What am I *doing*?" Kerr asked himself. A couple mornings later, he simply stopped reading the newspaper.

Within days of their sit-down, Kerr started to notice KD looking at his iPhone in the locker room a little less. Despite the burner account, despite the incessant noise about his "soft" move to join the Warriors and his ability to coexist with Steph the shooter and Draymond the alpha dog, KD found *Fuck it* to be the best advice he'd ever received. "The way you handle the backlash kind of determines your fate, so, on the court, he couldn't have handled the backlash any better," Kerr told me. "But in this modern life, it's easy to get caught up in all the other stuff, and I thought that put a lot of stress on Kevin, just feeling that constant criticism."

Draymond Green also lived by the mantra of *Fuck it*. After he was suspended for swiping at LeBron's balls in the 2016 Finals, he'd immediately sought advice from Kobe, who told him the same thing that Kerr taught KD, and he learned not to let anyone define him but himself. "But that's one of those things that anybody can say," Draymond reminded me. "If you don't live it, it really means nothing."

Two titles later, by the middle of the 2018–2019 season, Kerr's advice wasn't working anymore, and KD could recognize a separation between desire and distraction. "I came in every single day and kept my head down, I didn't say much, I wasn't too excited about much, so my coaches and my teammates thought something was wrong with me," he said. "And my methods may not be, like, welcoming to other people, but it's just how I do things." His looming free-agency decision weighed on the Warriors locker room, rankling Draymond especially. The media seemed to ask KD more questions about playing for the Knicks the next season than the Warriors at that moment. He came to the Bay because he wanted the pressure, but it was also part of the reason he quit the best team in his profession. Kerr kept trying to bring back the joy—who knew what next year might bring?—but then KD got hurt, and then came the thwap of his Achilles, and the Warriors dynasty was fucked.

"I tried, but I failed," Kerr admitted to me, before the Warriors played the Nets in 2020. "I could see the strain on his face every day, especially that third year, just *all* day. But it was, really, he was staring into that phone all the time."

KD hadn't seen many of his former teammates since the Finals, because he'd never bothered returning to the Bay after surgery—his staff had moved him out, and he'd never fully explained why he'd left. But the mellowest guy at Barclays Center had mellowed even more, enjoying his "me time" in Brooklyn detached from the media and fans. On the Brooklyn bench in the fourth quarter, he caught Steph's eye on the other end of the Barclays court, and they pointed at their watches, counting down to the Nets' forty-one-point win. As the buzzer sounded, they sprung up in matching black blazers, and Kerr could barely get a hug in edgewise before KD moved on to Steph for a waltzy back-slapper of a wraparound embrace. Draymond came over and gave Steph faux-shit for greeting the enemy, then left them to it.

The VIP MVPs kept talking, until the cleaning staff had just about finished scrubbing down the court and all the other players were off to worry about where they might live tomorrow. "*Never* come back, bro," Spencer advised his pal Alec with a laugh, as Steph Curry went to eat some popcorn in the locker room, and KD was finally content, doing nothing more than he wanted to.

<hr/>

📷 **JANUARY 25, 2019**

Weston, Massachusetts

THE NIGHT BEFORE the Warriors played the Celtics on network television, Kyrie invited KD to dinner at his mansion, a seven-bedroom spread in the woods of suburban Boston that did not feel particularly lived in. Kyrie had been pointing fingers at his

Celtics teammates in public all month, especially around a loss in Brooklyn. He was battling the flu, but that didn't stop the wine from flowing; Kyrie was preparing to make his power move and move out.

The Warriors' road trip had brought KD to Boston from Washington, and he told Kyrie how—since there was certainly no invitation from Trump this time either—the players had visited with Barack Obama for an hour in private at his office. Steph had set it up, because Obama and Steph were continuing their work on an initiative launched in the wake of the death of Trayvon Martin, to empower young Black men. Obama was a hooper, but in the Warriors meeting he had talked golf with Steph and given props to Klay Thompson for still reading the newspaper every morning. The former president remembered texting KD after his first championship in 2017—KD still found it strange that Obama had complimented, of all things, his defense. Mostly, though, the president had gotten animated around his conference-room table the other day when he heard that KD had just opened his after-school facility, at home in PG County, Maryland. KD had noticed an Obama quote on the wall at The Durant Center: *Change will not come if we wait for some other person or if we wait for some other time. We are the ones we've been waiting for. We are the change that we seek.*

Going home and doing good had been lingering in Kyrie's mind, and the Brooklyn Nets were a team he and KD could control—two max-salary slots, a flexible general manager, a few pieces—while Kyrie built a house in Jersey for his daughter, and perhaps more children yet, to grow up in. KD told a confidant that he didn't think the Warriors would get any better if Kerr couldn't hold Draymond accountable for his outbursts, and that he was occasionally irked when Steph got so much attention from the media and from the fans. Steph clearly felt the love from Obama, too. KD and Kyrie, on the cusp of their free agency, shared a loner's longing to settle down but look straight ahead.

"He didn't like what his situation was," KD said, "and me either in Golden State. And it was just like, 'Hey, man, let's just see how this would work. Let's try it out.' And DJ wanted to play with us to be that center for us that can kinda hold it down, and play for something, really—play for a team that's going somewhere, not just keep moving around and bouncing around to leave."

After leaving OKC nearly three years earlier and experiencing the rage of its fans upon his return with the Warriors, KD didn't feel as bad about bailing on a franchise and its fan base. As he advised the All-Star Gordon Hayward on his 2017 free-agency choice to leave behind the team that drafted him, "You don't owe anybody anything." And by 2019, KD's own Warriors teammate Andre Iguodala had transformed the *Fuck it* mantra into guilt-free advice for his friend. "At this point, fuck *everybody*," Andre told him. "That's including management, anybody—from this team to that team, fans, whoever. Do whatever makes you happy, man, and don't feel like you're letting anybody down with any decision that you make."

KD didn't care about being the king of New York. He didn't want to be the savior of the Knicks. He would follow Kyrie's lead. That night in the suburbs, he even ate a vegan burger for the first time. "I could fuck with this," he said. A super-team was starting to be formed, over a side of kale salad and . . . *clink*: Brooklyn.

KD and Kyrie went upstairs to the playroom, shared a vegan smoothie, shot a Nerf ball into a toy hoop and played *NBA2K*. Controlling miniature versions of themselves and their teammates, like marionettes, they wondered how else they could string together a team that was going somewhere. "And from that point," Kyrie said, "we took the power back and put it in our hands."

FEBRUARY 24, 2020 ⏭

Brooklyn

ON THE MORNING OF Kobe's memorial out in Los Angeles, the Nets held a shootaround at Barclays Center. Kenny Atkinson was already up at dawn every day, looking at scouting data as he worked out on a stationary bike, but the head coach found these game-day practices at the arena to be a waste of vanishing time, vestiges of an old-school NBA that overtrained players who should, according to the data, be resting their bodies. Atkinson considered himself a disruptor of sorts, one who took risks with tinkered lineups, who pushed overperformers to perform even harder. But this season had brought one unpredictable flip of the hourglass after another, and there was still no word to define this team on his fill-in-the-blank whiteboard at HQ. *Resilient*, he tried for a while. *Defense. Scrappiness.* Maybe *flexible* was more like it. "Right now," he decided, "that's our identity." Atkinson's haircut and tan from a surprisingly sunny All-Star Weekend holed up at his cottage in Quogue—a straight shot east on the Long Island Expressway—had overstayed their welcome, and the age had returned under his 52-year-old eyes, bunkers in an unwinnable forever war against corporate expectation and celebrity superintendence. His five-o'clock shadow was well past eight, at ten-fifteen.

The team finished reviewing preparations for the Orlando Magic that night, and KD strolled onto the Barclays court with his housemate Randy, reeking of weed, for a forty-five-minute rehab session, one of his most intense yet. They kept the rookies and second-year players around to grind for extra work and to try guarding the most unguardable man in the NBA, who was returning to form at long last.

Atkinson said a brief hello to his superstar, put on a winter beanie and climbed atop his white bicycle, riding out through the arena's side door. Across the street, an abandoned storefront on Flatbush Avenue had been wiped clean, after serving for six weeks as the canvas for a twenty-five-foot mural of Kyrie and a wallful of Illuminati eyes, and then, overnight, one of Kobe and his daughter. Atkinson used the solo commute from Downtown Brooklyn to his brownstone in nearby Cobble Hill as a form of therapy, and he tried to take a different path every time, past townhouses and housing projects, hipster bars and barbershops, yoga studios, mosques, middle schoolers in Brooklyn jerseys: *DURANT 7.* His wife, Laura, had been forcing Kenny to spend more time relaxing with the kids, eating dinner before the game and attempting sleep after it, instead of another long night with more basketball and nice French wine. When it came to work-life balance, the head coach said, "I'm in a better place." But if all this—China and Kobe, injuries and egos, heaven knew what else this minor hell had in store—had gone down during his first year on the job, Atkinson told me, "you'd have found me under a bridge on the L.I.E."

Kyrie's cortisone shot, which seemed for two months to glue the franchise together even as Spencer almost single-handedly kept the Nets in playoff contention, had worn off. Not many people in the franchise had seen Kyrie all month, as he'd traveled to California to get in time with his fiancée and at a local gym, to the Bahamas with the executive committee of the players' union, to Miami for his friend's birthday, to more doctors, until the bothersome days for his shoulder had simply outnumbered the good ones for too long. The entire organization could agree that shutting down Kyrie would transfer the Nets from an undulating daily uncertainty to, finally and not without its own drama, a standstill.

After fourth and fifth opinions while Jay-Z's agency negotiated personalities and parameters, Kyrie finally felt comfortable going under the knife. "You have to create some trust—but that doesn't always happen," the Nets medical director, Dr. Riley Williams, told me. "Inevitably, they come back like, 'Yeah, you were right. Let's do this.'"

Kyrie Irving was done for the season—with the basketball part, anyway.

Despite the team's excitement for Kyrie's recovery in time for summer workouts with KD, however, he was still putting off the operation. In mourning in L.A., he attempted to schedule a light workout back at Kobe's Sports Academy before surgery in New York with Dr. Williams. Like so many potential power moves and spiritual symmetries throughout a season spent hopscotching on quicksand, however, Kyrie's intentions were better than his follow-through: Priorities at The Sports Academy had shifted toward supporting the Bryant family for the memorial at Staples Center.

The afternoon ceremony for Kobe was the biggest collection of the most famous people in America, outside of an award ceremony, in quite some time. Kyrie sat next to Draymond Green and behind James Harden, Russ Westbrook and Bill Russell. After Beyoncé performed and Michael Jordan and Shaq had fished for needed laughter onstage, Kyrie found the teenage girls of Team Mamba outside on the sidewalk. It had been their tenth straight memorial, after the ceremonies for Alyssa, who was 14, and her parents; for Payton, who was 13, and her mom; for Coach Christina; for the pilot. The girls told Kyrie how they'd just played in a tournament for the first time since the accident, and he took the next twenty minutes to listen to their teenage grief with intention. "I'm willing to spend the time," he told Kobe's team, "to carry on his legacy. Just let me know."

Back in Brooklyn, Spencer hadn't been traded after all, but he had no time to watch the memorial during his game-day ritual. He'd already pledged proceeds from his new signature shoe to the crash-victim family fund—one of a handful of NBA players, KD and MJ among the first, to write an early check—and he needed a nap. Spencer was tired of carrying the Nets upon his broad shoulders, whenever it was convenient to the franchise. He said that Atkinson's coaching staff avoided playing his highlights in the locker room after he led the team to victory, in favor of lowlights during a study session at practice. And the head coach, he thought, was too busy nitpicking instead of focusing on team hierarchy. Spencer felt treated a bit like a young James Harden, who had played third wheel, rather than third star, to KD and Russ in OKC. Spencer wondered why Atkinson couldn't simply run the whole team through him, so long as KD, Kyrie and Caris LeVert were still on the injured list. But it was precisely because he was not a superstar, Spencer told me, that "I do become a whipping boy, a scapegoat."

The Nets blew a twenty-four-point lead that night to the Magic, a team chasing them for the final playoff spot in the Eastern Conference, with seven weeks left in the regular season. They took off for an eight-day road trip together, though Spencer began to sense infighting. "Winning can mask things, and losing definitely puts on a spotlight," he said. "But if everybody's not on the same page, or your stars primarily aren't on the same page with the coach, then, like, something's *gonna* change—I don't know *when* it's gonna happen, I don't know *what's* gonna happen."

As the bottom fell out of Brooklyn's February into America's

March, time seemed to vanish quickly, and slowly, and sometimes not at all.

The first night of the trip, in Washington, Spencer missed a
game-winning shot, which prompted Caris, who had returned
from his thumb surgery with bucket-getting abandon, to shred
the neckline off his jersey with his teeth. "We gotta wear those
the rest of this trip, you know," said the equipment manager, Joe
Cuomo, stuffing the last of the team's sneakers into a compart-
mentalized duffel bag that served as a flying shoe closet.

Pulling a spare hair tie over his usual black rubber gloves,
Brooklyn's equipment manager tightened his man-bun and as-
suaged a passing concern about whether the team traveled with
enough disinfectant wipes. "On it," he said. "No need to freak
out about Corona."

That evening, February 26, I asked Atkinson if the Nets
were preparing for scenarios in which the coronavirus got worse.
The Nets coaching staff hadn't talked specifically to the players
about anything related to the virus, he said, beyond casual conversation. There were only fifteen reported cases of Covid-19 in
the entire country, largely contained to the West Coast, and he'd
been too busy forcing difficult conversations in the locker room.
The coach was "dumbfounded," he said, by "infantile mistakes"
and "abysmal" play in D.C., and then his team lost its next game
by twenty-three. The coach was exhausted, and moved right
along from the existential.

KD traveled to watch the Nets lose their fourth straight in
Miami, on the day New York City confirmed its first positive
case of Covid-19 and the NBA sent a memo to teams, instruct-
ing them to start discussing contingency plans with local city
officials and medical centers. Atkinson ran his team through
a grueling workout at the University of Miami on March 2,
when the league office sent another memo, encouraging players

to fist-bump fans instead of high-fiving and to sign autographs with team-issued Sharpies, but otherwise to continue washing their hands and waiting on the experts. The following night, on national TV in Boston, Atkinson benched the entire starting lineup in the fourth quarter, except Caris and some of the coach's newest experiments from The Program. They came back to win, but Spencer was livid. On a plane ride back to New York, Garrett recoiled at Wilson, who'd been fighting a cold: "Get away from us, Will! You're too close!" This was, in the early days of March 2020, still a joke.

Wilson would eventually test negative for the virus, but executives and doctors from the franchise had been doing their homework all week, wondering what might happen if a player did test positive—if an outbreak could spread not just across their entire team but their seventeen-thousand-seat arena. Across Brooklyn. Across the world and back again.

Joe Tsai and the Nets' interim CEO, Oliver Weisberg, lived in Hong Kong and had helped lead their companies through SARS— another strain of sudden, respiratory-attacking coronavirus—in 2003. When an Alibaba employee tested positive for SARS after traveling back from a conference, the nascent company had successfully quarantined its entire staff, even as it had been on the brink of launching its e-commerce platform. Online shopping exploded when China was forced inside by that virus, and Joe Tsai launched upon his way to becoming a multibillionaire. "I've been through SARS," Weisberg, who sat on Alibaba's board and ran Tsai's private-equity portfolio, told me the first week of March, "so I kinda *get* this." His and Tsai's connections helped identify UV-light and air-filtration systems to disinfect the arena and Nets HQ. But this strain of coronavirus was much, much different than SARS—American scientists in China would soon learn that Covid-19 could spread in public, without anybody knowing they were sick. Weisberg's advice to the players in the locker room remained: *Just wash your fucking hands.*

"They totally downplayed it," said a senior franchise executive who felt uncomfortable being forced to make employees keep coming into work at Nets HQ, even when a staffer tested positive in early March. "Nobody wanted to make a call, and they were just like, 'Let's see what everyone else does.'"

Dr. Michael Farber, the Nets team physician who ran the franchise's coronavirus response, said that the in-office infection led to an early form of contact-tracing and that it did not spread. DeAndre would stop at a faux-freaked-out distance whenever he saw Brooklyn's doomsayer in the hallway, but some players expressed skepticism to the team doctor as to whether Covid-19 was even real. "Trust takes years to develop, and it can be lost in a sentence," Dr. Farber told me. "So we had to be prepared to answer, as best we could, the unknown."

MARCH 4, 2020 ⏩
Brooklyn

EVER SINCE KD AND KYRIE first arrived in Brooklyn, Sean Marks worried about overcrowding his franchise players. Despite protestations from marketing executives, the Nets general manager decided, from the beginning, not to put Kevin Durant front and center on the banner over the entranceway to Barclays Center. All season long, half of KD's world-famous, twenty-foot face peered out from behind the Afro of Jarrett Allen, who remained a fan favorite. "A lot of the things we did, Kevin is in the background, which is kind of exactly where he's been," Marks told me. "That doesn't mean he hasn't had a say in how we do things, but it's a subtle reminder that the big dog's coming back—and watch out."

KD was watching when the Nets returned home to play the Memphis Grizzlies. Sandwich boards with his face were draped on the seats behind him, as the franchise was finally approved to sell against his and Kyrie's likeness with a season-ticket campaign for next year: *KINGS OF NEW YORK*, went the slogan. KD even paid his first visit to the in-game broadcasters on the local sports network. "I'm just looking at the game from a different lens," he said, squeezing behind the courtside scorer's table. He was studying lineup switches and preparation routines, "trying to figure out what's best for myself and the rest of the team." He wandered back toward his teammates, then over to the exercise bike behind the bench, to give some notes to Joe Harris, the sharpshooter whose career was saved from the scrap heap by Atkinson—and who was seething, as Brooklyn's stars were relegated to the bench once more.

"What the *fuck*," Joe asked KD, "is going on here?"

KD tried to explain that it was nothing nefarious, just a difficult stretch. He returned to his seat on the bench, next to Garrett and DeAndre, pretending to hide from Joe as he smiled with a palm stretched above his eyes, in a familiar windshield sunguard from the spotlight.

"Man," KD winced to his friends, "I never seen Joe get *hot* like that."

He did not mean hot, as in shooting-hot. The Nets, clutching to their playoff position and playing one of the youngest teams in the league, were getting blown out by thirty-nine.

"You get your ass kicked," Joe later explained to me, "you're obviously going to discuss it for a while."

The Brooklyn Nets took their seats around the locker room, a horseshoe that looked like an Apple Store but felt, on this night, like a campfire of frustration. Kenny Atkinson pulled up a chair in the middle. "Let's talk," he said. "What's our problem?"

The coach asked Wilson to start. "A discussion needs to be had," Wilson told the room, not just about Atkinson's lineup tinkering but about players who got cold and distant off the court, like everyone knew Kyrie did, or else too hot and then disappeared on it, like teammates thought Spencer had.

"We need you to be aggressive to win," Garrett told Spencer.

"Oh-kayyy," Spencer said. "But we also have to *play* that way. We can't play every man for himself but: *Spencer, save us!* And then if it does work, *Hey, the team did great!* And if it doesn't work, *Hey, Spencer lost us the game!*"

For nearly a half hour, voices of dissent reverberated around the room, mostly from players who'd joined the team that season, and their criticism was increasingly directed at the head coach. The forum swung past Kyrie's empty locker to DeAndre, who sat atypically quiet. DeAndre was upset that Atkinson had decided to go with a smaller lineup that night during the flow of the game when he typically substituted in his backup center. Garrett spoke up for his fellow veteran: "A person like DeAndre, twelve years in the NBA, I think he's owed an explanation, or at least a heads-up: *We're not gonna go with you.*" That 21-year-old Jarrett Allen was still in the starting lineup at all, instead of an Olympic gold medalist who'd helped put this team together, had been a burning ember since September. Now it had lighter fluid.

Jarrett watched in shock at the insurrection before him. It was Atkinson who had pushed to draft him, who'd busted his knee for him on the practice court, who believed in him when the incoming Nets stars had not. "That's my guy, and I was ready to fight for him," Jarrett told me later. "I didn't really have a say in what was going on." Not in the lineups. Not in any revolt.

Nor, come the off-season, in his spot on this roster. Joe Harris agreed with the room that "we're sort of all over the place." Caris LeVert, who had maneuvered adeptly between The Clean Sweep corner of veterans and The Program's smoldering core in this corner of the locker room, felt uneasy that Atkinson's voice was being challenged so openly. "But we had a lot of new guys this year," he offered.

Spencer was pissed off. If Atkinson could barely distinguish between the Nets' big dogs and the flavor of the month by now, how would the coach ever properly allow the kings of New York to shine? Kyrie, though absent, sensed trouble brewing, too. "A hierarchy, that's what Ky was getting at," Spencer later acknowledged to me. He continued, of Atkinson's relationship with KD and Kyrie: "Him and the max guys weren't necessarily on the same page—but if we're all not on the same page, then *somebody's* gotta go, and it's not going to be *them*."

Kenny Atkinson had spent nearly four years working to gain the trust of men like the forgotten Spencer Dinwiddie and the post-Linsanity Jeremy Lin, urging these athletes to let the Nets surveil their bodies and transform them into somebodies. But all the employees and players who'd built The Program—scientists of sleep and scalpel, sneaker-packers and flight-schedulers, backup point guards with chips on their shoulders, the man who would become Jarrett Allen and the man Jarrett Allen would come to be, famous nobodies—did not matter as much as the max-contract guy walking in the front door.

Atkinson's latest project, the French forward Timothé Luwawu-Cabarrot, sat at the second-to-last pod around the horseshoe. His Sharpie eyebrows headed for his hairline as he spun his chin and his leather chair counterclockwise toward the final locker in the room. For so many months it was a sterile display case—one bottle of lotion and one spray can of deodorant down there on the ledge like props, below the rack for its owner's signature shoes, the hook for his sweat-free sweats and a placard permanently hanging above: *DURANT 7.*

This time, KD was present, and down sliced the scythe of The Silent Reaper.

"We don't work hard enough! Our *habits* aren't good enough!" A team had to be great every day, KD told the coaches and the players, and every night, to be great in the playoffs. A championship team like the Warriors held shootaround on game day. A championship mentality meant working as hard as he did. Blaming a lack of focus was not going to cut it anymore. And a game like this? A blowout to a bunch of kids on the *Grizzlies*? He'd seen games like this at least six or seven times from the Nets so far, while peering around Kenny Atkinson's timeouts, as if without a care in the world. But he cared deeply about this personalized dynasty, and there were consistencies that Atkinson, who'd never been an NBA hooper, simply could not comprehend. "This isn't new to me," KD told the room, and extinguished the meeting.

Atkinson listened to this raw final assessment, and, honestly, he thought it could have been worse. The coach disagreed with KD that the Nets did not believe in hard work; it was just that nobody in the NBA worked as hard as Kevin Durant, except for, maybe, LeBron James. "I regret that I don't spend more time with him," the coach had admitted to me, not long before that night. "I wish I could take a week here and just hang out with him and do his rehab or be by his side—really can't wait 'till the off-season, when I can just, you know, rent an apartment in wherever the heck he's gonna be and just be around him more."

After Atkinson's campfire on Wednesday night, Joe Tsai asked players about the vibe. The owner had been increasingly in contact with KD and Kyrie, though he and Spencer liked to nerd out, too. Spencer was not involved in the shadow conversations that week about the Nets' future—KD and the GM were shuffling around the tunnels of Barclays Center together more than usual—but Spencer didn't exactly stand up for the head coach either. Not that this head coach stood a chance anymore.

On Saturday morning, there was a change to the world map outside the front office at Nets HQ. The map featured a name plate for each employee and their hometown, a display of the franchise's global ambitions and family values. Each staffer got a thin black magnet, from Jersey (*KYRIE IRVING, WEST ORANGE*) to way out in New Zealand (*SEAN MARKS*), while the owner had a special plate, notably thicker and notably gold (*JOE TSAI, HONG KONG*). That day, there was one magnet missing:

KENNY ATKINSON—BROOKLYN, NEW YORK.

The general manager texted the news to a group chat with the players—not *the* group chat, because Death Row was players only. The younger ones among them were shocked. So was the greater NBA community: "The only thing he's done there in the last two years," the Rockets head coach Mike D'Antoni said of his former colleague, "is overachieve." Formally, the Nets and their head coach had mutually agreed to part ways, but Atkinson saw his out and ran for it when he could. Still, he knew that he'd been fired, and he didn't completely understand why—if his high office with a potentially historic team could have been decided by majority vote, he maintained that he would have never lost. But basketball was not a democracy, and the office culture was always window dressing.

As the Nets tipped off for the first time without him the next afternoon, Atkinson drew the blinds around his townhouse—three stories with toy trains on the sill, the type of place you could cozy up inside forever. He'd been living so hard for the game, one legend of Kenny went, that even while working out at home, the coach had instinctively raised his voice at his wife, when Laura failed to complete a perfect pass to him, in his perfect shooting pocket.

At the end of the first quarter, with the Nets losing, the Lakers and the Clippers were tipping off on ABC when Atkinson realized that he could simply . . . change the channel, away from the Nets to a championship-caliber game, without having to organize a scouting report. Laura ordered some organic burgers, and they settled in for a hoops marathon on the flat-screen in their living room. Kenny walked into the kitchen to get some plates for dinner and glanced up at the wall, full of square pictures of his children playing sports, like a printed-out version of the Instagram feed he'd never had time to start. He would rather have been anywhere that night but the crowded stadium up Atlantic Avenue, especially if anywhere was here, half-awake, on the couch with his family. Unfortunately, the rent was too damn high, so the Atkinsons would have to move out to their cottage on Long Island, as Kenny looked for a new job. They would miss Brooklyn. But they were happily stuck in the in-between, for a little while longer.

The marathon would continue. After the Lakers won in front of Jay-Z and his daughter, Kenny indulged in the OKC-Boston game, admiring the Celtics' rising stars and longing after a bottle of Bordeaux on the counter. The last of the sunset began to peer from the promenade through the window shades, and the coach's wife began to shut the door.

"Sleep?" Laura asked.

"Yeah," said the coach, "I think we can do that now."

11

TIMEOUT

KD EXTENDED HIS ELBOW to a passerby—a newfound gesture from the fist-bump region of a suddenly handshake-free universe—and stepped up onto the Staples Center hardwood. Turning his back to the game just underway, he looked out and above the gathered masses, at two oversize jerseys—*BRYANT 8*, *BRYANT 24*—reflecting a spotlight along the rafters, as if the full moon over Los Angeles had made its way inside.

In the eighty-five hours since the Nets officially fired their head coach, the NBA had forced teams to crack down on off-the-court contact and restrict access to the locker room, such that Joe Harris had to give his pregame interview at a safer distance, behind the dais of a UCLA classroom, so that nobody might risk a spread of the coronavirus. "One person gets it in the NBA," he said, "it seems like everybody will probably get it."

But there was KD in his trademark black blazer, surrounded

by assistant coaches in the huddle, as one joked to the interim head coach: "Put him in there!" And there was the paparazzi, pouncing into KD's path at halftime—"These guys are *assholes*," he said to me—as he offered a pound to two teenage fans and pulled in close for custom shakes with celebrity friends in the front row. During Brooklyn's final timeout, KD grabbed the game ball, palmed it, feigned a behind-the-back pass to the Laker Girls, flicked in a layup and high-fived five Nets players. After Spencer hit the go-ahead shot, KD and his teammates on the bench screamed so loudly and in such unison in the face of Anthony Davis, not six feet away on the three-point line, that the Lakers star missed the game-winner and Brooklyn's distraction went viral.

KD woke up the next morning, groggy from a postgame night out with Drake, and got in some half-court three-on-three, followed by full runs in stride on his Achilles with Garrett and the rookies. On their ride back to the team hotel in Beverly Hills, KD's housemate Randy was going off about an outbreak.

"Shit might be shut down! Once they find out somebody in the league got it, this season about to be *over*! Or at least for a few months . . ."

"Randy, stop playin'," said one of the bench players on the bus, "or *you* gonna get The Covid!"

"Man, they just need to go ahead and shut down the season right now," KD told his teammates, exasperated by 2020 as it was. "Suspend the season."

A few hours later, the Nets flew from LAX to the Bay to play the Warriors. But they would have to leave part of their traveling party—wives, girlfriends and children accompanying the team for a week-long California road trip, and even the inactive KD—behind in Los Angeles, as inessential personnel. Because while KD was partying with Drake overnight, San Francisco city officials had banned gatherings of more than a thousand people, meaning that Thursday's contest was about to become the NBA's first ever . . . without any fans invited.

Brooklyn had coped with daily uncertainty throughout the China trip—*Are we playing on Thursday? Will anyone else be there?*—but NBA owners considered, on their conference call during the team's flight from Los Angeles, that a game of echoes and empty seats should become the temporary new normal. It was Wednesday, March 11, and there were twenty-three newly reported cases of Covid-19 in California. Steph Curry's test for the virus, thought to be the first administered on an NBA player, had come back negative—he'd only contracted the flu—but there were forty-four new cases discovered back in New York for the day, and counting. That Wednesday, The Covid had become, officially, a pandemic.

About an hour after touchdown, Garrett was unpacking in his room at the St. Regis San Francisco when his mom called, urging him to turn on the television immediately. "The Utah game hasn't started yet! I think one of 'em has it!" On Fox, the former Republican vice-presidential candidate Sarah Palin was dancing to "Baby Got Back" in a pink bear costume on a show called *The Masked Singer*. On Fox News, Trump was banning all travel from Europe. Garrett started watching ESPN, and over the next half hour, the Jazz-Thunder game in OKC began to look like a zombie documentary: A team medical staffer sprinted onto the court to prevent tip-off. Chris Paul walked toward the Utah Jazz bench to ask, "What's wrong with Rudy?"—but he was warned to keep away. The public-address announcer informed some eighteen thousand impatient Thunder fans that the game was being postponed—*You are all safe*, he assured them, inciting an instinctive Oklahoma boo, and a long shriek, like a housecat sprung from a catapult, and a man shouting, *Why?!*

Garrett texted his former teammate, the Jazz point guard Mike Conley Jr., who replied with a selfie of a face mask resting atop his beard and blue surgical gloves stuck to his hands: *We locked in this locker room right now.*

Rudy Gobert, the All-Star center for the Jazz, was Player Zero. Over the past several days, he had touched teammates' belongings. He had patted reporters' microphones as if they were Bongo drums. He had clapped teammates on the back when I watched him at practice a week earlier in New York. And he had rubbed the head of his fellow Utah star Donovan Mitchell during an interview on camera, to celebrate their last win. His team had flown to OKC on the same Delta plane that two NBA franchises chartered right afterward. And that night, Rudy, a Frenchman, had tested positive ahead of a regularly scheduled primetime basketball game in the middle of America, for a virus that so many millions of fans considered to be foreign, transferred by hand and near impossible for a young athlete to contract. The end of invincibility had arrived.

This shit, Garrett texted back, *is crazy.*

Within forty-six minutes of Rudy's lab result, the NBA suspended its season indefinitely. Within the next twenty-four hours, the NHL, the Final Four, baseball, Broadway, concerts, Disneyland . . . all of the entertainment business went the way of the NBA. American culture, officially and as we knew it, existed in an indefinite timeout.

Chris Paul sent beers to the Jazz locker room, since they might be sleeping in it; the Nets, stuck in San Francisco, broke out Spencer's favorite tequila. During a meeting scattered about the St. Regis restaurant, Nets players spotted on Twitter that Tom Hanks—Tom Hanks!—had gotten The Covid. They heard that one Nets coach had just taken the subway from the hotel to his off-season home—"This dude took the BART, man," Randy said, "and I *know* he got it!"—then learned that another coach was on his way to visit the Warriors' Klay Thompson across town. Sean Marks, observing the hysteria, instructed Brooklyn's traveling party to stay close.

Over dinner, teammates listened to Spencer's soliloquy on how the NBA could avoid cancelling the season altogether, how the players might get paid in escrow in the meantime, how the shitshow from that one tweet in China was already leading to a $400 million revenue shortfall and how the economics were about to become a sinkhole: There were fifty-five thousand workers in the NBA, and millions more workers beyond the basketball industry—mothers and fathers, hoopers and entrepreneurs—who wanted to be like them when they grew up, who needed their jobs and their health care a lot more than the Nets did.

Garrett was concerned about his family: Kára was trapped down in L.A.—and she was pregnant. "I don't want her flying commercial right now, 'cuz that's a fuckin' cesspool," he said. KD quickly arranged for the stranded wives, girlfriends and children of the franchise to fly private up to the Bay so that they could join the team. Their traveling party complete, the Nets boarded a charter plane home on Friday morning. Noses ran, coughs were covered up and everybody onboard received a hastily printed-out questionnaire about symptoms and sick family members. Dr. Farber, the team physician, looked at the responses and immediately started texting with a lab. "It was," he said, "alarming."

MARCH 14, 2020 💬
DAY 3 WITHOUT BASKETBALL
Brooklyn

ONE BY ONE, the Nets moved to the front of the line at HQ, where a long swab got shoved up each player's nose and into the back of the throat. A test of the tongue, too. Some blood. Not every staffer in the traveling party was offered one of the tests, which the medical team procured from a private diagnostics company in Missouri, but KD's entourage was taken care of.

The players waited for three anxious days. They figured a couple franchise employees might have the virus, but not them, right? *Right?* Jarrett dreamt that he was rubbernecking past a car accident, worried that he knew somebody inside. DeAndre, against the advice of team doctors, went out into the real world to stock up on his immunity-boosting, plant-based diet at Whole Foods—the aisles were packed, because New York City was shuttering restaurants and bars, and the schools, too.

The Nets' results arrived, and four of the players tested positive—four of one hundred eighty-two new cases counted in the city that day. The team's Death Row group chat switched into a group FaceTime, with a dozen famous heads floating about; each time another man on edge would join the video chat, a new face bubbled toward the front of the screen.

"So, who's got it?"

KD, as if to pierce the awkwardness, spoke up first. "Yo," he said, his scraggling goatee and neck hair enlarging on everyone's phone: "I got it, man."

His teammates thought KD was joking. "Nahhh. No you *don't*, man. Get outta here."

Some of the Nets had mentioned flu-like symptoms, but KD was for real. "Man, I didn't even know I had it," they heard him groan. "I ain't got *no* symptoms, but this shit is fucked *up*."

Theo Pinson, the happy-go-lucky backup guard, remained quiet on the group chat, for once. He, too, had The Covid. "It was one of those moments where, like, it can hit anybody," Theo told me. "You would think K is one of those guys that don't get it, 'cuz that's Kevin *Durant*—it's just how it *is!*—but that was big for me, for him to just come out and say it. It helped out everybody."

Team doctors and trainers warned KD to stay home, because the superstar had the potential to be a super-spreader. His entourage would have to inform Drake, and everyone they'd been in contact with, that KD had tested positive. Notoriously curious, KD asked Rich, his fixer and agent, to call even fancier doctors. They thought of all the dap-ups, the ushers and the fans—the culture of closeness and embrace that came with being a person who is loved, or wants to be. They listened to some Jay-Z: *It was all good just a week ago / Last week I had everything.* They decided to push back the release of KD's new shoe, and they quickly decided to break with the Nets' code of silence to get out the word on his lab result—to help out everybody—in a statement to the town crier of the NBA media, Shams Charania: *Everyone be careful, take care of yourself and quarantine. We're going to get through this.*

Were we? And what did Kevin Durant know? He was the most famous very healthy person on the planet who'd admitted to having a world-eating virus, but the Nets had procured immediate testing and, with it, certainty about their good fortune. The untested masses found this to be villainous, and charmed, and wrong. For the first time ever, and not for their play, KD and Kyrie's super-team was on the front page of *The New York Times*, under the banner of *At the Front of the Test Line: A Lot of A-Listers.* The mayor of New York City, Bill DeBlasio, tweeted: *an entire NBA team should NOT get tested for COVID-19 while there are critically ill patients waiting to be tested. Tests should not be for the wealthy, but for the sick.* At a White House task-force briefing, the president was asked if well-connected athletes like the asymptomatic Brooklyn Nets should receive access to testing while the sick wait in line. "No, I wouldn't say so," Trump responded, "but perhaps that's been the story of life."

Leaders around the NBA thought the Nets' privilege of first response was a story not of celebrity class warfare but political disregard, as Washington's absent guidance over the previous two months slowed the United States from distributing Covid-19 tests to its non-millionaire fans and citizens. On the day the Nets roster got tested, there were five hundred and eleven tests performed in New York City and forty-two thousand in the United States—about 2 percent of the tests that all of South Korea was administering, despite the same outbreak timeline. "The problem," said the NBA players' union chief Michele Roberts, "rests at the foot of the federal government. They were responsible . . . and they failed."

Too much of what the world was hearing midway through March sounded either depressing (*social distance, shelter-in-place*) or scary (*morbidity rate, The Curve*). Basketball's phrase in the new parlance, however, promised a beginning of the end of the end of the world: *return to play*. Commissioner Adam Silver beamed in live from his apartment to pregame shows—pregame shows without any games to follow—and reiterated that the NBA, as "part of the psyche of the country," listened to science. Obama's surgeon general, Dr. Vivek Murthy, had been advising the league since 2016, and he delivered the owners a bleak picture of infection rates—despite Trump's sleight of hand, this thing was airborne—and eventually suggested that the sporting world "rethink spectators." But Dr. Murthy offered a seedling of hope that the 2019–2020 NBA season, and with it the joy of basketball, might return from hiatus, without fans, in June.

A world trapped inside yearned for distraction, and epidemiologists badly needed a culture on pause to help remind the ignorant, still-clustered masses and the young, still-partying people that if their contemporary idols could get sick, so could they. On TV, Trump's surgeon general name-checked KD and Kylie Jenner, of the Kardashians. "We need to get our social-media influencers out there," he said, "helping folks understand that, look, this is serious." The Kardashian did just that, to her more than two hundred twenty-five million followers, that day.

KD, a reluctant influencer, decided to be a dude of the people: His first public appearance of the pandemic was on a desperate first attempt at live programming by ESPN, playing video games, as he did for seven or eight hours a day during an initial quarantine phase spent at his place in Manhattan.

"I wish I could ball so bad," KD said to his opponent in ESPN's *NBA2K* tournament of the stars. He crossed his legs by the window, chose to play as the Los Angeles Clippers and mumbled his way through the e-sport awkwardness. "You heard what they said?" he asked the slam-dunking scrub from the Miami Heat during a break. "They might send everybody to Vegas?"

Despite the sudden relocation of KD's rehab to his couch, some Nets executives wondered if the hiatus might last just long enough for him to return . . . this season, if the season did. Vegas had doubled the odds of a 2020 Brooklyn championship, and Vegas might be where it all went down, remodeled as a campus built for sports and seclusion and little else. It could be a return to the simpler life KD had enjoyed at the University of Texas, the baller's life, chilling with Randy, his go-anywhere bowling ball of a housemate from Austin and OKC. "Hand Kevin a backpack and stick him on a court," Randy liked to say, "and he'd still be happy as hell."

On March 30, as he and KD completed their fourteen-day penthouse isolation, Randy wiped the sweat from his brow and, as he did every afternoon at cardio time, walked through KD's canyon of a dining room to look out the wraparound windows. This time, Randy spotted a big-ass white barge, more than three city blocks long, gliding slowly uptown along the Hudson River. Randy was, on many days, one of the happiest men in New York City—a paid friend—and this boat was great content for the 'Gram. But as it passed KD's apartment building, Randy saw the mark of the Red Cross on its side: The USNS *Comfort* was a floating navy hospital built for war, with a thousand beds onboard. The sight could stir empathy from Beelzebub. All over the city, Randy and KD would come to realize, doctors and nurses had been drawing up plans for an onslaught. The disease experts in Washington said more than a hundred thousand people could die, just in America. There was little defense for this virus, basketball was no savior, and the real heroes didn't wear Brooklyn Nets uniforms anymore.

MARCH 31, 2020 ⏩

DAY 20 WITHOUT BASKETBALL
Baton Rouge

GARRETT TEMPLE'S BROTHER could see the dying, but he still couldn't smell the hospital disinfectant. Elliott hadn't been able to taste anything either, since a week ago lunchtime. The doctors had tested him, but, since Elliott was just 38 years old and had no shortness of breath—and since rapid results were not yet available, even in a state that had rapidly become one of America's biggest virus hotspots outside Brooklyn—they had sent him home. By the next morning, he could hardly breathe. That night, the doctors in the Baton Rouge General ICU told Elliott, his lungs were collapsing; they needed him on a ventilator, stat. He could barely walk ten feet to the bathroom before he got bone tired. And that's when Elliott saw the dying, out across the hospital floor, through the clear glass wall: Doctors and nurses, half a dozen of them, sprinting into the room before him, to care for another patient, a man or a woman, he was not quite sure. Then a single nurse, wheeling the patient out of the room, a man or a woman Elliott Temple would never know, because the patient's body was covered in a white bedsheet. Elliott hadn't talked to his entire family yet, didn't want to freak them out, but he called his older brother, coughing, in the middle of the night, frightened awake. "I don't think I'm gonna make it, man."

His other brother, the dormant NBA basketball player, woke up a little later these days, up in Brooklyn. Garrett fed Basil, his English chocolate Lab, made himself and Kára a smoothie and still drove himself to the Nets practice facility for treatment, now that the teamwide quarantine was complete. He had a bad knee, so the Nets were technically permitted to let him inside for rehab, at a distance from his masked and gloved coaches and caretakers. Garrett could make it to Nets HQ in nearly five minutes flat, because there wasn't any traffic on the Brooklyn-Queens Expressway—because there wasn't any traffic anywhere. In the parking lot across the street from the gym, the city planned to wheel in refrigerated trucks for a makeshift morgue.

Garrett arrived back home from HQ in time to watch Andrew Cuomo's daily lunchtime briefing on CNN. He and Kára found these midday check-ins grimly soothing. But the governor had more bad news, that seventy-five thousand New Yorkers had tested positive, that New York was approaching a biological ambush at the apex of The Curve: There were more reported cases here, in Brooklyn, than in nearly any entire state in the nation, and the city would witness more death that coming month than it had on 9/11. "Never underestimate your opponent," Cuomo said. "You don't win playing catch-up. Plan forward."

Then Garrett's father gave him more bad news: "Elliott's got The Covid."

Garrett called his brother, asking Elliott why he hadn't told him sooner and whether Garrett and Kára should drive on down to Louisiana—his teammates had already begun to flee NYC. Elliott insisted that his family not worry; he had some scarring on his lungs, but he was out of the ICU and smelling things a little better. The family had bigger things to worry about at the group homes they ran for foster kids and developmentally disabled adults, one of whom had just tested positive. Besides, Elliott said, it was best for Kára to stay home in Brooklyn— there was another Temple on the way, and hoops could wait.

The NBA hiatus, however, could not stop the Nets' ambition: Every morning, a text and a temperature check-in. Staffers delivered groceries and precooked meals to each player's doorstep. Every man on the roster got an exercise bike, a dumbbell, a jump rope. Strength coaches created three custom workouts a week and required the completion of at least one. Several of the Nets, stuck in their apartments, did not so much as touch a basketball for weeks, but you could be on the moon, Garrett joked, and this franchise would find a way to make sure you stayed in shape. When DeAndre claimed he couldn't figure out how to log in to a boxing session on this new video-conferencing app called Zoom, the Death Row group chat knew he simply wasn't up for the work-from-home grind. "You don't have no fuckin' hands," Theo Pinson told him. "That's why you can't get on."

It felt, to Garrett, more like an off-season, the cognitive dissonance encroaching upon the social distance. He had more time to walk Basil, with his eyes as open as the neighborhood was closed, down to the Red Hook pier. From this side of the New York Harbor, he could look at the Statue of Liberty and turn the dog back home to see, on a clear day over in Manhattan, the World Trade Center. He thought how surreal it had become to notice another dog owner strolling down the sidewalk and, even when he could spot two cheeks rising under a mask and assume it meant a smile, to have to scamper the other way. He thought about his brother. He thought about his future son. He imagined how historic that first game back in front of the fans at Barclays Center might be, here in the middle of it all. And, hot damn, that first trip back to the barbershop!

But he thought more and more about doing something else.

Garrett wondered if he was doing what he was good at for a living, when he could be doing more of what he should.

He jumped on another Zoom meeting with Kyrie and the executive committee of the players' union, making sure the paychecks didn't stop, hearing out every scenario for a potential return to play. He kept harping on tests—how you couldn't even begin to organize this quarantined basketball orgy, with all that essential personnel holed up in some Las Vegas hotel, if you still couldn't tell whether the man guarding you on the perimeter might also kill you. Roberts, the union boss, was starting to think that a surveilled, family-free "bubble" sounded a lot like incarceration to her. But Trump would speak with the pro sports commissioners, and urge asses back in seats ASAP, and even this Dr. Fauci guy, the former point guard from Brooklyn who'd been the voice of science in what Garrett otherwise thought was a laughable White House response, figured that basketball in a bubble could be better than nothing: "Buy a gazillion tests," Dr. Fauci said. Still, the governor would warn, when Garrett watched his press conference, "I would love to see sports back— help with cabin fever—but this is not about hopes and dreams and aspirations and what you would like to see."

Trump seized upon sports as a cudgel for reopening the culture and thus the economy—and thus his reelection campaign. With or without the president, though, the NBA's persistence once again became the barometer for progress, for better and, in the midst of a plague, for much worse. Progress would be difficult to come by, in 2020. The safe return of basketball would require leadership and science of the highest profile and precision. But distraction with all the necessary capital could be worth the risk, even of that very real possibility that the NBA might trigger its own outbreak for all the world to see. Or maybe sports would just be gone, like hugs were.

Even if the season got cancelled, Garrett hoped the following season might get pushed back well past Kára's due date in September—he dreamt of spending so much time with their newborn. Plus, he aspired to schedule a different kind of test: That movie *Just Mercy* really had inspired him to become a lawyer, so Garrett began attacking his problem sets for the LSAT, three hours each night during quarantine. His law-school entry exam score would hold up for five years. By then, Garrett figured, he'd be on track to become a general manager—KD had been saying how the league needed more former players, Black players, in the front office—or maybe the president of a university. Or perhaps our politics might require someone measured and mature like him again, when he retired from roundball in three or four seasons, when this other tangerine blob in his life wouldn't be on the television anymore, suggesting that the American people drink bleach for dinner.

Garrett and Kára cuddled into their gray sectional couch and watched that Netflix documentary everyone was talking about, the one with the man who owned a hundred and seventy-six tigers, and look at the latest printout of the ultrasound. For her sonogram with a Nets-recommended OB-GYN, Kára had been forced to travel alone—The Covid turned fathers into nonessential personnel—but they looked at their boy, at fifteen weeks, and they realized: This baby ain't gonna remember *any* of this year. He wouldn't remember Donald Trump. And he wouldn't remember when Daddy put on surgical gloves to walk down the stoop and throw out the trash at their doorstep, in the middle of The Great Big Timeout of 2020, when the kid walking down their block in the Brooklyn Nets shirt burst with hopes and dreams—*Hey! You're Garrett Temple!*—and rushed up to shake his hand, and Daddy had to let him down easy. "You can't really do that, little man. Not right now."

12

THE ROAR OF THE CROWD

APRIL 3, 2020 💬

DAY 23 WITHOUT BASKETBALL
Brooklyn

FAHAD SALEEM'S iPHONE was blowing up: His brother, his friends, even co-workers from his internship who never messaged him on Instagram were all sending this 18-year-old Nets super-fan the same post from @SportsCenter that, minutes earlier, had started going viral. The photo showed his old bedroom. The wallpaper was black with smoke. An alarm clock rested on the rubble. His bedpost was the only belonging that remained . . . except for a basketball jersey sagging on two hooks in the sunshine: *IRVING 11*. His missing Kyrie jersey.

A month earlier, Fahad's neighbor from across the street had FaceTimed him: "Yo, your house is on fire." Fahad began laughing, until the camera flipped from selfie mode to reality and revealed his childhood home, engulfed. He rushed back to Sheepshead Bay, where FDNY trucks, five of them, jammed his block, blasting so much water upon the blaze that the wooden floor collapsed upstairs. An investigator joined him and explained that the outlets next to his bed had likely set the mattress aflame, then the carpet, and within seconds the smoke was everywhere. The fireman pointed through Fahad's door. "Holy shit," they said in unison. Neither could believe that this jersey had survived fully intact. Fahad took a quick photograph and brought the uniform downstairs to his garage. It was cold to the touch, freezing over from the hoses, and it smelled as rancid as the rest of his remaining clothes.

Each day in March, even as the virus encroached, Fahad had called over his best friends to help him piece back together a bedside shrine to their favorite team. But his Caris LeVert bobblehead was incinerated. It seemed like the Spencer Dinwiddie jerseys were gone, too. When they'd gotten surprised with free sympathy tickets to a game on March 6, Fahad had nothing left to wear, let alone Nets merch. So one of his friends lent him sweatpants, the other a hoodie, and Fahad sat down at Barclays Center, two nights after the inferno, in an alternate reality. Brooklyn was up big. Caris was on fire. Was that Dr. J in the house? In Fahad's old normal, trauma never happened, his room was still bright orange, and basketball went on forever.

"Yo, after the game, let's go hang at my place," he said to his friends.

They almost laughed.

"Oh, shit," Fahad said. He remembered the five red trucks on his sidewalk. "Yeah."

In the third quarter, a Nets staffer found the boys. Kyrie had heard about the miraculous jersey and wanted to autograph it. Fahad handed over his prized possession, and the staffer instructed him to meet up after the game—the Nets had a special guest. Once Fahad and his friends made their way past security, the guest emerged from the home locker room: Spencer, not

Kyrie. He asked how the fire started, how Fahad's family was doing, and said the team would replace those two *DINWIDDIE* jerseys he couldn't recover from the ashes. That Kyrie's uniform had prevailed from his collection—and that Spencer's hadn't— was not lost on either of them.

Kyrie had been too busy for the kid then—frantic, between the surgery and the casting-away of his head coach—but the lives of the rich and famous began to slow down, once coronavirus took hold, and celebrities could reconnect online with their followers in the shared safety and self-absorption of isolating at home. Adam Mosseri, the head of Instagram, told me his advice to athletes during the height of the pandemic's screenfluencer curve was: "You can't show your hundred-percent authentic self, but be as authentic as you *can* be, because that's what people want." Indeed, posts on Instagram related to coronavirus and its attendant hashtags from influencers—classified as talent, brands and professional "creators" whose business of boredom was booming—had nearly three billion impressions by the end of March, with more engagement than usual.

Social media had mouse-trapped social life: To fans, NBA Twitter's latest GOAT debates outlasted the political bickering of catchups with aunts and uncles on Zoom. Kyrie showed up on the TikTok account of his 12-year-old half-sister, dancing all over the family porch. Facebook had become recently and entirely old-fashioned, like cigarettes, but Instagram's new Live Q&A feature could salve the callus of binge-watching with split-screen A-lister salons, materializing around happy hour from the accounts of basketball players in particular, as Carmelo Anthony drank wine with actors and athletes, or KD dropped in on a high schooler's graduation day, or Dr. Fauci chatted in front of the hoop in his Washington office with Steph Curry, while Donald Trump called up the baseball player Alex Rodriguez for advice on a plague from the Oval Office, and a DJ named Nice threw a dance party on IG Live for D-Wade and Drake, Joe Biden and Kim Kardashian, and you and me.

Never late to a trend, Kyrie materialized again, on a Live hosted by a high-school friend during the week that Fahad's phone was blowing up, for a DJ battle of his own, head-bobbing in a home office decorated with paintings of himself, philosophizing about how he would no longer play it safe in speaking his mind. "Safe is cool for some people, but at the same time, activists before us came talking about change in our society, and changed the way we see race, social class, the way we see our climate, as just *humans*, the way we treat each other," he said. "Our generation being in this unique position where we saw technology grow, we got movements starting just on the *internet* now. You could tell two hundred people to pull up in Central Park tonight if you so chose"—Kyrie was not, he clarified to his friend and their followers, encouraging a super-spreader event in Central Park, which was at the moment a gigantic field hospital— "but I'm saying, like, you have that type of reach, and if you're on here and you're utilizing your voice and utilizing this platform for spreading the goodness, and spreading the faith, man, you're doing some good things."

Kyrie's personal brand worked to contribute to the mass of celebrity altruism in the feed: meals and vegan burgers for virus-stricken communities in New York, solar-water kiosks in Ghana, pallets of food lined up outside a high school on the reservation of the Standing Rock Sioux, where the kids had been breaking into the rec center to eat, because the nearest grocery store wasn't for forty-five miles.

When a coach from Kyrie's high school heard about Fahad, he put out the word on Instagram and Facebook, then started rounding up clothes from Jersey to the city and Westchester and back again. Kyrie's prospect protégé Jon Kuminga, gym-less and busy studying so he could qualify to get into the NBA faster, asked what size shoe the kid wore. The coach got Fahad's address, dropped two bags of sneakers and gym clothes at his doorstep, and walked away. "You don't take pictures or anything for the clout," the coach said.

Now Fahad had something to wear to class and to work—until classes and workplaces shut down. His mom's two jobs, at his former school and as a part-time makeup artist on Broadway, had been vaporized by the virus. The Saleems would be forced to #StayHome, but first they needed to find one. Except there was nobody working at the real-estate firm down the block, nor anybody answering the claims line at the insurance company. Fahad lucked out finding a place by his brother's apartment, then moved out of the Best Western, went to Target for cleaning supplies, took his classes on Zoom and, in sports withdrawal, either played as the Nets on *2K* or watched their highlights on YouTube: a compilation of Spencer's game-winners, Kyrie's fifty-point game on opening night.

As much as Fahad appreciated the outpouring of support, he worried that Kyrie had forgotten about him, that his lucky No. 11 jersey would never be signed or seen again. After weeks of searching through the last of his belongings, Fahad stared at another bag of clothes strewn across his old lawn, charred and unwearable . . . except for something poking out from the bottom of the pile: *DINWIDDIE 8.* It was the first Nets jersey that Fahad had been able to afford with his own money. When Spencer changed his number, retiring it for Kobe, many play-ers had done the same, but Spencer came up with another idea for his fans: If you already owned the old No. 8 uniform, he'd send you a brand-new autographed No. 26, for free. But 26 had burned. And from the rubble, Kobe's old number emerged, the only treasure from Fahad's fandom—the only thing he could track down, anyway.

Fahad gripped his phone for any fresh hint about the NBA possibly coming back, but so much of the news in his Twitter feed was full of depressing numbers: Sixty-five hundred Americans had died from the virus; The Curve in New York City looked more like the face of El Capitan. He was finding his first year of college to be pretty depressing itself, compared to how much fun everyone seemed to be having on Instagram. Then, at the beginning of freshman calculus, came the dings: *Let's go Fahad* 💜 and so many more direct messages, from friends and family, sharing what looked like the photo he'd taken of his bedroom and posted to his hundred followers. Except it had been shared to *SportsCenter*'s sixteen million. *Who took that pic? Is that you?* He wasn't sure—this ESPN post had extra photos, too, of a Kyrie uniform with an autograph and a handwritten note: *TO WHOM MUCH IS GIVEN, EVEN MORE IS REQUIRED. WITH PEACE AND LOVE, WE ALL CAN HEAL FROM LIFE'S UNEXPECTED EVENTS.*

It was a strange feeling, going professionally viral in the middle of math class. Especially when his prized possession wasn't even *in* his possession: Kyrie's digital-content team at Roc Nation had prepared ESPN with their photos the day before and set a 9:30 a.m. news embargo, but the Nets had not yet shipped back the jersey to its very rightful owner. Fahad only learned that this autographed jersey did, in fact, belong to him when the *Bleacher Report* app buzzed in his hand and Fahad saw his own name in the alert. "I was hoping it was, like, more of a surprise," he told me. "I didn't expect to find out through social media." Fahad sat through attendance, then immediately logged out of the virtual lecture and put away his phone.

He had a headache. The curse of growing up at the time—in

the avalanche of 'Gram-dunks and memes, filterized selfies and TikTok dance routines—was to be constantly grasping at unnecessary influence and a faux-tangible fame, all by oneself already, in a free solo. Even as Fahad felt closer now than ever to the top of the feed, the virus only made life in isolation that much more lonely, masked up and eyes down, promless and dormitory-free, for Generation Zoom.

Two days later, Fahad peeled open a package from FedEx. Immediately, that stench—a whiff of shuddering old smoke—began to fill his new bedroom. He stuffed Kyrie's gift in a plastic bag and hid it in the closet. "It brought back so much bad shit," he said. "That smell, I hate it."

APRIL 27, 2020 🔜

DAY 47 WITHOUT BASKETBALL
Manhattan

THE DREADED COMMUTE. Miguel Gonzalez preferred taking the Q train the other way, Brooklyn-bound toward Barclays Center, where his cheer sparked the die-hards of The BK Block, as a sort of human firework from the crowd splashing down upon the concentration of a visiting team's free-throw shooter: *Sommmme-body BOO this guy!!* He'd been in attendance at Jay-Z's inaugural show on the arena's opening night, hollering along with a soon-familiar chant: *BROOOOOOK-LYN!* They held tryouts to join their group up in Section 114, for free season tickets and friends for life. Miguel had committed to attending every Nets home game this year, even after exhausting himself with the 6 a.m. shift, and with picking up the kids, and then exhausting himself some more with the overtime shift. But overtime taught him how to scrub down the operating room and gown up the doctors with personal protective equipment at New York–Presbyterian Hospital. By the second half of the season, Miguel, Brooklyn-born and bred for 38 years, had transformed his career from deli worker to hospital housekeeper to medical materials manager, a job that got him off by five o'clock, which meant he could still make it to Barclays in time for a few Modelos before tip-off.

The L train screeched more lightly than usual that Monday morning, westward into the city. Hardly a soul transferred at Union Square from the L to the northbound Q, and the underground cars felt the opposite of a crowd. The city was planning to stop the subway system overnight, its first shutdown since Superstorm Sandy in 2012, the catastrophe that had delayed the debut of NBA basketball in Brooklyn. They'd *just* finished fixing the damage Sandy had done to the L, but the city that never sleeps, Miguel thought, might be safer as a ghost town for now.

Miguel had stayed up late the night before with his 14-year-old son, Chris, to watch *The Last Dance*, a ten-part documentary series about Michael Jordan and the Bulls on ESPN. For two hours each Sunday, this became the sole television activity for American sports fans, a programming alternative to counting new cases of the virus. He finished building a gaming rig for Chris, maxing out the final hours of a week-long vacation that he'd scheduled for his daughter's sweet sixteen but had morphed into a reprieve from the front lines. He watched his son watch MJ clips for the first time. What Chris really loved, though, was watching the shoes—the night before, ESPN had showed the Jordan 7 Bordeauxs from '92, and Chris thought it was dope that his dad used to have the originals.

Shoes were underestimated at the hospital, Miguel believed. The little blue baggies covering his Jordans were scrunchy and disposable, but they'd become his top order in the days since basketball stopped, along with the N95 masks and gloves.

Miguel ordered hospital gear all day long, but he'd been ordering so many shoe coverings that he felt like he was working for Macy's at Christmas.

Before he took the week off to spend with family, Miguel pulled twelve-hour shifts to prep the tenth floor for a virus overflow. He and his colleague Eddie had cleared out another OR to become yet another ICU—the one downstairs was filling up. Miguel wheeled away stretchers upstairs meant for recovery from minor surgery, and he converted hallways so that Covid-19 patients could be hooked up, even two at a time, to whatever ventilators his colleagues might yet track down, even from China. He appreciated that Joe and Clara Tsai had tracked down two thousand ventilators from way over there, for $7 million, but those were meant for less fancy NYC hospitals than his to use. There'd been more than four thousand reported new cases in the city on the day Miguel went on vacation, and nearly nine hundred hospitalizations. New York–Presbyterian could have about nine hundred ICU beds ready if necessary—double the hospital's usual capacity—but Miguel didn't know what to expect upon his return.

Having withstood that morning's commute, fresh off his week at home, Miguel walked east from the Q to the hospital, past the ambulances and upstairs to change. He kept a Nets bandana in his cubby. But when he emerged from the hospital locker room, out into the halls of the tenth floor, there were no New Yorkers on their deathbeds, no ventilator traffic jams, no patients to be found.

At lunch, he brought his Chipotle back to the tenth-floor break room. He and Eddie used to keep on ESPN in here, when it was full of hospital workers with time on their hands. Now the TV was stuck to CNN—something about how the vice president thought the pandemic would be "largely" over by Memorial Day—so they got stuck talking about MJ and Netflix. The binge-watch conversation fizzled out, and Miguel listened to the halogen hum of an empty hospital floor, stupefied.

"Yo, Eddie," he said through a mouthful of burrito, "what's up with this? What they planning on ten?"

"Supposedly in two weeks," Eddie responded, "they're gonna start doing elective surgery again."

The tenth floor was gowning down, preparing for liposuction—a ghost town, Miguel decided, in a good way. The country was passing a million cases. There was no way the government was going to open up the city for a while. But The Curve had flattened, while Miguel had been distracted by Jordan highlights.

On his way home from another twelve-hour shift, Miguel passed an ER doctor he'd gotten to know, by talking sports, and asked what he'd missed on vacation.

"My man," the doctor told him, "we're not getting cases right now."

This had to be, Miguel thought to himself, as normal a day as he could remember.

He started walking back toward the Q train, past the ambulance parking lot, and gaped at the high-rises of the city. A video had gone viral last month—*Entire Brooklyn neighborhood sings "Juicy" by Biggie while on Coronavirus lockdown*—and it was pure joy, the harmony of New Yorkers uniting in song out the window. Pure joy until it was revealed that the video was fake news—those windows were closed, and that sing-a-long audio was from an old Jay-Z show at Yankee Stadium. But now, as Miguel commuted home from the hospital, the New Yorkers emerged from their apartments for real, and the roar of the crowd began again. *Woooo! Yeaaaaahh!* He pirouetted around the street corner and listened to all of First Avenue: balconies clanging, keys jangling, pots and pans and every species of kitchen appliance bang-gadanging together, and then someone lit a firecracker into the sky. Miguel loved this new ritual, the nightly applause for the first responders—the doctors and nurses, the Uber drivers and pizza guys, the shelf-stockers at the supermarket and even Miguel himself, the *somebody-BOO-this-guy* guy who also happened to be the shelf-stocker at New York–Presbyterian. The people were rooting harder for him than he used to root for the NBA.

MAY 15, 2020 ⏭

DAY 65 WITHOUT BASKETBALL
Fulshear, Texas

SPENCER WAS TWEETING AGAIN, into the half-moonlight of what was apparently a weekend, but who could even tell anymore? Like so many NBA players, and people of privilege, he'd escaped the city—Brooklyn had become the deadliest county in America, with more than four thousand people lost to coronavirus. In quarantine from his girlfriend's family home, though, Spencer had become the mayor of NBA Twitter, indulging in trade rumors about himself while smoking short ribs, volunteering to become the new general manager of the Chicago Bulls before watching cartoons with his son, arguing about the GOAT and gun control and Trump while preparing to test the limits of The League.

He already wondered if it was worth finishing *this* season, and he was becoming increasingly sure that the Nets would try to deal him away before *next* season. He couldn't control much before 2021, when he planned to opt out of his contract and become a free agent. But technically, Spencer realized, he could then agree to sign a one-year contract, make a list of five franchises, settle for a cheap deal that an already stacked contender could still afford . . . and let his *followers* decide his next team, charging *fans* to endorse his free agency in exchange for *their* democratic decision.

The next morning, Spencer set up a GoFundMe page to crowd-source himself, complete with photos of his head and shoulders in a Nets jersey, and a Lakers jersey, and a Clippers jersey. Under that, his asking price: $24,632,600, nearly as much as the reigning MVP, Giannis Antetokounmpo, was making—which, he realized, was ridiculous. But so was everything in the longest spring. Worst case, he'd give the money to charity.

This scheme was slightly less ambitious than The Spencer Dinwiddie Plan to Save the 2019–2020 NBA Season, for which he'd opened a Google Docs spreadsheet and typed out a bracket: twenty-eight teams, ranked top to bottom, play-in games, no separate conferences necessary, winner take all—March Madness for the pros. Fans would go nuts for his tournament, and The League could recoup its leaking millions. *I'll be giving away my ideas all month for free*, he tweeted. *Don't sue me @nba.* The players' union forwarded along Spencer's bracket pitch to league officials; after all, the commissioner *had* said it was time to get creative with broadcasts and empty stands.

A week earlier, on a league-wide call with players, Adam Silver had also said that there were "a series of bad options" for restarting a basketball season in the throes of a global pandemic. Chris Paul, the union president, thought "the virus was in control" of their ultimate decision-making, but he set up a superstars-only call—LeBron, Giannis, Steph, Kawhi Leonard, Anthony Davis, Russ Westbrook, even the injured KD—for a united front: *We want to play.* Spencer had been a little busy the day of the A-list meeting, explaining the asymmetrical yield curve of trading a LeBron James token for a Serena Williams token at a virtual cryptocurrency conference; in his spare time, he offered tweet-of-consciousness concepts of how, even though The League really ought to wait for a vaccine, owners and players *could* make some extra money from in-game fan trivia, or even—wait for it—live gambling in the NBA app.

Basketball power brokers were as desperate as couch potatoes for the NBA to lead the comeback of sports and culture, responsibly, as league-wide revenue losses cratered above $1 billion, between the shuttered arenas and unfulfilled television contracts. Chinese state TV still refused to air NBA games, and Trump's dog whistle of the "China virus" wasn't helping Joe Tsai's back channel. The Nets owner had felt the president's anti-Asian racism trickle down to his neighborhood outside San Diego, during his regular quarantine run: Tsai spotted a pickup truck ahead of him, and as a steady jog brought him closer to it, he realized that the truck driver was slowing down. When the pickup stopped him in his tracks, Tsai saw the driver's face in the mirror—the face of a white man—waiting for him to pass by, with the windows down. It was the first time, the billionaire immigrant said privately, that he'd felt his physical security at risk in the United States. He thought the two white people in the pickup truck might yell epithets, or jump out to confront him. He thought they might have a gun. Joe Tsai turned around and jogged home.

Internally, the Nets had done the math: Despite surrendering 40 percent of revenues from game nights at Barclays Center, they could break even if the owners decided to cancel the season, because Tsai wouldn't have to pay the players—incentives, like the million bucks KD was due to "earn" if the Nets made the playoffs without him, would have sent them over the top. And without KD, they wouldn't contend for a championship in the playoffs. "If you look at the Los Angeles Lakers or the Milwaukee Bucks, they're in first place when the season got suspended—of *course* they want to play," Tsai said. "Then there's other teams that, if you're in twenty-eighth place, maybe this season isn't that important. So there's a difference in opinion among the owners."

Silver and his resident scientists, though, were beginning to feel comfortable with an innovative "campus environment": Quarantine would be required upon arrival, for all players and essential personnel, at a resort to be determined, followed by the end of the regular season and a full playoff schedule, monitored with fifteen thousand tests and conducted without fans present, before crowning a champion of 2020 and going home. There was a pandemic raging outside, but the NBA could show the world how to survive and succeed inside, in The Bubble.

"The alternative," Silver said, "is to stay on the sidelines—to, in essence, give in to the virus."

A decision from on high was imminent, and the return of American entertainment would be up to Adam Silver, not Donald Trump. "He truly showed leadership that we didn't get from the government," Mark Cuban, the Dallas Mavericks owner from whom Trump once sought economic council, told me. "I truly believe if we hadn't shut down the NBA," Cuban continued, "there would have been thousands more deaths." Two months after Silver called timeout, the commissioner asked the owners a risky question about potentially moving forward: Could The Bubble remain intact, even after the inevitable first positive result threatened to pop it? "We followed the science," Cuban said. "He didn't have to take any special steps."

Spencer thought this entire hiatus had only reinforced the rarified company of decision-makers. Were the players *actually* going to get paid in this handshake deal? And was anybody *really* asking if it was *kind* of a bad look to confine more than three hundred successful men in their hotel rooms for that long? Had anybody considered their families left behind? Their mental health? The resort staff? Hadn't everybody *just* watched the video of the pickup truck slowing down in front of the jogger, and stopping him in his tracks? The one where the two white men jumped out yelling and, as the jogger passed by, gunned him down? Ahmaud Arbery was 25, and he could not turn around and jog home, because Ahmaud Arbery was jogging in Georgia while Black. And everybody was *about* to see another video go viral, of a white woman walking her dog off-leash in Central Park then calling the cops on a Black man . . . for bird-watching. Was basketball going to represent a better way of life, or was it all about reestablishing a status quo?

"Why don't you create a task force with the union and the league," a friend asked Spencer, "and help make changes?"

"Y'all know damn well they ain't listening to me," he said. "I sat down with the NBA almost a year ago, and they looked at me like I had three heads."

After lawyers for The League had stalled out his block-chain vehicle from the previous off-season and deep into 2020, investors in Fan Shares had pulled out during the virus-induced recession. "If they hadn't disenfranchised me back then, all these ideas would go straight to Adam Silver," Spencer told me. "If I had a pipeline to him and thought we could effect real change, then why wouldn't I?"

The NBA *did* end up considering Spencer's bracket play-in games for its playoff plan, and a players' working group did take into account the optics and housekeepers of The Bubble, while Disney World emerged as the enormous experiment's location of choice. Amy the dog walker *did* face charges of a year in jail, although her charges would be dismissed after court-ordered racism lessons. And Georgia law enforcement felt increasing pressure to arrest one of its own, as soon as celebrities started saying Ahmaud Arbery's name. *We're literally hunted EVERY-DAY*, LeBron wrote.

Spencer watched as LeBron presided over a graduation ceremony for America's lonely high-school seniors—a streaming celebrity feel-good-a-thon that Obama declined to host. Good for LeBron, Spencer thought. "He's gonna get to do that stuff without much backlash, and it's also more of a traditional lane," he told me the next day. "Fans, and especially me being me and not necessarily a LeBron, they're gonna come a little more negative than they would if I was one of those guys." Contagion or not, the success of A-list brands was irrepressible, and the continued bastardization of unpopular dissent, Spencer still believed, "says a lot about how legacy systems operate: They see something that could *potentially*, maybe, *some*what be a threat . . . it's *scary* for the NBA. But they're starting to get it now—now that they're in a crisis."

He was preparing to launch his own platform—the blockchain IPO of his contract had been a pilot for a new app that would leverage the world of social "creators" to buy and sell tokens in a "galaxy" for actual interactions with trendsetters, rather than celebrity voyeurism. "People love the platforms, but oftentimes big business gets greedy, and the reason why personal liberation is so in vogue is because of people's mistrust—of management, government, Apple, Google," he said. "If you look at the trends, and where things are going, a lot of the things I'm talking about are new, yes, but they're not completely radical. It's just how you package 'em and sell 'em."

Late that Saturday night, Spencer checked an alert from his GoFundMe app: Another donation to help crowd-source his free agency had just arrived, and it was the largest to date. It was for $69, from a user named "Knicks are Poopiepoopbuttbuttsoup Doo doo." Spencer laughed, and he watched another episode of the Jordan documentary—the one in which Steve Kerr hits the game-winner and MJ still gets the last word—and realized this little experiment of his had run its course.

13

A REVOLUTION ON TOP

WHEN THE VIDEO OF George Floyd first appeared in his Instagram Explore tab on Memorial Day, Eric Garner Jr. did not believe his eyes. The cell-phone footage, of cops gathered on a drab sidewalk in Minneapolis, looked shaky to him. Grainy. Unmodern. "I thought it was one of them fake news, but then I seen everybody posting it, and then I went back and looked at the video, and I was just, like, heartbroken," he said. "It was like just watching my Pops die all over again."

Unlike so many mothers and children of Black Americans lost to police violence who continue to fight for criminal justice and policing reform, Eric Jr. was an apprehensive activist. He went by a different last name and lived alone in Brooklyn, depressed and unemployed. He'd given up hooping and recently quit a job at Whole Foods, after overhearing a white co-worker rant about his father resisting arrest. "The last couple years," he said, "I've just been tryna find some way to cope."

This time, he was fed up. Everyone was fed up from watching eight minutes and forty-six seconds of George Floyd gasping "I can't breathe" on his way to heaven, as a white police officer knelt onto his neck outside a grocery store, for buying a pack of cigarettes with an allegedly counterfeit $20 bill. Eric Jr. wanted to get out in the streets, like he had for his first protest at Barclays Center in December 2014, the night LeBron and Kyrie wore his father's last words on T-shirts. Except he suffered from the same asthmatic condition that his father had died from, and he couldn't risk contracting Covid-19 at a march—he was only 25, but he'd seen Kevin Durant, his favorite basketball player, test positive, and the American death count from coronavirus had just passed one hundred thousand. Eric Jr. turned on the TV instead.

On CNN, and MSNBC, and all over social media beginning that Friday night, anyone watching could see Barclays Center become an epicenter of mass demonstration: A phalanx of three-hundred-plus NYPD cops formed a perimeter around the empty arena, as if defending it. Thousands of peaceful protesters in masks and bandanas streamed up Flatbush Avenue and congregated at the arena's front plaza: *George Floyd! No justice, no peace! Fuck the police!* Officers pepper-sprayed a local politician who'd spoken to the crowd and handcuffed another one. They clubbed young men on the sidewalk and shoved a young woman, head-first, into the street. An empty NYPD van was set on fire. Officers attempted to round up arrested New Yorkers onto a public bus, but the bus driver refused to drive it away. Even if by geographically central default, Barclays Center had become, as one reporter called it, Brooklyn's accidental new town square.

Eric Jr. wasn't watching Fox News Channel, on which the demonstrations were framed as *RIOTS 2020*, and a protest leader named Ace Burns was portrayed as a terrorist, despite calling for policy change (and maybe a little petroleum) with an acoustic guitar on his back, in front of the banner of Kyrie, KD and the Nets. The next night, Ace dispersed thousands of marchers at Barclays—white and Black, Latino, Asian, lesbian, gay, bisexual, transgender and young, very young—then got confronted up the block by NYPD officers, who proceeded to beat the shit out of him and arrest him on charges of making terrorist threats. He got out on $5,000 bail and began a week-long slumber party outside the arena. This 2020 moment of resistance would be defined by a generation connected by the feed of frustration and death they'd grown up in, Ace argued, as he prepared to guide another group of teenage activists and hipster moms from Barclays Center to city hall, megaphoning on rollerblades about defunding the police. The movement—fractured, as ever, between the OG compromisers and those youthful revolutionaries on the come-up—was expanding quickly now. And if the self-declared influencers or celebrity allies wanted in, Ace believed, they could not expect to be followed as leaders of change anymore, simply because they played the game.

"Jay-Z and Black athletes are living their best life. Get off your fuckin' ass and hit the streets," he said. "I support LeBron and a lot of these guys who are actively putting media out that influences the movement. But you know what we need? We need bodies on the ground. That is *everything* to us. That is the life-blood of the revolution—that shows more influence."

Ace was impressed when he looked at Twitter, on that very first Saturday after George Floyd's death, and saw the rising NBA stars Jaylen Brown and Malcolm Brogdon down in the streets of Atlanta, actively *leading* a march. Jaylen, who had studied under the same professor as Colin Kaepernick at Berkeley— who might have taken a knee four seasons earlier were it not for his rookie contract with the Celtics, who had clashed with Kyrie and negotiated a better deal—drove fifteen hours through the night to his hometown, then tweeted at his followers to meet him for a peaceful protest. Malcolm, the former NBA Rookie of the Year, was from Atlanta, too—his grandfather marched alongside Dr. King—and he had a fat new contract with the Indiana Pacers. But he was no influencer. "I didn't know how to protest," he said. Malcolm called up his college teammate Justin Anderson across town; he didn't either, but they'd both seen Jaylen's tweet, and they wanted to learn.

Justin had played with the Brooklyn Nets on a ten-day contract and led their minor-league squad, before the pandemic arrived. At 26, he was on his fourth franchise, and he was concentrated on making the team again, in The Bubble. Any NBA player could opt out of the season restart, for whatever reason he pleased, so opting in developed into a finesse of mind, body and bank account. Justin had always stayed "politically correct" on Twitter, not because he wanted to but because he could not take the financial risk of losing out on a longer contract—because he had been afraid of speaking out a little too loud. But that week, as he followed his fellow NBA players and even the carefully curated accounts of high-school basketball prospects out across the nation, Justin saw these young people like him demanding justice up and down his feed and sideways, too. He felt liberated, and the cry for liberation was spreading into demonstrations worldwide. "I wanted to actually take action," he said. "Tweeting didn't mean anything to me anymore."

In the middle of Atlanta's basketball protest, empty police buses creeping alongside him, 23-year-old Jaylen Brown broadcast live to Instagram from Auburn Avenue. "Being a celebrity, being an NBA player doesn't exclude me from no conversation at *all,*" he said. "As a young person, you gotta listen to our perspective. Our voices need to be heard."

The march paused, and Malcolm Brogdon was handed the megaphone. Justin always thought his friend from the University of Virginia sounded like Obama when he talked loud and he talked with rhythm, but he could hear a nervousness in Malcolm. Justin grabbed his shoulder. *Talk, man,* he whispered in his friend's ear. *Talk!* Like that, Malcolm spoke up, and he spoke out: "I got brothers, I got sisters, I got friends, that are in the streets, that are out here, that haven't made it to this level, that are experiencing it, that are getting pulled over, just discrimination, day after day, dealing with the same bullshit, and this is *systematic,*" he said on the mic. "We have leverage right now. We have a moment in time. . . . We need more leaders."

Justin felt that Malcolm had said enough for them to keep marching on. He was also concerned that his presence itself, standing in the background with his aviator sunglasses on, in solidarity with his brother, might still get him in trouble if Malcolm's speech went viral, which he knew it would. "My ass is gonna be in *Israel* playing next year because of this," he told his friends. "My ass is gonna be in *France!*" But marching those Atlanta streets had made Justin appreciate something powerful about his priorities—that he would be a Black man longer than he bounced any basketball—and he decided to rededicate himself to community work back home in Virginia, where they were finally preparing to remove a slave auction block from a street corner downtown.

That evening in Atlanta, two college students were driving back from the protests when the cops smashed in a window, tased them and ripped the woman from the car.

"There are no more cheeks to turn," Jaylen said. "Being a bystander is no longer acceptable."

It had been less than a week since George Floyd's sense-less killing, and the Nets were too spread out around the country to march together in Brooklyn. But the faces of the NBA and the WNBA were at once everywhere—L.A., N.C., Philly, D.C., Dallas, Boston—and nowhere: That Sunday, the 25-year-old Nets forward Timothé Luwawu-Cabarrot made his way to a protest wrapped around Barclays Center, wearing a heavy-duty mask of anonymity—the Nets would be flying to Disney World in a month, and he needed to stay as safe as possible. That was cool by him. Because, yeah, Jarrett Allen stood out above the marchers taking over the Brooklyn Bridge, but Tim loved that he could blend in with a crowd.

"It's good to have symbols *and* heroes, like Colin—like LeBron," he told me at another march days later, holding a *GEORGE FLOYD* sign as he dribbled one of two hundred basketballs bouncing past the Marcy Houses where Jay-Z grew up. "But NBA players, for people to see that we can come down in these streets, along with anybody else, and be the change? *Then* you move on to the next step, which is: *Do* something, *get* something. And that's what we're going to talk about in The Bubble, and we know we can do that down there."

The NBA, however, saved its righteous agita for when money was on the line.

A community organizer working with the Nets easily pushed the league office to support a revised Black history curriculum in schools, courtesy of the Smithsonian museum in Washington—the one that KD and the Warriors had visited. "That being said," the organizer, James Mcdougal, told me, "the NBA, it's all a business. So some of the policies you can't get to the NBA are police reform—that's not safe. Defunding the police will hurt their bottom line." The Tsais were the second-richest owners in the NBA, and Clara Wu Tsai began speaking with activists at length—about how to address overt racism by killer cops by using her pick-up-the-phone power, to uproot covertly racist institutions like the NYPD. "But," Mcdougal said, "they're also gonna put the phone *down* and say we don't wanna have nothing to do with this at *all*. In activism, like politics, there's a middle ground."

The owners prepared a statement declaring that enough was enough, as did seemingly every franchise in American pro sports. Wu Tsai organized long calls for franchise employees and the team with Bill Clinton and Van Jones, the former Obama adviser turned CNN commentator who worked with her and Jay-Z on a criminal-justice-reform initiative. "I felt like I was looking at a bunch of people in those little Zoom squares, any one of whom might be able to save a life, pass a bill, green-light an economic project," Jones told me. "They had zero idea how powerful they were." NBA players didn't need to have all the answers, Jones reminded the Nets, so much as questions—Jay-Z didn't know the penal code of Minnesota, but he'd asked what was going to happen when an old white local county attorney drew the George Floyd case, and then Jay-Z picked up the phone and asked the governor to install the trusted Black attorney general instead. Nets players logged out of their little Zoom squares after a few minutes; they were not Jay-Z, nor were they signing up for his version of the good fight, a benevolent march of The Hovites.

Even as demonstrators began to congregate elsewhere around the city, Joe Tsai told *The New York Daily News* that peaceful assembly at Barclays Center "from residents to businesses to police alike" was "good with me"—a comment that upset his employees, since Joe Tsai did not own the nearly thirty-nine-thousand-square-foot "town square" plaza outside the arena; the people of Brooklyn did.

One morning in June, a new billboard appeared along the exit to the Barclays Center subway station, at the top of the escalator: *I am no longer accepting the things I cannot change. I am changing the things I can no longer accept.* The sign attributed this message to the great activist Angela Davis, but the inspiration of a radical appeared to be fake activism approved by the NBA franchise itself: The origins of the quote were in dispute.

JUNE 2, 2020 ⏭

DAY 83 WITHOUT BASKETBALL
Thousand Oaks, California

KEVIN DURANT WARMED UP in Kobe's old gym, spry as spring. Coronavirus had set back his Achilles rehab at first, but he'd been camped out at a new temporary mansion in L.A. for more than a month, and while he didn't plan on leaving anytime soon, he was seeking a change of scenery.

After Wilson Chandler's own isolation in a Manhattan apartment had stressed him out, he had craved a little sunshine and found his way to The Sports Academy, where Kobe used to coach his girls and teach All-Stars how to become better teammates, as its courts partially reopened for private training. Over the last week, KD had joined him up here at Kobe's gym—as had Kyrie.

The Nets superstars played socially distant basketball as best they could inside The Sports Academy. But this was not permitted under the NBA's guidelines for a return to play, which limited teams to working out at their own practice facilities without coaches, and Sean Marks was slightly paranoid about getting found out.

The general manager, watching from court to court alongside trainers and assistant coaches, was so impressed with KD's domination in this gym that he'd allowed for the possibility that KD might actually complete rehab in time to play in The Bubble.

So did Kevin Durant himself. It had been nearly a year since the most talented player in the game played in a game that mattered, and it would be at least another six months before the next NBA season could safely begin. He had always imagined making his debut in the black-and-white, in Brooklyn, in front of his fans. But the Nets could make a fan-free playoff drive for the ages in Disney World, the conquering return of a forgotten hero.

Alas, KD would have to wait.

"Even though he wasn't cleared, he still wanted to go," KD's housemate and bodyguard, Antjuan Lambert, told me. "But it was just a lot, and the team shut it down."

"We don't want you at ninety percent," a doctor had said.

Dejected but determined, KD thought the least he could do for his teammates was try to enter The Bubble as a fan on the bench, but the Nets decided that wasn't worth it either.

Kyrie was looking healthy, too, except he'd been all-out on The Bubble since the entire idea of it began in March. He'd been out on this lost season since well before that. Kyrie had spent his springtime quarantine rehabbing alone on both coasts, driving solo to his middle school in New Jersey, running wind sprints and revving up his drills as the paint chipped in that empty old gym. But he'd been in a headspace separate from sport, meditating on his Sioux prayer rug every morning as the sage floated high, and he'd been thinking about the oppression of his people. He tried going to therapy. He thought about Kobe and how he could pass down the wisdom of his elders—Native history, Black history—to kids in the cities and the suburbs, where he'd been taught that Columbus Day and MLK Day were long weekends. He worked on some pretty decent Basquiat-style paintings, crowns and all, and he rapped a little at his friend's new studio. But mostly he read—Angela Davis, Assata Shakur—and told friends and family and his fiancée that he was willing to put down his ego to try listening again. He felt a strong Black pride, and he could feel almost balanced, once he joined his best basketball friends, back on the court.

There but for the approval of the NBA did these veterans of The Clean Sweep corner decide with Marks to set up shop in Mamba Land. The team tried to rent out Kobe's gym for the month and considered bringing out the whole squad for training camp before Disney World. But air travel still had its risks, and Marks didn't know what the Nets roster might look like down there, or if they could even be competitive. Their best player left was Caris LeVert, the shooting guard formerly known as Baby Durant, but Kyrie and KD were apparently trying to convince him to opt out of The Bubble, too. *Wait 'till next year* was the prerogative of the truly empowered. Here in California, KD and Kyrie could play one-on-one while helping to construct and observe the rest of a squad that would soon be sequestered in Orlando. "We want to see the level we can get to now, sharing it with a person that we believe in," Kyrie would later tell KD. "As well as other people, but it started with us being at the foundation."

The energy in Kobe's gym had been flat all week after the killing of George Floyd. For Kyrie, real life was forcing him to question whether any game mattered anymore, and as that morning's workout began, he'd gone missing again. His teammates stretched and waited, kept peeking past the indoor beach volleyball court toward the door.

"Where the fuck is Ky?"

In the parking lot outside, Wilson pulled up and spotted the elusive Kyrie Irving in his car, on his iPhone, typing into Instagram. Everywhere in Kyrie's feed—everywhere in everyone's feeds—there were black boxes. They looked like the square that DeAndre had posted six years earlier, when he was left with nothing to say about Donald Sterling, no caption necessary since the owner's racism was so obvious. But this Tuesday was officially #BlackoutTuesday. Every brand and every influencer was trying desperately to say something about social justice by saying nothing, and yet they seemed to say, in their thirsty allyship, even less. "I'm not with the blackout post," Wilson told me, that day he passed Kyrie in the parking lot. "It's not even just the NBA. I feel like people, and corporations in general, are just using it for a brand name. Like, it's a *thing* now: The symbolization of Black Lives Matters is a thing now." He skipped #BlackoutTuesday, posting a video of James Baldwin instead, and thought Kyrie might just be on the phone with his fiancée or something in the car.

As Wilson headed into Kobe's gym to find some hand sanitizer and catch up with the morning workout, Kyrie finished tapping away at another manifesto, subverting his black-box Instagram post with a screen-filling caption:

> I am calling on all my People of Color, Leaders of Change, and all those that are aware of what is happening, what has happened, and are ready for solutions. ✊🏼 ✊🏾 ✊🏿 ✊🏾 . . . I am sick of this idea of letting things balance out and talk it out bullshit. . . . We know all this talking and protesting will get us maybe a few law changes and conversations, but at this point it's bigger than that. It's time we take all our Native Indigenous Black culture, business, ideas to a new place as a collective and protect it just like other cultures have done. Build our own! . . . This is for Our Future Kids kids. We are the generation that will change this!

Out here in Mamba Land, Kyrie could talk every day after workouts with Wilson, who found the unbearable whiteness of wokeness, its convenient reckoning, to be exhausting. Wilson watched mobs of armed white men hold his Michigan statehouse "hostage," only for Trump to call them "very good people"—some of whom would later be charged with plotting to kidnap the governor—and then he saw that Trump had said that unarmed Black people, peacefully protesting state killings in the streets of America, were *THUGS* who could be met with martial law. But at least the cops were kneeling in the streets, too! Wilson saw the Michigan militia hang a doll from a flagpole, and he saw Covid-19 continue to disproportionately affect Black and brown people, and then he saw the NFL and NASCAR decide that racism was bad. Wilson was done with marching: "Shit is same old, same old." In The Bubble, Wilson was sure there would be more and better T-shirts, more talk at postgame press conferences, more LeBron. But the familiar symbolism inherent to athlete activism would only spin around and around, like a basketball wobbling on a fingertip, until the momentum ran out, and it fell off again. "It won't be powerful," Wilson declared. "Just the NBA and Nike capitalizing off another tragedy. Branding at its finest." Stef Rizzo and the Nets' human-performance staff at Kobe's gym told Wilson they wanted to teach him how to swim in Disney World. But he refused to be treated as part of a human experiment, only for ESPN and the YES Network to cash in, while Adam Silver nodded to some token scholarship program. "Shit is a plantation," Wilson said, and decided to opt out for the rest of the year, so he could spend time with his grandmother and his kids and his elusive peace of mind. In a way, he thought, George Floyd was his family, too. George Floyd was 46 years old.

After George's death, Kyrie began speaking regularly with

Stephen Jackson—a retired NBA "journeyman" known to friends as Stack, who was notorious for punching a fan in the stands during The Malice at The Palace in 2004 and known to a new generation of fans as the co-host of a popular player- and celebrity-interview podcast, *All the Smoke*. Stack had been longtime friends with George Floyd from growing up in Houston's Third Ward—"my twin," he called him—and now Stack, at 42, was becoming an activist. "I had no idea what I was doin'," he told me, "but from all the police killings I've seen in the past, no one had a celebrity to speak up for them."

On #BlackoutTuesday, Stack was in the streets of downtown Minneapolis with six-year-old Gianna Floyd—George's daughter, like Kobe's, was called Gigi—when the gap-toothed little girl said she was tired of walking from protest to protest, interview to interview. Uncle Stack hoisted her upon his shoulders and started spinning 'round and 'round. Up from the six-foot-eight view of things, Gigi could see posters of her father's face in every direction: "Look at my daddy, Unc! Look at my daddy, Unc! Look at my daddy, Unc!"

"Yeah, you see? Your daddy changed the world," said Uncle Stack.

Stack piggybacked her a few more steps, and she cheered: "Daddy changed the *world*!"

"He did what?" a friend asked the girl, filming on his phone.

Stack stretched out Gigi's hands in his, like wings. "Daddy changed the *world*!"

Millions of views and several protests later, Stack hadn't heard from the NBA in any official capacity, or from the players' union. Steve Kerr called. The head coach in Minnesota texted, and his guy Jimmy Butler down in Miami, too. LeBron reposted one of Stack's Instagram posts to @KingJames—Stack messaged to thank him, because George had been a huge LeBron fan, and

LeBron promised not to let Stack down—but Kyrie kept peppering Stack with questions by FaceTime and text: *Whatchu doin' next? What's next?* When Stack traveled to the streets of Milwaukee and Philly and Kalamazoo, Kyrie made sure his elder got in a nap. Kyrie wanted to learn how to be an all-of-a-sudden activist, too, instead of an all-the-time basketball player. Perhaps the extra effort could at least make him a better leader. At best, Kyrie might begin transforming from heady to full-on humanitarian. Perhaps the lifeblood of revolution was inside the athletes already.

"I wasn't one of the players that was one of the NBA's favorites," Stack said, "but with me being on the front lines, being a face of a civil rights movement of eighteen countries and all fifty states—me being the leader of it, an NBA player, that's never been done before—then I would expect the NBA to get behind me and support me. But having Kyrie, being a vice-president of the players' association . . . that meant the world. Because what I'm doing, I'm doin' it at the surface, and he's doin' it at that *top* level."

The day after Kyrie's Instagram manifesto, however, came word that The Bubble was on. The movement in the streets of Brooklyn and beyond had gotten Kyrie's mind racing about systemic racism, but the streets couldn't keep up with the big business of the NBA, even as Adam Silver said the league could have "more of an impact on this issue than almost any organization in the world." The sequencing was off; the science experiment was already underway. *So the NBA's inviting 22 teams to Orlando*, tweeted the all-seeing ESPN reporter Adrian Wojnarowski. *Vote tomorrow to ratify. The NBA's back.*

Kyrie only wanted to dissent more. He joined a rally near UCLA the next afternoon—not his first rally of the week—and, in the morning, dialed in to the players' union call to ask mundane but probing questions about logistics, like the availability of high-end booze in Disney World hotel rooms. Not that it necessarily mattered to Kyrie—he wasn't even going. He cast his ballot for a return to play as The Bubble was approved unanimously, but he had veered off to his own turnpike by then. "There's so many issues that you wanna tackle—that *I* wanna tackle," Kyrie would tell KD. "And, honestly, it's so hard to do it without having a destination, and my destination at this point is not to be the Greatest Basketball Player to ever play the game. Like, what the fuck does that title mean? It's so small."

Kyrie's change in focus had become particularly activated by the case of Breonna Taylor. He, like so many millions of Americans, was gut-wrenched to hear how the emergency room technician, a Black woman on the front lines in Louisville who was trying to have a baby with her boyfriend, had been awakened from her sleep by undercover officers in a drug raid gone horribly wrong. Kyrie opened up Instagram and instructed his thirteen million followers to email the mayor and the attorney general, calling for them to fire, arrest and charge the Louisville officers who still roamed the streets, nearly three months after they shot Breonna Taylor five times in her bed. Breonna Taylor was 26.

"Black lives matter, but this is more than a movement—this is a revolution that has been underground, and now it's on top," Kyrie would soon reflect. "Justice can exist in many different ways, but specifically for me, it's doing my part, not just being this six-time NBA All-Star, or this NBA champion, or everything I identify with or what I thought my legacy was gonna be about. This has taken a whole new turn."

There was always another workout, or another pickup game, and, yes, the president was having the streets cleared with tear gas, for a photo op with himself and the Bible outside the White House. But Kyrie Irving was busy putting a quarter-million-dollar down payment on a big new house in Houston for George Floyd's daughter and her mom—their first home, a permanent mansion, in one of the fanciest parts of town.

JUNE 8, 2020 🌙

DAY 89 WITHOUT BASKETBALL
Montclair, New Jersey

KYRIE HAD BEEN HEARING from players throughout the NBA—and the WNBA—who were questioning The Great Sports Comeback of 2020. They had concerns about abandoning the momentum of a social-justice movement for the friendly confines of Disney World; younger and underpaid athletes were worried about not getting compensated if they refused to go. Despite voting alongside the leadership of the players' union three days earlier to resume the season, Kyrie was frustrated that its twenty-eight team representatives spoke for four hundred fifty players. Union chief Michele Roberts had been hurrying to canvass teams about a restart, but the rebels needed a champion for their cause. "Kyrie was and is known among the players as someone who is *not* shy," she told me. "I'm not threatened by opposition or opposing voices. That's what democracy is all about."

A mass boycott of The Bubble had a minor groundswell. An informal coalition of the potentially unwilling, dozens strong and growing, was born.

At Kyrie's invitation, members of the coalition opened up a Zoom meeting and saw a wisened harbinger with a familiar fist, Dr. John Carlos. He'd been disappointed by NBA players for missing their moment of reckoning during the 2014 Donald Sterling scandal, not solely to invent a profound symbol but to make demands upon ownership. Still, the Los Angeles Clippers had put the world on notice that athletes could collapse the culture instantaneously, and not since then had Dr. Carlos sensed in the sporting community such "a nucleus of individuals" as he did now in the NBA's empowered hoopers, who could force structural change, with their followings and especially by hitting billionaire owners in the pocketbooks.

Dr. Carlos left the basketball players with advice similar to what he'd told Colin Kaepernick when the two generational pioneers first met: "You have jumped into the pool of humanitarianism, and this is not in-the-moment—this is in-the-*movement*. You're in the *movement* now. And now is not the time to go dormant with your voice. Now's the time to turn the volume *up* and *keep* it turned up, because you jumped out there to speak up for the voiceless."

Kyrie and his Bubble-busters would have to come together as one unit, Dr. Carlos reminded players on the call, which included several title-hunters from LeBron's Lakers, their starting point guard Avery Bradley and the veteran Dwight Howard among them. "He said this opportunity might not be available for *another* fifty years after this," Avery told me, of John Carlos. "There was so much pressure—other NBA players said we were crazy—but we had to find a way to reprogram everyone's way of thinking and not just moving fast. Because this job moves fast, and some of it is on purpose, to not give you an opportunity to think, and just make impulse decisions instead. . . . There's systemic racism going on in our job."

Spencer, in Kyrie's ear again that week, encouraged the rebels to get numbers and strike while the nation was hot. "Bro, I know how this story turns out," he advised his teammate. "They're gonna throw out disinformation to discredit you. And if you're not resolute, then the movement's going to die. Ky, you need the ayes."

Kyrie and Avery scrambled to find player cell-phone numbers and text out a mass invite for a video-conference call that Friday night: *Because of our competitive nature, there has been an unnecessary division amongst us. In joining together we have the ability to empower one another. We reach out to you because we want all of your voices to be heard.* The eye-rolling was almost immediate, even across the court from Kyrie, KD, Wilson and Caris that day at Kobe's gym, where the Lakers forward Kyle Kuzma took a break from training and from suddenly tweeting daily about race and politics to make clear to his followers that *some of us want to hoop and compete, don't get that twisted.*

Dwight Howard, at home with his family in suburban Atlanta, sent the invite to Natasha Cloud, a star of the WNBA's Washington Mystics, and asked her to spread the good word. Natasha, too, was sick of talking logistics for the so-called Wubble on hour-and-a-half-long WNBA union calls, so she'd interrupted restart negotiations to say their names: George Floyd. Breonna Taylor. "I kinda got pushed as the radical leader," she said. "I was the Kyrie of the WNBA."

Natasha clicked on the invitation and saw, in the seventy-five-plus boxes of the Zoom, the NBA's modern-day thought-leadership hall of fame. Superstars, like Chris Paul and Russ Westbrook. Veterans, like Carmelo Anthony, Andre Iguodala and Mike Conley Jr. The next superstars, like Joel Embiid, Donovan Mitchell and Malcolm Brogdon. And several Brooklyn Nets, including Kevin Durant. No LeBron. The host was a user named Ky Birving.

Kyrie's opening remarks, from in front of a laptop at a friend's house in North Jersey, were less rambling than usual. If everyone on the call wanted justice, he asked, how could players best unite in being present, for the movement and their Black communities? His presence from The Bubble, of course, would be one of absence. He was hurt, officially, and remained skeptical of the types of NBA medical experts responsible for the league's coronavirus response. But Kyrie believed Black players needed to put health and safety at a premium in order to fully articulate that their lives mattered. Covid-19 cases in Florida were on the uptick, and entertainers at Disney World were nonessential workers in a pandemic. They could be revolutionaries instead.

Chris Paul, as union president, warned players not to get too specific about new plans for negotiations on the call, because he knew that such details would leak to the press. But he and Roberts were already working to guarantee financial commitments from ownership for social justice and voting rights . . . while simultaneously recouping a couple billion dollars in player revenue lost to the virus.

If this coalition was rallying for a boycott or a strike, Carmelo asked, "What do we stand for?" Were NBA stars going to march in their home cities instead? Fight for reform in state legislatures?

"Unity," Kyrie kept saying.

Garrett found Kyrie's entire insurrection to be rushed and relatively unnecessary. He reminded players on the call that the world was at a standstill. Baseball's return had been stalling, the Dallas Cowboys were testing positive, and college athletes were bringing coronavirus back to campus. The Bubble would offer time to discuss more demands, while players could pour their paychecks back into their communities and set an example for what Black generational wealth looked like. By the time the games began, Garrett said, people would *have* to watch basketball and listen to their message; the NBA would be the only thing on.

Andre Iguodala could navigate between compromisers and freedom-fighters alike, a 2020 version of Stokely Carmichael if he'd invested early in Zoom, as Andre had. After KD left the Warriors, Andre flexed his player empowerment by holding out from the season for four months, until Miami had emerged as a title contender so he could finesse his trade of choice to the Heat, and he served on the union's executive committee with Chris, Garrett and Kyrie. In 2014, Andre had prepared the Warriors to go on strike during their playoff series with the Clippers, an act of unity to help protest the vile bigot Donald Sterling. He'd encouraged Chris and the Clips to boycott with a firm stance: "Man, don't show up. *That's* powerful, right?" It was a true team-mate's duty, however, to do what was in the best interest of the group, and the internal priorities of the NBA in 2020 remained making back money. "I can't always be so militant," Andre told me. "But at the same time, I can slowly get that information to the guys and say, 'OK, when we *really* ready, this is how we do it.' You got to slowly bring them along."

Spencer chimed in on Kyrie's call: If a mass of players opted out of returning *this* season, the owners could lock them out, right after The Bubble. Ownership could even hold back those long-awaited paychecks from their work in Disney World as le-verage to cancel *next* season, if not *two* seasons, demanding that the players give up their fifty-fifty split of NBA revenue shares. A total of $1.2 billion in player salaries was in jeopardy.

"I'm willing to give up everything I have," Kyrie said. If a coalition of players had to compensate those who wanted to opt out of The Bubble, he figured, the top earners could cover the little guys.

"I didn't believe him," Garrett told me. "It's easy to say that when you've made what you've made and you've got the Nike money. If you're coming into the league and haven't made a dime yet, then that would be a totally different story—and you had other big guys randomly just start talking about social justice, and it seems convenient because they have tens of millions of dollars in the bank." Even if Kyrie could support the paycheck-to-paycheck players who wanted to work on social justice, rookies and grinders like Justin Anderson were still working to earn a spot in the league as their workplace reopened early. They deserved the option to conjoin protest and play. By the end of the back-and-forth, Garrett said, "there *was* no new plan, because most guys that didn't want to play did not have a plan. They just said, 'We'll sit out, and something will happen.'"

Toward the end of the call, Renee Montgomery's Zoom box filled the screen. The women of the WNBA had led for so long—she and the Minnesota Lynx had T-shirts for Philando Castile and Alton Sterling back in 2016, and had already refused to talk about anything else in media appearances—but they didn't appear, to many non-believers, to have the same hit-'em-in-the-pocket power as players in the NBA. Renee now played for the Atlanta Dream, which was co-owned by the Republican senator Kelly Loeffler, who used her own team's activism as a race-baiting reelection tool. Women were on the front lines of the movement in the world at large and the sports world, once again, as the Dream and the WNBA players' union tried to force out the owner. Renee was willing to risk her season to get out there on CNN and MSNBC talking about racial injustice, instead of going to The Wubble to finish the season and get paid—and she only made $109,000 a year.

Kyrie was shocked to learn more about the wage gap in the WNBA, where the maximum salary was $215,000 and players often had to work a double season by playing abroad, and he was willing to ante up for them, too. "We need to protect our Queens," Kyrie said.

"It was like a Black Panther call, in the best way," Natasha Cloud told me later, "because we were empowering one another as Kings and Queens. As the NBA and the WNBA, we've been separated for far too long. We've been completely separated. They didn't want us in communication."

The call may have had a bit *too* much communication, because the revolution had been tweeted by reporters within minutes, spewed back out to fans who considered Kyrie a forever villain. Some players accused ESPN of bias for wanting sports back on TV for its bottom line, and so for labeling Kyrie as The Disruptor.

Closing the laptop at his friend's house, Kyrie ate a sandwich and laughed a familiar, fed-up laugh at Twitter. A radical on top was on the right track, he believed, when the system was trying this hard to sabotage your best intentions underground. "It won't happen to Kyrie, but it's similar to what happened to Kap with that narrative," Andre said. "It's almost like they're infiltrating our system—like what happened to the Black Panther Party."

Kyrie and Avery Bradley remained disappointed, though not surprised, that their insurrection failed. They did not exactly convince anyone new that evening to join their mass boycott, and they felt that their list of demands—for franchises to hire more diversely in front offices and coaching staffs, to partner with Black-owned arena vendors and local businesses, to donate a lot more money—went largely unread at the time.

John Carlos had told players in the coalition to expect that it might take the media and fans decades to realize they were right, but the rebels never reported back to the wise man. "I'm a bit embarrassed of how we handled that entire situation," Avery said, "because I don't feel like we did what he wanted us to do. The opportunity for us to take advantage of that situation was *there*, and we missed out on it—we didn't know who was together. And I know everyone's pushing for change, but the NBA had a big opportunity, because everybody else woulda followed suit—every other sport—if we made the right move."

Dwight Howard called Craig Hodges, the freedom-fighter blackballed by the Bulls and the NBA after he'd been up in Michael Jordan's business thirty years earlier, and confessed to his elder that he felt lonely and confused in picking up the mantle of athlete activism. Craig told him to go win a championship with the Lakers then come back to his Atlanta community in the off-season. "This generation, you don't *have* to boycott," Craig said. "You can have your social media to put on heavy, *heavy* pressure, and you can still play the game.

"But what *is* the game?" Craig asked. "Our goal has to be defined *by* us who have been part of the oppressed community, but now it's time to redress it to the point of solutions. The only thing that this white power structure realizes and considers is somebody pulling their tail economically. *Slavery* was economics. Going down to The *Bubble* is economics. Opening up the *economy* is economics. The bottom line is the green . . . and this whole structure don't wanna look at the power that underlies *their* power. The NBA's power structure is Black athletes, but they don't wanna give those Black athletes equity. When you go down to The Bubble to play, Black people are still being murdered, *today*, when you're opening up your season. So what has really changed?"

Later the night of Kyrie's call, at a Wendy's parking lot in Atlanta, Rayshard Brooks fell asleep in his car, woke up to police officers questioning him and, after resisting arrest, was shot by one of them twice in the back. Rayshard Brooks was 27 years old.

Kyrie was fired up. "Sport is a distraction," he told a coach at Duke. "We run the industry," he would go on to say. "Without us, there is no industry!" On the Nets' player group chat, several of Kyrie's teammates found this line of thinking a bit out there—

even for him, even if the ideas were not all that new—and one of them leaked to the *Daily News* that Kyrie believed NBA players could start their own league someday. His remaining friends and protégés on the team stood by him, but Kyrie abandoned the season-long group chat, and several players on the Nets never heard from Kyrie again.

That was the end of Death Row, a lifeline of laughs and links about dunking and dinner, China and childcare, love and basketball, Kap and Kobe, and ultimately far too much division and death. By the time the Brooklyn Nets drifted apart for the year, these players who'd defined themselves as stronger than any franchise culture or cultural schism—*us versus everybody else*—hadn't proved as resilient together as they were balanced out on their own, an archipelago of individuals.

"Nobody likes a radical, nobody wants nobody thinking outside the box, 'cuz that's a threat to the government, to the establishment," Wilson told me. "People try to discredit Ky, like, *Oh, he's not a good teammate*, like that has something to do with Black men getting murdered. Like, he said the Earth was flat. I don't care if he said the Earth was a *rectangle*—he had the backbone to say what he felt: He don't think we should play, and I don't think he should be left on an island for saying that."

At his new family home, under construction in Jersey, Kyrie welcomed Natasha Cloud, the Kyrie of the WNBA. Yes, Kyrie made $31 million a year from the Nets and $11 million a year from Nike. "But," she said, "what do those owners make? They make billions of dollars off Kyrie's name and likeness, off of Kevin Durant's name and likeness. And that's what people still can't wrap their heads around: Some systems can be seen as new-age slavery." She and Kyrie talked about how to change the system—how to use the system back, with a seat at "the head of the table"—for more Black female executives, more Black coaches, more Black generational wealth, more Black Power. "Man," Natasha said, "can you *imagine* if both of our leagues said, *Fuck y'all, we're not playin'*? Can you imagine the power and the spotlight that would then be on both of our leagues?" Then Kyrie said all that Natasha needed to hear: "I'm pulling out your chair at the table and I'm pushing it in."

Kyrie FaceTimed with Jewell Loyd, a fellow Kobe disciple who'd been nicknamed The Gold Mamba by their mentor and was headed to The Wubble in Bradenton, Florida, to go win a championship with the Seattle Storm. They talked about education, not just paying off tuitions at high schools and historically Black colleges and universities but rewriting the history books, with Kyrie starring in videos about the Tulsa massacre at Black Wall Street and the early resistance of The Little Rock Nine. Jewell was repeatedly struck by how many questions Kyrie asked: *Would you be down for something bold? What do you need? Do you need a platform? Do you need some financial freedom?*

"That's something that Ky did *all* the time," Jewell said. "And that's what Kobe did: He sat down and listened. It wasn't always him telling me what to do, how to do it—the reality is that you can empower *other* people. And that's what Ky's been able to—that's what Kobe taught us to do—is give back."

Kyrie pitched to Natasha and Jewell a financial empowerment initiative for the dozen-plus players in the WNBA opting out of The Great Sports Comeback of 2020 in order to fight social injustice, or pursue a second career, or take care of their own families and well-being during a time of epochal threats to the human body—to live their lives instead. He offered $1.5 million.

The Disruptor hadn't been there for his teammates, hadn't been present for much of his homecoming season, because he was looking for something that was not in a locker room, or on a basketball court. "I *haven't* done the job that I've wanted to do in my responsibility to speak up on these things, but now that I do, I'm here in full force to *be* that voice, to *be* that platform," Kyrie told his Queens. "I'm gonna be there, and I'm gonna be present for you, and I'm gonna show up."

14

THE TOOTHPASTE IS OUT OF THE TUBE

JULY 14, 2020 ⏩
DAY 125 WITHOUT BASKETBALL
Golden Oak, Florida

AT THE END OF QUARANTINE, The Bubble Nets could breathe the swampy air again at last. The NBA had locked them up for days inside the Grand Floridian Resort & Spa, and this was no place like home: The franchise provided an exercise bike in each player's hotel room, along with a book about mass incarceration. Pictures of their families, who were not permitted unless the team survived into the second round of the playoffs, hung inside the door. Mandatory bracelets functioned as both hall pass and hall monitor, in addition to the former special-ops guards providing extra security around the walls of "campus." The NBA had, in a matter of weeks, transformed the theme park formerly known as Disney World into a science fiction come true: Coronavirus was under near-complete control in here, any team could be a Cinderella, and fans got to watch the entire bizarre spectacle all by their lonesome, live on television all day and all night, while real life on the outside continued at an inexorable standstill.

With another two weeks of practice remaining until the last eight games of the regular season restarted, the Nets had an off-day to get to know each other . . . again. The young guys went fishing, but Garrett Temple received his daily rapid test, snuck in a round of golf and a swim, then finished up his nightly LSAT prep before a long FaceTime call with Kára, who was seven months pregnant in Brooklyn. "It's like a dorm room," he said, except it still wasn't safe to play doubles ping-pong in the dining hall.

The next afternoon, Garrett hopped off the team's bus and into its designated gym, a nineteen-thousand-square-foot converted ballroom typically reserved for weddings and family reunions. Behind the muffle of a mask, he welcomed the roster's late arrivals to Disney World, demonstrating a stripped-down playbook for Jamal Crawford—the 40-year-old point guard who'd guided Kyrie back up the mountaintop with Bill Russell—and teaching some isolation moves to yet *another* backup point guard. There were four of them now, and one might have to play power forward. The other twenty-one teams competing around Orlando were busy preparing for the playoffs, but that afternoon was the first time The Bubble Nets had enough active hoopers on the floor to play five-on-five basketball. Brooklyn had been forced to sign four replacement players to make up for suddenly vacant roster spots, in what multiple players perceived as a public tryout for the super-team of 2021, pitting the vestiges of Kenny Atkinson's development system against a revolving door of devolving veterans who were favored by KD and Kyrie. Just the other morning, KD's friend from Stink's unstoppable team on the teenage circuit in Maryland, Mike Beasley, got the call from GM Sean Marks to his Bubble Nets hotel-room quarantine . . .

that he would need yet another test. No wonder Mike couldn't taste the microwave salmon from The Bubble kitchen; after regurgitating it for an hour and a half, the former No. 2 draft pick was taken to the hospital with food poisoning, shortness of breath and a case of Covid-19, destined never to return to The Bubble or the NBA again.

Garrett knew he'd have to lead more than ever down here: Damn near half the Brooklyn Nets were missing, and several more of them had gotten coronavirus.

KD and Kyrie were already MIA by design. Then the team had decided to make players detour from their summer homes back to New York City in late June before The Bubble, and the test results for DeAndre and Taurean had come back positive. They were both asymptomatic, but they hadn't really been feeling The Bubble to begin with—DeAndre had asthma and was getting pretty good at the electric guitar, while Taurean, having recorded his first single in the studio, was spending more time than ever with his kids, at the first home of his own. When Spencer came down with a mild case of the virus, bedridden and unable to work out for a week with sinus headaches, he still wanted to fly to Orlando and play on. Team doctors told him not to bother, not for this season. Garrett was, of course, concerned for these teammates and their families—nearly one hundred thirty thousand Americans were reported to have died of Covid-19 in the three months since the NBA's first positive test. He also heard that the Rockets franchise players James Harden and Russ Westbrook had tested positive just before The Bubble, and then he watched them compete hard for their shot at an historic championship. "If guys wanted to come to The Bubble," Garrett said of his teammates, "they could have."

Even the Nets' coaches had, after the death of George Floyd in Minneapolis, wondered if it was worth going to Disney World.

"We talked early on as a coaching staff, as an organization, how do we—*do* we go back to playing basketball? Or, fuck it—do we spend all our time trying to make change?" the development coach Ryan Forehan-Kelly explained late one night in his hotel room. His grandfather, the first Black carpenter at Disneyland, had sued Disney for discriminating against him in 1969 and won, emboldening the coach to protest as a student in Berkeley. In 2020, there'd been murmurs that KD and Kyrie were backing the legendary Gregg Popovich as their new head coach—or even the Hall of Fame point guard Steve Nash as a first-time head coach. Atkinson's lame-duck staffers were essentially trying out for the superstars, too. But they agreed on a plan to spend their time in Orlando as educators, coaching Black history to ensure that "I'm not educated enough," which a 31-year-old LeBron had blamed for failing to condemn the police killing of a 12-year-old boy in Cleveland, would never be a good enough excuse for the next generation of hoopers.

The Bubble Nets, the interim head coach Jacque Vaughn told his players, were there to compete, not complain. JV saw in them a team of the time: imperfect, vulnerable and accepting of its own differences. Before going on to play at Kansas and in the NBA, he'd been a sophomore in high school at the alma mater of Jackie Robinson and Rodney King during the L.A. riots. "The week after that," he said, "a lot of those places I had grown up walking to—stores, establishments that were really native to my upbringing—weren't there anymore." As those memories reverberated at 46 years old, JV would take advantage of his dwindling summer as one of only seven Black head coaches in the league, in part by beginning every practice in Disney World with a message of equality: The Nets could get back to hooping as a full unit that afternoon, but first they would have to review the Minneapolis policing conditions that had set off the movement again. And in a few days, he would make sure they all registered to vote.

No matter where he traveled around the NBA campus, from his hotel room to the makeshift gyms, JV carried with him a prized possession he'd purchased across the street from Barclays Center, encased in glass.

"Yo, coach!" said Justin Anderson, who'd made the team after risking his career for public protest and, on his way to The Bubble, become the *ninth* Nets player to test positive for Covid-19. "Coach, why are you carrying that plant everywhere?"

"Bamboo," JV responded. "Bamboo." The coach petted his foot-tall stem in its vase. "It's the most resilient plant that doesn't require much. Doesn't need much sun, doesn't need much water. You can *give* it sun, and you can *give* it water, but it doesn't need much. And it's going to continue to grow."

Resilience was the corny motto of the franchise, stickered on the wall in the Nets' hotel block. But the coach said that it applied as much to a flexible mind as a well-trained body, and that the Nets should no longer be afraid to speak up. Nobody in the NBA was, as players all over The Bubble turned the league's platform into their own megaphone for racial justice. Jaylen Brown of the Celtics, who'd been leading in the streets of Atlanta with Justin, kept telling like-minded friends on campus to "keep it hot."

From New Jersey, Kyrie produced a low-rated special on Breonna Taylor for his startup network. On a call organized by the players' union, Breonna's mother popped up in a Zoom box, and players in The Bubble were encouraged to bring up her daughter's unresolved death and too-short life in public. Many began using their nationally televised interviews to talk about arresting the cops who killed Breonna Taylor and nothing else. Celtics beat reporters would begin to ask about team defense, and their shooting guard Marcus Smart would say: "Justice for Breonna Taylor."

The union boss, Michele Roberts, who is Black, thought that a player merely saying Breonna Taylor's name at a press conference remained a minor achievement. She figured that if *one* Boston fan who had never heard of Breonna Taylor's case kept hearing half the Celtics' starting lineup say her name, then talked about it for ten minutes with *another* fan, then that was still progress. "Anyone who suggests that the players should be intending to create revolutionaries out of their fans—that's an incredibly naive assumption," she told the veteran NBA journalist David Aldridge. If a conglomerate "spends billions of dollars in marketing, to make you buy Colgate," she continued, "they want you to know the name, and have a positive affiliation, learn something, try the product. And if it makes you enjoy Colgate, all the better."

But many NBA players had grown sick, over the past decade, of the increasing burden to market brand-name wokeness. Toothpaste Activism felt older and more corporate than ever to many of these athletes, even to the more pragmatic messengers among them. Within the seal of The Bubble, hoopers wanted badly to get a taste of being the change—to squeeze the toothpaste out of the tube.

"There's a generational piece that's going on there," Roberts explained to me. "But not everybody is Malcolm X, and not everybody is Martin Luther King or Huey P. Newton. We do what we do, as best we can, and as much as we can. And so if all a player wants to do is say, 'I support Black Lives Matter—that's all I'm prepared to do,' rather than say, 'Well, fuck you, that's not enough,' my response is: Do what you can do, as long as you're part of this conversation and this movement."

Garrett understood that for every conversation in the Nets'

hotel swimming pool about the redistribution of Black generational wealth, or every time he explained defunding the police on TV, there would be players going viral for guzzling beers on a sopping wet deck nearby. When he and more than two dozen players gathered for a social-justice check-in on July 16, he thought they would continue talking about tangible action like The Foundation, a ten-year, $300 million commitment from owners and players to empower Black communities. But players soon overwhelmed the call with the theatrics of kneeling: *Is everyone gonna pull a Kaepernick during the anthem? Coaches, too? Will the refs go along?*

Jacque Vaughn decided to start Nets practice that Saturday with a message of gratitude, in honor of a man who spent his life fighting for an equality he never saw. A man who'd been taking a knee for going on six decades. The coaches wheeled in a television intended for game tape and played a clip of John Lewis, the congressman and giant of justice who had passed away on Friday evening. Taking the stage at the March on Washington, Mr. Lewis looked determined to speak, yet just as nervous as the basketball players had been in the streets of Atlanta in May 2020. The Nets stood watching the famous 1963 address, some European players for the first time, and they could see how much Mr. Lewis admired the civil rights movement in action before him, its sheer youthfulness and volume, and how being a part of the next generation inspired him to speak a little louder, too: *We do not want our freedom gradually, but we want to be free now!* Jarrett Allen stood high and tall above his teammates, finding the sea of humanity on the screen as unfathomably vast himself as John Lewis did then, and he watched the great leader continue. *We must say: "Wake up, America! Wake up!" For we cannot stop, and we will not and cannot be patient.*

"Twenty-three years old when he gave that speech," JV said,

as the video faded back into practice. The head coach pointed at one backup point guard. "How old are you?"

"Twenty-four."

He pointed at another backup point guard. "How old are you?"

"Twenty-four."

He pointed up and to the back, at Jarrett. "How old are you?"

"Twenty-two."

"And you get to play basketball today," the coach said.

He swiftly approached his team to form a huddle, meeting their fists in the air with his. He called out a team leader to break the huddle with a mission of the moment, as Kenny Atkinson had, back when *Death Row on three* was automatic.

"What we got, GT?"

"Hoo-eeee," Garrett Temple said, shaking off the goosebumps. "*Grateful on three. One, two, three, grateful!*"

◖◗ MARCH 22, 2018

Sacramento

GARRETT WAS ON the massage table, receiving treatment for a sprained ankle in the Sacramento Kings training room deep inside Golden 1 Center, when he flipped on the news. Stepping into his walking boot, he quickly realized that this arena *was* the news: A human barricade—hundreds of demonstrators, maybe a thousand—had started to surround the entranceways. *You shoot us down, we shut it down! You shoot us down, we shut it down!*

There were only forty-five minutes before tip-off, and all sorts of Sacramento grassroots organizations had picked up extra marchers from city hall, from along the freeway overpass and toward the gates of the game. A twenty-first-century civil rights movement that had bubbled and simmered and boiled, ever since the death of Trayvon Martin, had finally come knocking for the NBA. Garrett wanted to hobble up the aisles the wrong way and out the turnstiles—to join them in protest, linking arms with hundreds, to make sure that millions heard the name of another unarmed young Black man in America, on ESPN.

Garrett had been involved as a mentor and donor at Sac High, in the underfunded nearby neighborhood of Oak Park, and four nights earlier, one of the school's former football players, Stephon Clark, had been chased into his grandmother's yard. The cops were suspicious that Stephon looked like a man who'd been breaking car windows around Oak Park, and that he had a gun. His "gun" was an iPhone. The cops fired twenty times. Eight bullets hit Stephon Clark, three in the back. They handcuffed his lifeless body before muting their body cameras as backup arrived. Stephon Clark was 22.

Now, an hour after Garrett's massage, there was a demonstrator at every door: *A game is not a life! Fuck your game!* Nonveteran players asked why the crowd outside was trying to stop their game from starting. "They're not protesting the game," Garrett told them. "They're protesting the situation." Once arena security delayed tip-off, Garrett thought Adam Silver might have to postpone the proceedings entirely, which only made Garrett think even harder about heading out to join the demonstration and grab the megaphone. But his father had always taught him to think before he acted, off the court, upon his competitive impulses. "You're getting paid eight million dollars a year, and an NBA owner, the people who have to coach, the general manager—they're not interested in being in the middle of some civil unrest," Collis Temple recalls advising his son that week. "But you've got to put everything on the table now, and it can't be driven by no money."

Garrett worried about reinjuring his ankle if he joined the barricade of his team's game and marched onward from there. He worried about getting suspended and scapegoated, which would mean sacrificing his platform—the relationship with Sacramento's first Black police chief and the closed-door town halls with kids and cops—for the clout. "If I would have walked outside," he told me, "Black people in Sacramento would have been like, 'That's what's up! He's standing for us!' But what tangible thing would have come from that? Would any legislation have been changed because Garrett Temple walked outside? I think not."

Word came that the commissioner's office had been on the phone: The game would go on. Security sealed the doors, and the PA announcer invited ticket holders who'd made it in early—two thousand at most—to stream down the aisles into the lower bowl, claim some free hot dogs and spread out as they pleased. There would be no national anthem, no starting-lineup introductions. The vibe felt almost like fan appreciation day or a scrimmage, Garrett thought. He'd played in front of more people for the state championship in high school.

Garrett sat on the bench in his walking boot and turned to his Kings teammate Vince Carter: "Should we really be playing right now?" It was never too late to go on strike.

At 41, Vince was an elder-statesman superstar and Hall of Famer in waiting, comfortable with his role as a role model to up-and-comers. He wasn't a politics guy, but he'd been reading about the protests of the police all week. This being the NBA, he also found himself talking politics with members of the Atlanta Hawks, like Taurean Prince, around the free-throw line in the middle of a late-season game. Vince Carter did not, that evening, give a damn about the score.

At halftime, suits from the franchise approached Garrett and

Vince, asking if they wanted to say something about the situation to the pseudo-crowd after the game. But Garrett and Vince figured Melo, Chris, D-Wade and LeBron had said their piece onstage at the ESPY Awards back in 2016. Just a month earlier, in an ad that went very, very viral, LeBron had said Donald Trump "don't give a fuck about the people," and KD said, "Our team as a country is not run by a great coach"—talk that had only led to a Fox News host race-baiting them to . . . *shut up and dribble*. LeBron may have leveraged the stick-to-sports slur for his new More Than an Athlete™ brand, but the rhetoric on replay, re-'Gram and retweet hadn't accomplished much of anything but more polarization. Not so far. And that was *LeBron*.

"No," Garrett told the suits. "We think Vivek should do it."

Sacramento Kings chairman Vivek Ranadivé had taken a hard line on Donald Sterling in 2014: "We have to have zero tolerance," he told Silver, and it was Michael Jordan, one of the NBA's only other two owners of color, who'd come up to Ranadivé in a board meeting and reassured him, "I got your back." Tonight, in a near-empty arena, where the protesters outside outnumbered the beers sold on the inside, Ranadivé was more trepidacious. The Silicon Valley billionaire looked up at his stars: "You guys want *me* to say something?"

"You need to be the one that says it," Garrett responded.

"I'm happy to do that," Ranadivé said, "but tell me what you want me to communicate."

"This is not just business as usual," Vince told his boss.

The game continued, and the demonstrators began dispersing. Berry Accius, however, was still on the megaphone outside when a Kings radio announcer spotted the 38-year-old community organizer; they'd met on social media earlier that day. Berry wondered if he was about to get arrested, but he was invited inside to meet the owner, at least for a few minutes of pleasantries, thoughts and prayers. From the bench, Garrett flashed a raised fist toward the activist—he wanted to meet Berry after the game.

Once the final buzzer sounded, Garrett, Vince and the Kings players stood behind Ranadivé on the court. The owner stumbled through the players' talking points so awkwardly as to be perhaps more authentic than any tech executive with a microphone and an ill-fitting sweater has ever seemed on camera: "We at the Kings recognize . . . your . . . people's . . . ability to . . . protest peacefully, and we respect that," Ranadivé said. "We recognize that it's not just business as usual, and we are gonna work *really* hard to bring everybody together to make the world a better place, starting with our own community, and we're going to work *really* hard to prevent this kind of a tragedy from happening again." The remaining fans seemed to appreciate his speech, and Garrett and Vince whispered to the owner that they did, too. But Garrett still wanted to talk to that activist. So he stood outside the locker room with Berry and two Black broadcasters for about forty-five minutes, asking how best to keep investing in Sacramento's Black communities. Vince finished showering and responding to the press and joined them, feeling slightly vulnerable and more than a little guilty. "I'm willing to use my voice," he said. Berry headed back out the tunnel, knowing that he had spontaneous leverage—he was fucking up that owner's revenue stream, and he was *loving* it—and that Vince Carter didn't know what the hell to do. The activist figured the NBA and this marched-upon franchise would do anything he asked of them for, oh, about a month.

Before the Kings' next game against Boston, Garrett got some #StephonClark T-shirts made and filmed a PSA including Vince and the 21-year-old Celtics backup Jaylen Brown. "We will *not* stick to sports," Garrett said to the camera. The owner's speech had gone viral—Obama texted that he was proud—and

Ranadivé would eventually meet with Stephon Clark's mother, Se'Quette, a huge Kings fan, about trying to work together, and the team invited her to a game. The Kings decided on a multi-year commitment to Berry's organization, with the local chapter of Black Lives Matter™. Vince even showed up to their event, hesitant at first but finding himself, within less than five minutes, comfortable as an ally for mainstream activism. "And then they got the Kings to build a court and do all this publicity stuff," Se'Quette Clark said, "so I guess in a *sense* it went to our community, but no one *goes* there." The Kings tried to make fighting the good fight "go viral to the other teams," Ranadivé told me, including an annual cops-and-kids summit with the Milwaukee Bucks. Both teams would visit Folsom Prison. "Most people would say that really ain't shit, but it's *something*," Garrett said. "And I did all of that without 'protesting.'"

None of the somethings stopped the pain inside Stephon Clark's brother, as he took over the Sacramento city council meeting two nights later, jumping on the dais, demanding to be heard. The politicians who refused to listen could not stop the demonstrators from marching onward to Golden 1 Center once more, barricading the gates of the Kings' following game.

"Why are they here again?" asked a player in the locker room.

"They're doing it so you don't get shot, bro! This is *you* out there," his teammate responded.

Franchise executives tried to negotiate with activists, as if the arena were being held for ransom, to let the game begin. Fans asked why security guards were locking the doors already, with only four thousand people inside, just so the NBA could start its show on time.

You ain't seeing no game tonight, demonstrators responded. *Join us or go home!*

The city was hot, and Stephon's funeral was approaching. The

Kings' former All-Star center, DeMarcus Cousins, had paid for the whole thing. Matt Barnes, a former Kings player and Sacramento native, put up the family in hotel rooms for the week, and when Stephon's brother tore one up in anger, Matt covered the damages and organized a rally. "It was a small gesture," he told me, "but you could see how much the family appreciated it—appreciated that I knew Stephon Clark was someone walking the same streets I walked, that it could have been me, that it really touched me and *bothered* me." Garrett knew this would be a good fight for the players, but a long one for the game: After the franchise took its woker alternative for action, Stephon Clark's mom never sat at the table with the Kings again.

"With the NBA, during the first wave, they're *awesome*," she said. "But where are they now?"

JULY 31, 2020 📧
Kissimmee, Florida

THEY HAD REHEARSED the routine, more or less, already: When the lights go down, flank the far out-of-bounds stripe, the one across from the cameras. Head coaches at center court, players lining either side, trainers and referees at the far end. Everyone kneel, arms interlocked.

Garrett had texted his teammates that every NBA franchise in The Bubble was preparing for this ceremony of solidarity for the national anthem and that the commissioner was choosing to look the other way. The Bubble Nets had reviewed their places at practice two mornings earlier, conferred over the pregame playbook in the Brooklyn meal room to double-check—left knee, not right—and taken their cues by watching LeBron James lead the way. Basketball had returned the night before, and it was a whole vibe of kumbaya. "I hope we made Kap proud," LeBron said.

Toward the egg-yellow sports castle of an arena in Disney's ESPN Wide World of Sports Complex, Garrett led the way off the bus. Each player wore a mask, and almost all of their T-shirts read *BLACK LIVES MATTER*. That was the messaging painted on the hardwood inside as well, which had been a matter of some contention with players who supported the movement but less so Black Lives Matter the brand name. There were no fans in here, and not many advertisements, just a smattering of reporters and camera operators and play-by-play announcers, who were almost all white, and safety personnel. It was a stage, not a stadium.

In the darkness before tip-off, Garrett heard his own voice boom over the loud speakers, in a video featuring the new NBA thought-leaders: "I'm a Black man, I'm fed up, tired. I want change—now." He had chills, and he was fighting off a tear as the American flag began to light up the screen behind him, as planned.

Then Garrett broke the human chain—and raised his right fist in the air.

He and his new "replacement player" teammate Lance Thomas had made a pledge to each other: For as long as they were in The Bubble, the two would take a knee lined up next to one another, but they would plan to stand out. The fist was that "extra *extra* emphasis," Garrett told me, "not to be just strictly uniform."

John Carlos watched in Atlanta, proud of the Black Power and excellence being expressed throughout the NBA and the WNBA; hell, even baseball players were holding up their fists in empty stadiums all over America by now. Garrett's father watched on television from Louisiana, where in 1969 the governor had talked him into becoming a weapon of progress, to integrate a basketball team against his will; Collis Temple wondered when his son might complete law school and, perhaps, go on to become the governor of Louisiana himself. Garrett finished praying, and Kára sang out from their couch in Brooklyn as the camera cut to her man: *ba-ah-annnner yet waaaaaay-ayaaaaaave. . . .* Garrett usually prayed for peace and health for his family. Now he prayed for his teammates to test negative and for Joe Biden to win the election. Garrett Temple prayed for policy change, for heaven's sake, and for divisiveness to give way to common ground.

Garrett opened his eyes, the players rose up from their knees, and the lights came on. As he was heading back to the huddle, he heard that a player on the Orlando Magic named Jonathan Isaac—a Trump-supporting, All Lives Matter fundamentalist—had been standing up throughout the anthem in his jersey, instead of kneeling in another NBA-issued Black Lives Matter shirt. The Nets rolled their eyes at this misbegotten counter-protest and got back to hooping, for their first game in a hundred and forty-three days.

From the socially distanced bench with his mask back on, Garrett watched his teammates remove the T-shirts and reveal brand-new jerseys. Their last names were missing from the back, each replaced with an NBA-approved phrase. *SÍ SE PUEDE* won the jump ball, tipping it to *SAY HER NAME*. Then *BLACK LIVES MATTER* missed a three-point shot, but *EQUALITY* raced back in transition to hit a thirteen-footer over *JUSTICE NOW*. Garrett substituted into the game not as Temple but as *EDUCATION REFORM*—he had formed a productive group chat with players around the league who chose the same phrase—and played terribly. When he checked back in, in the third quarter, he looked up at the wraparound screens and saw the "virtual fans" flickering in and out from their laptops at home, silently cheering in augmented reality. The crowd noise was pumped in straight from the soundtrack of *NBA2K*, but Garrett could hear the actual sneaker-squeaking and the play-calling in here a little too clearly, and the lights were far too bright; he made a three-pointer, feeling like his own character in the video game. The Bubble Nets fought hard, but they lost, and walked back to their quarters, as the cleaning staff mopped the backboard and sanitized the floor.

Two days later, Garrett and Justin Anderson remember, they were catching up, facedown on massage tables in the Nets hotel block, six feet apart and exhausted by their experience.

"Hey, GT, did you notice anything *across* the court from us, while you were kneeling for the anthem?"

"Nah," Garrett said. "I'm usually praying. Doing my pre-game rituals. Why? What's up?"

"I usually am, too," Justin said, "but I kinda just peeked up at the environment, when we all took the knee together."

Back when Colin Kaepernick had a day job, and especially once a mass of NFL players and even owners started watering down his gesture, Justin always noticed the cameramen on the football broadcasts racing past the knees. They were clearing cables out of the shot and listening to their headsets, as the sound guys held boom mics overhead. He thought something was off—it upset him that these members of the production crew, who seemed pretty much always white, couldn't take a moment to respect America, or the pain and sacrifice of the Black men before them. The Bubble offered him an uncluttered view of this perceived ignorance. On the one side of the court that you could not see on television, the people producing the show were sitting down or milling about. Behind a wall of Plexiglas, the media schlubs and the front-office suits tweeted and checked their watches—Justin could not see a single person on the other side standing at attention or kneeling for equality. Michele Roberts applauded, but otherwise Justin felt part of a performative silence. He used to be scared of speaking out for fear of not making the league; now that he'd seen the fight in the streets, he wasn't sure he wanted to be a part of the NBA's same woketastic spectacle, rebranded for catastrophe as a #WholeNewGame.

"I recognized," Justin told Garrett, "that this is for TV. But what is for TV, and what do I actually have to *deal* with, every day? What's going *on*? At some point, you have to draw the line: That whole situation with Kaepernick, we're taking *away* from what he was doing. Now it's almost like we're making this shit *cool*. Like, alright, *every*body's kneeling. It's cool."

"At the end of the day, man," Garrett said, "just because something becomes a trend doesn't mean that you shouldn't do it."

"But we all had that opportunity to kneel with Kaepernick when it was happening!" Justin said. "We *all* did. And now it's become: Every game we're gonna kneel, and everybody's gonna wear T-shirts. Is this all for the movement, or for the hashtag? What is *happening* here?"

"I think a lot of people nowadays, especially younger people," Garrett told me later, "we always want to go against the grain. We want to be rebellious: If everybody else is doing it, it must not mean anything. And I can understand that—I was like that, too. But the more people are doing it, then the more eyes are wide."

It was not influential to be rebellious, they agreed, for the sake of being a rebel. But history didn't always come with a plan.

Before they played the Milwaukee Bucks the next afternoon, the Nets prepared for the new normal of pregame rituals. Equipment managers handed out fresh white towels, for the players to protect their kneecaps and cruciate ligaments. "Nah, I'm OK," Justin said. If George Floyd had to suffer the pain of a killer cop's knee for eight minutes and forty-six seconds, he thought, then he could skip the towel and endure two minutes of hardwood and "The Star-Spangled Banner" in order to honor Black lives. As the anthem finished, Garrett opened his eyes to see the media and the executives milling about behind the see-through dividers on the other side of the stage, and he smiled at Justin. "You're absolutely right, bro."

Justin felt empowered, and he proved it with his play. He dunked on Giannis Antetokounmpo, the MVP, and got into a shoving match with the veteran George Hill, as the Nets beat the Bucks, the best team in the league. "The Bubble Nets goin' crazy," Garrett said, hop-stepping through the tunnel. Brooklyn's team of replacements won five of its seven final regular-season games—the fifth-best record in Disney World—and the Nets made the postseason for the second year in a row. Kevin Durant wasn't there to cheer them on, but he received his million-dollar playoff bonus nonetheless.

AUGUST 23, 2020 ⊠

Golden Oak, Florida

THE BROOKLYN NETS PACKED UP their masks and extra sneakers, the barbells and the bamboo, more than ready to leave basketball behind. Their starting small forward, Joe Harris, had exited The Bubble four days earlier; his grandmother was dying. "Go take care of family business," said Garrett, who'd been worried about having to rush home to Brooklyn himself, for the birth of his son. Kára wasn't due for more than three weeks, though, and the Nets, trailing three games to none in their first-round playoff series against the defending champion Toronto Raptors, were resigned to elimination day.

The Nets and Raptors had both been distracted by that week's release of body-camera footage from a deputy sheriff working security for the Warriors at the previous season's NBA Finals, shoving the Raptors president Masai Ujiri as he tried to join his team in its championship celebration on the court. The worst part, Garrett thought, was that he hadn't been surprised when the white cop *sued* the Black executive for alleged assault on *him*. But the teams played on, and Garrett made a three-pointer to start Game Four.

Outside The Bubble, Spencer watched from his house in Los Angeles as he got dressed for his aunt's seventieth birthday dinner. He saw Caris LeVert score twenty-six points in the first half, emerging as a championship-caliber scorer—Caris was a better friend of KD and Kyrie than Spencer was by now, or perhaps an increasingly strong asset to get dealt away instead of Spencer for a third superstar. In any case, Spencer had heard more of the trade rumors about himself, and he felt pushed out already. "My time in Brooklyn is obviously short, and I'm at peace with that," he said.

KD, on the beach, had been getting reports from Sean Marks to better assess the new kids and the OGs, while getting back to full strength at a high-school gym in Beverly Hills that he and Draymond Green, after rekindling at a nearby restaurant, liked to share. Brooklyn's star and GM thought this Chris Chiozza kid looked promising as the new backup point guard, even as Cheeze missed another defensive coverage in the third quarter and the Nets began to let the game slip away.

In Jersey, Kyrie put the finishing touches on a video tribute he'd been writing for Instagram—it was Kobe's birthday, and Kyrie was convinced more than ever, he intoned to his followers, that the *real* player empowerment had revealed itself to him: "It isn't so much just about the word *empowerment*. It's just through the action. Seeing the disparity in wages, and already knowing the wealth gap in a lot of communities when we're talking about race, it can't be continued without us joining forces and coming together to make sure that our next generation is taken care of." Kyrie saw that Toronto's Serge Ibaka was dropping three-pointers all over The Bubble Nets; even though Serge had been guarding KD when he injured his Achilles in the first place, Kyrie and KD had thought about recruiting him for next year's team, all year long. The NBA was still a brotherhood, after all.

The Bubble Nets wanted to escape the season with at least one playoff win, for the memories, but 2020 wasn't giving you any more hope than it had to. Justin Anderson chucked in a bank shot as time began to run out on the basketball Cinderellas of Disney World, and they lost Game Four bad, real bad, by twenty-eight. Brooklyn's endless season was over, in a clean sweep.

The NBA had instructed teams eliminated from contention to shower at their designated hotel, receive a final meal and take a team bus to the airport. The remnants of Death Row smoked cigars and reminisced about how fun the last month and a half had been, compared to the last year and a half. Geopolitical chaos by tweet, racial inequality by cell-phone video, the scientific methods of innovators and unqualified presidents alike—these were not distractions from their game, The Bubble Nets concluded, but real life, moving real fast all around them. Sports had been the interruption.

Most of the Nets were grateful to have been able to play basketball safely together in this parallel universe. But Garrett made sure to thank his teammates for standing up for what they believed in, even when Trump called NBA players "very dumb" and said "there was a nastiness about the NBA" in not standing for the anthem—in not "doing what they're supposed to be doing." LeBron had dismissed "that guy" all month, and gotten more upset about right-wing advocacy groups discouraging mail-in voting during the pandemic with fake news that featured his likeness, as the Lakers kept rolling through to the second round. Garrett was intent, once he'd established some distance from paternity leave, on catching up with local officials back in Louisiana. "With the *little* celebrity some of us have, and the *big* celebrity that others of us have," he said, "policies aren't as far away—or as distant—as we make them out to be."

While the Nets were shooting the shit on their final night together, a video started going viral of a police officer pointing a gun at a Black man in Kenosha, Wisconsin. The cops were responding to a 9-1-1 call, claiming that the man refused to give his girlfriend her car keys. There had been a warrant out for his arrest on a charge of felony sexual assault in a domestic-abuse case, which was later dropped. But as police were arriving, neighbors say they saw the man breaking up a fight between two women arguing on the sidewalk. The officer stalked him toward his car door, where the man reached for something—there was a knife on the floorboard—and shot him seven times in the back. Jacob Blake, whose three sons were sitting in the back seat, survived.

In the morning, the Nets traveling party underwent mandatory Covid-19 testing—since play had resumed, there had not been, nor would there be, *any* positive results among active players in The Bubble—and walked out the front door of Disney World, back into the real world. Some players took car services home to various parts of the South, and some prepared to fly back to Europe. They would see each other again, on the other side of all this, likely on opposing teams, at uninhabited arenas. Perhaps there would be a vaccine by then, but likely not. Garrett, clambering aboard the team plane to New York and leaning back in a relative comfort, could not wait to get home.

He hugged his mom as soon as he arrived in Brooklyn and thanked her for staying up North over the past week when Kára had a bit of a pregnancy scare. Garrett and Kára sat on the back porch, in the maskless fresh air, to grill a beer-can chicken. They had some catching up to do on *Grey's Anatomy*, while waiting for their first child to be born.

Kára had been brought to tears after the death of George Floyd, concerned about bringing a Black boy into the United States, and now this Jacob Blake video was blowing up. She and her fiancé switched past the Republican convention's message of doom to catch the end of the Lakers game on TNT; LeBron was talking about the latest tragedy. "Quite frankly, it's just fucked up," LeBron said. "We are scared as Black people, in America. Black men, Black women, Black kids. We are *terrified*."

The next day, Garrett watched a video from the Jacob Blake protests in Wisconsin: A 17-year-old white boy shot a demonstrator in the chest and in the heart, after having killed someone else, too, and walked free, by walking toward the cops with the weapon—an AR-15 style assault rifle—dangling from his shoulders.

One of Garrett's best friends in the league, George Hill, watched it, too, while sequestered back in Disney World. George was not a superstar, not nearly: Having played in the 2018 Finals alongside LeBron, the 34-year-old was getting close to a ring with Giannis and Milwaukee—the Bucks, his sixth team, were the odds-on favorites to face the Lakers for the championship in a month. He'd gone big-game hunting near his ranch in Texas during the NBA's pandemic pause, so George was no ordinary liberal. But this kid with the AR-15 was sending him over the edge. "We shouldn't even have come to this damn place," he said from The Bubble. "Coming here just took all the focal points off what the issues are—we can't do anything from right here."

What good was money, George wondered, if you could not showcase your humanity?

Concern and confusion began to escalate at full tilt again, at the NBA's highest levels, about a potential work stoppage. Kyrie and Avery Bradley were among many players welcomed to a call with the players' union, and they made their presence felt. Avery wondered if the league office might be worried that The Disruptors had something to do with this latest looming resistance—and if anything productive would come of second-guessing inside The Bubble.

"Do we have a plan?" Avery asked his fellow players.

They didn't.

On Wednesday, August 26, the fourth anniversary of Colin Kaepernick protesting the national anthem in the name of brutalized racial injustice, George Hill took his coaches on the Milwaukee Bucks to breakfast. Over a bacon-egg-and-cheese and hash browns, he told them he would not be playing in Game Five of their playoff series that afternoon. Basketball did not matter, he believed, not that day.

The incidental activist would not—could not, any longer—be alone.

George's 25-year-old teammate Sterling Brown had been on a date in Milwaukee in 2018, when he parked quickly, too quickly, across two handicapped spaces, for a trip into the pharmacy; he returned to half-a-dozen squad cars, a Taser and a knee on his neck. Sterling was having the same conversations about police brutality in the Bucks locker room in 2020 that he'd had in the holding cell that night with another Black man, around his age, who had blood all over his face. Sterling still thought it was bullshit—the cops using power to their constant advantage, the keep-calm-and-carry-on mentality in a shoot-to-kill country—and he was ready to do something about it, out front.

"If you're one of those guys who do things for the cameras, do things for views and clout, then it's gonna show," he'd told me earlier that season, at Barclays Center. "But if you're one of those authentic guys, then it'll show within your experience, in what you come from, in what you're doing—not even just an obligation. It's something you *want* to do." Sterling was going to sit this one out alongside George, he told the Bucks in their locker room . . . in fucking Disney World.

"I'm not playing this game," added Giannis, the Milwaukee megastar. Nobody was.

George and his teammates may not have had a plan, but they represented Wisconsin, and Jacob Blake was paralyzed in the intensive-care unit, ten minutes from their silent stadium. The team felt *thisclose* to a nation's recurring pain, and so these athletes were compelled to answer the latest call to the responsibilities of the recognizable, before the moment could sink back into the divide of what Kyrie called, simply, Racist America. The Milwaukee Bucks thought they would just forfeit a game, except the toothpaste was out of the tube now: As the opening buzzer rang out on an empty court, they had declared the first real boycott in NBA history.

"We can't just not play this game and then go back to our room," one of the Bucks said, "and play cards or video games."

"What are we gonna do?"

The athletes' next step was to utilize their leverage, immediately, and they weren't leaving the locker room until they acted—they were already wearing custom T-shirts. They used the coaches' whiteboard for policy ideas instead of *X*'s and *O*'s. Ownership helped get the lieutenant governor of Wisconsin on speakerphone, and he reminded the team that the state legislature had not passed a single piece of legislation since April, but a police-reform bill had been introduced for a vote, and they could keep applying pressure.

The Bucks remained in the locker room for more than three hours, as LeBron James woke up from a nap and the Lakers agreed to postpone their game; so did every other team in the NBA, the WNBA, Major League Baseball and Major League Soccer. This was a full-on strike for justice.

Huddling around an iPhone again, the Bucks cried together as Jacob Blake's parents poured love upon the team's influence. "We don't know exactly what the future holds—we're not sure exactly what our plan is going forward—but we're doing the right thing," said the Milwaukee shooting guard Kyle Korver. "This is the right thing."

Just before midnight in Brooklyn, Garrett Temple was dozing off. The two biggest trending topics of the day had been *Milwaukee Bucks* and *Kyrie*—as in *Kyrie was right after all*, after calling out the GAME and *LIFE* the previous year, after calling for a boycott two months earlier, after calling on all hoopers to break the cycle. At the end of the day the sports world stopped, Garrett wondered if the 2019–2020 season would end for good.

The bleepedy-deep-bleep-bleep of FaceTime stirred him awake: His group chat of old friends from the Sacramento Kings—including George Hill—had an urgent update for Garrett and Vince from The Bubble, where another three-hour meeting, full of every player and a lot of coaches still down there, had just concluded.

The former teammates talked about how painful the video of that lunatic walking home untouched, down the middle of the damn street with an AR-15, still felt. How the onslaught of white supremacy refused to relent. And by the way, LeBron had really laid into George down in the packed hotel ballroom: Did George realize what he'd just *done?* Without *telling* anybody? Without a *plan?* Chris Paul and the union leaders made clear the momentousness of the choice ahead: Boycott the season—

risking the NBA's entire fight to bring back sports from the brink already, as well as next season, all so they could fight the good fight—or play. Andre Iguodala and Jaylen Brown challenged the rest of the gathering, the largest gathering that most of them had attended in five and a half months: If the players were to remain on strike, would they head to the front lines of Wisconsin . . . or home to their kids after being stuck in Disney World for seven weeks? Would they actually book meetings at city hall this time, instead of massages in the Bahamas? The Bubble, at least, afforded the last man on the bench a platform—not to mention he was getting paid—and the Bucks, Jaylen told the ballroom, did not owe anybody an apology, least of all LeBron James.

George Hill explained to his former Sacramento teammates on FaceTime that the coaches had left the room, the players gathered with their teammates, and everyone took an informal vote. "I was surprised," George said, thinking back on a very long Wednesday for the Milwaukee Bucks. "We already decided *not* to play today, and after all that, we voted to *stay!*"

"Who all voted to leave?" Vince asked the old friends.

They told Vince and Garrett that many players in Disney World, especially LeBron, were concerned that if the NBA just restarted again the next day—without demanding that ownership be held accountable for their promises to work *really* hard in the community to magically end racism—then this historic moment might look like it was for nothing. Like it was cool. "If we don't have a plan," LeBron recalled saying, "then what are we talking about? Why are we still here?" Almost every team had agreed to stay, but then it was the Clippers and the *Lakers* who had voted to exit The Bubble. LeBron couldn't believe the Bucks had flip-flopped; the room couldn't believe he seemed ready to go. He was reminded that his vote alone still mattered more than that of his teammates or any majority, if the game was to go on. "We're out," King James said. With that, LeBron marched his team straight out the doors of the Coronado Ballroom, a protest of the protest, into chaos.

"Wow," Garrett said. "*Wow.*"

"We left the meeting with basically nothing done," George told his best basketball friends, "and no progress." He had to jump off the call. People down there wanted answers. The only plan was for more meetings in the morning.

"It's gonna end up being a shitshow," Garrett said, "one way or another."

George Hill's face blooped off their screens and disappeared back into The Bubble, but the rest of the old friends stayed on the line. They were proud of George. It had taken his raw and truly authentic disruption to make LeBron James even consider threatening to abandon the NBA, and to do it with another championship in his sights. A decade earlier, such radical action was all but forbidden, especially by such a luminary of the mainstream economy. If LeBron really decided to boycott the season that night, though? In 2020? And institutions like the NBA and Nike *didn't* back him? "They'd be crucified," Vince said. That's why you couldn't skip steps like this strike, he believed, before composing structural demands—this step made superstars realize they had more power than they thought. From that vote, though, in the team-by-team clusters of the massive ballroom meeting in The Bubble, the Sacramento OGs on FaceTime could still tell that NBA players wanted to stay the course.

Influence was, Garrett maintained, a process of the subconscious conscience, teaching fans how to think about education reform while they watched the Brooklyn Nets, or about banning no-knock police raids while they brushed their teeth. And hindsight in 2020 told him that the non-superstars of the NBA had become better ambassadors than ever, even if that headway had taken them a decade—had taken a pandemic—and even if the actionable change he sought might take the next decade or five. "And the younger generation that we have to teach," Vince would say, "they're not afraid. They like, 'We ain't *standin'* for this. We front-*linin'*.'"

Late into the evening of the strike, Chris Paul and Andre Iguodala stayed up with players from many teams, discussing how to make the most of the spontaneous leverage thrust upon them. But mostly they sat with LeBron, trying to bend around the corner of history without progressing in circles. They picked up the phone, along with Carmelo Anthony and Russ Westbrook, and received an offer for a plan that was straight out of the community organizer's playbook, to help translate impulses for seeking social justice into something concrete. It came from Barack Obama.

"Y'all need to set up a more permanent structure," the former president joked, "so that you don't call me at midnight."

An office of staff attorneys and communications experts, Obama suggested, could help NBA players get into specifics with ownership, pooling player resources and political passions to stay one step ahead of, rather than immediately following, the next still-inevitable tragedy. "It's not going to be solved overnight," he recalled saying. "This is something that you've got to stay on. You gotta keep on moving."

LeBron woke up on the right side of the bed the next morning. After an all-players meeting back in the ballroom and a huddle in the afternoon, player representatives presented their demands to ownership on Zoom. Michael Jordan, taking rare but confident control of a Board of Governors call, told his fellow owners to do more listening than talking, and he made clear to players that enough really was enough with all that talking: The adamant non-activist, as flawed as yesterdays will always be, found himself ready to implement LeBron and Obama's plan. LeBron wanted Obama's social-justice committee in place, he wanted Black people in positions of power throughout the NBA, and he wanted everybody, everywhere, to vote. The A-list claimed victory again: The players would play.

Obama thought there had been "a suspension of activism" in sports, since the days of Ali and Russell and Arthur Ashe until LeBron's wave of influence took over, as Black athletes focused on contractual and sponsorship ascendance—he'd been disappointed when Jordan, consumed by living up to his own image, joked about Republicans buying sneakers, too. But it was precisely because players had become more sophisticated as businesspeople, Obama believed, that they could leverage not only today's platforms but entire superstructures, from Nike and the National Basketball Association to statehouses and the United States Senate, with a strategic leadership in civil rights and social good that had become so suddenly suspended in Washington. "And that," Obama would conclude, "is the next evolution: translating this not just from protest but then also understanding how they can use their *power*, which is significant—formidable, more than it was probably twenty or thirty years ago." Basketball players especially, he later reminded LeBron, had set a new tone for young people: Hopeful hoopers big and small had begun to realize, in their moment, that the superstardom of tomorrow was no longer a scorer's game. You had to pass it on.

On the night of the NBA's decision to come back to life, Kára felt her stomach ache. She'd gotten a prenatal massage that day and was concerned that her baby might arrive early because of it, except she didn't know what contractions felt like. Garrett kept handing her saltines for the nausea, until he dozed off again, watching Netflix 'till dawn. But a new day rolled around, and there was no planning for it: Little man was on his way.

They drove to New York–Presbyterian Hospital and took the elevator upstairs. Miguel, the Nets super-fan, was ordering masks and gloves from a converted virus ward on the third floor. Garrett put on some Whitney Houston and ignored his cell-phone alerts, while Kára got in the zone. At 5:59 p.m., standing twenty inches tall, at seven pounds and ten ounces, from *Brooklyn*, Garrett Temple Jr.—Two, they called him—began his rookie year.

The basketball player looked at his son for the first time and felt a rush of joy greater than any crowd of twenty thousand could ever deliver. He continued to love that the baby could not possibly remember a season so burdened by hate and sorrow, and that he could offer his boy such undivided attention. Garrett looked at Kára, and into their baby's curious eyes, and he believed that 2020 might end up becoming the best year of their lives, despite everything. The next generation was just getting started.

ENCORE

THE SNEAKER STORES outside Barclays Center were boarding up their windows again, looking forward to a celebration or a riot. Tourists took selfies before the mural of Kobe and Gigi Bryant. Posters of George Floyd and Breonna Taylor, plastered on the scaffolding walls of skyscraping construction projects nearby, peeled around the edges. There was a longer line for takeout at Shake Shack than across the street at the arena, where, for the first time, ballots were being cast. It was Election Day, and Colin Kaepernick's birthday, and even the cops on the barricaded plaza talked shit about Donald Trump. The closing campaign message at the president's rally the night before had been: *LeBron James sucks!*

Inside, voting booths awaited the people where the ticket-takers had. The Nets owners, in addition to a ten-year, $50 million commitment to "address systemic imbalances and root causes that produce racial gaps in education, health and wealth," had kept paying their ushers and roadies. But the seats had been empty for eight months, and the only sound a passerby could hear, standing on the covered-up court, was the murmur of *Monday Night Football* highlights on loop in the luxury boxes, where the franchise was trying to safely return its fans as soon as possible.

There was, that day, possibility milling about. A poll worker named Pamela Jones waited for drop-off ballots at a folding table, telling stories about the Freedom Riders. "We're here in Barclays Center because they stood up and said, 'I'll go through whatever I have to go through to vote,'" she said behind her mask, recalling how she'd stepped off the bus—*the* bus—to a burly bigot with a shotgun, how he said that she'd be at the bottom of the Mississippi by the end of the night, at the bus stop in the summer of '61. "Now it's still a battle, but it's not as overwhelming. There's just such an idiot in the White House—it's just *me me me*—and the big question is: Why do some people buy into that? Why are all those people at the rallies?" Another poll worker stood listening to Pamela on top of a sticker that reminded voters to keep six feet away from one another. The young white woman hoped that nobody would vote third-party for Kanye West that day, but she appreciated that she and Pamela would not have been here together were it not for LeBron's More Than an Athlete™ brand spawning More Than a Vote™, his campaign—emboldened by the NBA players' strike two and a half months earlier—to transform twenty-two NBA arenas into coliseums of democracy: "Whatever LeBron says, goes."

When Jay-Z challenged LeBron during his 2010 free-agency pitch to do what was best for him, it was, as Dr. J said, a move in service to oneself. Jay-Z had gotten in trouble, in a subsequent interview, upon defining his bond with the young king. "Our stories is the *same* thing—it's pushing the culture forward in another way," he said. Seconds later, Jay-Z spoke up for his class of superstar in response to the 1960s artist and activist Harry Belafonte, who'd accused high-profile celebrities including Hova himself of having "turned their back on social responsibility." To which Jay-Z said: "This is going to sound arrogant, but my *presence* is charity. Just who I am, just like Obama's is. Obama provides hope. Whether he does *any*thing, the hope that he provides for a nation, and outside of America, is *enough*."

At a charity event during NBA All-Star Weekend that next season, Jay-Z and LeBron talked about how Muhammad Ali was seen as arrogant when he said he was pretty. When he said he was talented. When The Greatest decided he would not fight a war that was not worth fighting, while providing confidence— maybe even air cover—for Bill Russell and Mahmoud Abdul-Rauf to refuse to shut up and dribble, for John Carlos and Tommie Smith to raise their fists in the air. There was a distinction, though, between confidence and authenticity: When he was with LeBron that weekend in 2011, Jay-Z emphasized that once you got to the mountaintop, you need not be some mythical character beyond the grasp of real-life fans. And Hova was, back then at least, the keeper of the real. But there was an even bigger distinction, which LeBron had come to appreciate in the years since, between worrying that the masses agreed with you while you were doing something real—maybe even historic— and staying focused on a mission for change, with the same determination as the quest for a championship. His presence had become progress, and the mission—the action—had become social responsibility itself.

When I asked LeBron, at All-Star Weekend in February 2020, how the American athlete had evolved as a role model during the Trump administration, despite an even more polarized country, he stood up straight, adjusted his personal brand's varsity jacket and said: "Just having a voice, having control over your own narrative, being passionate about what you believe in, no matter if other people don't approve of it, or disapprove of it—so, for me, it was never just about basketball for me. I know my inspiration, and I know how many more people that I inspire that don't even play the game of basketball. So I just felt like I could give so much more than just dribbling a basketball, you know?"

He smiled, because the rhetoric of *shut up and dribble* seemed like ages ago, and that was before the rest of 2020 put some serious gray in his beard. "So I just try to continue to inspire the youth, inspire as many people as I can all over the world. Make as much of an impact as I can. And then . . . and then live with the results after that." He was not always the hero we wanted him to be. But LeBron seemed to appreciate that he could be the leader America needed, when we were all desperate enough for somebody, anybody, to tell it like it was. King James could brand love.

LeBron and the Lakers defeated the Miami Heat for the championship three weeks before Election Day, an inevitable conquering. He just thought it was too bad they couldn't have a victory parade in the streets. The Bubble, though, was a certified win for scientists and tycoons—the NBA recouped $1.5 billion for its efforts, and Chinese state TV even broadcast the last two games—while a majority of Americans finally supported athletes kneeling during the anthem, especially the country's growing population of diverse basketball fans. Not that such inevitabilities stopped conservatives from inventing a #GetWokeGoBroke meme to blame the NBA's low playoff ratings on its players' devotion to social justice, and on that one damn tweet surrounding the Lakers and Nets' trip to China.

The more Spencer Dinwiddie thought about it, with Brooklyn's 2019–2020 campaign having left him behind, he still saw LeBron as the future, with a politician's diligent care in tending to the next wave of his influence, while Kyrie Irving was stuck leading from the back and living in the now. "Big picture? LeBron is fully willing, able and capable to not only be a sports owner but also the president . . . like, of the United States," Spencer told me. "Especially with the state of the country the way it is, and he's loved globally. That's the type of vibe that you get from LeBron: He's gonna always make the *right* move. Even if there's maybe possibly a *more* right move, he's still going to make the *right* move. It's meticulous. It's calculated. Whereas Ky does whatever is in his soul. He does what his heart or his mind calls him to do. And so it's not as meticulously planned, but that's who he is—it's *outrageously* authentic, and it's *supremely* Kyrie. That's why he's willing to put his fist in the air: He's willing to be himself. He doesn't have any aspirations to be the president of the United States."

Like so many of the renaissance men caught in the revolving doors of the Brooklyn Nets and professional sports at large, Spencer was awaiting a fate beyond his control, unsure what the now might look like next, after a season unlike any other. Spencer Dinwiddie, of course, was exploring how to represent himself without a sports agent, but still: "Half the people that were on the team this year are gonna be gone, because that's the way it works—to fit around KD and Kyrie," he said. "The people that struggle with that the most and end up depressed are completely focused in their life and tied up in the NBA—and if I lived and died with the decision-making of those in power, I'd have been crushed a long time ago." Indeed, Wilson Chandler had arrived to play back in Zhejiang the week before; his absence from the United States and the NBA was, he said, a "leave of mind."

The National Basketball Association was hustling back to business as unusual. Adam Silver talked to players about forming "a legislative agenda" with ownership, even as he expected that they would return to the "tradition" of standing for "The Star-Spangled Banner"—and that these young, healthy people would not jump the lines for swiftly emerging coronavirus vaccines. But the commissioner was desperate to salvage as much as $1 billion in TV money, and he'd convinced the players' union to try starting back up with a truncated 2020–2021 NBA campaign on December 22, only ten weeks after the last exhaustible season had concluded.

Brooklyn had been waiting for next year all along.

Revitalized by the strength of his Achilles and the Covid-19 antibodies lingering within him, KD began to imagine a place he called NetsWorld. An elite hooper's sanctum, cordoned off from the sports media and social media and the mad, mad rest of the world. It would be a shared headspace, in which Kyrie could boycott the beat reporters and burn sage around the borders of the court. Their utopian team motto was already emerging: *Protect the group*, which applied to the virus, too. KD didn't have to imagine for very long, either, because NetsWorld was coming true right before his eyes at the West Coast hub of the franchise, inside The Sports Academy.

An unofficial, player-first training camp had broken out on Court No. 4, with DeAndre back in the mix, even as the sessions came to ignore official lineups in favor of invite-only, big-name pickup and roster roadkill. Taurean Prince and Caris LeVert joined the Sports Academy runs, but they knew that Sean Marks and the front office had been dangling them, along with Jarrett Allen and Spencer, as assets for a trade, for going on a year—and they knew that Brooklyn was still star-gazing.

On the morning of Election Day at Kobe's old gym, KD

and Kyrie played a top-secret game with Chris Paul and James Harden. Chris talked about how he'd led a march to the polls back home in North Carolina, after saving the NBA season at least twice. And James . . . well, James Harden was the league's back-to-back-to-back scoring champion, and his upper lip was now consumed by enough facial hair to serve as a near-medical-grade Covid mask. But he was unhappy, even if still under contract, with the Houston Rockets, and the runs in NetsWorld got him thinking about how to will the imagination into existence. James and KD hadn't hooped together seriously since they played in brushstrokes on the Thunder with Russ Westbrook, reading each other's minds at mesmerizing speed. "Go ahead," KD would tell James, encouraging him to take control of a game, sacrificing Durantian stardom to protect that group and cultivate The Beard. After Miami's super-team beat OKC's Big Three in the 2012 NBA Finals, James Harden had wanted more money, and so was traded by management. But in 2020 he was willing to forgo a contract extension of $50 million a year to tell management where he wanted to go instead, and James . . . well, James Harden wanted to play in Brooklyn.

KD and Kyrie and, yes, The Beard could already see the twinkling paths of their constellation, a bouncy flow that might look different on any given night, especially if one of them was injured or sidelined by coronavirus—either by contracting it or side-stepping the NBA's strict protocols on partying while fit and famous at the tail end of a plague. To unlock this unselfish brand of basketball, James would first have to be selfish enough to request a trade and become such a nuisance to his team, until the trade destination was to his liking, that the Rockets would be forced to settle for less. Such a blockbuster deal would, as Spencer had predicted, mean shipping half of Brooklyn's resilient roster to Houston and perhaps other places like Indianapolis, even Cleveland, if management could make it happen for KD, Kyrie and The Beard. But such a celestial trio would immediately relaunch the Nets into the Lakers' stratosphere for years to come. It was, James said, "a no-brainer," and it was ultimately, after a decade of undeniable player empowerment, up to him.

A couple hours after the inaugural run of Brooklyn's Big-Three-to-Be, Garrett was changing his son's diaper in the house that Jay-Z had suggested he buy for the long-term, way back when, at Kyrie's welcome-to-Brooklyn party. "Players have a *lot* of say nowadays in this league," he said. Garrett and Kyrie hadn't spoken since the instantly notorious Zoom call in June, on which they'd disagreed about boycotting The Bubble in front of so many of their peers. Suddenly, Garrett was starting to get the message from his agent that his pragmatic leadership had become a threat and that he might want to prepare a move to Chicago—he wasn't so sure anymore if the Nets would pick up his team option for the season ahead. "Players in the leadership, if you go against what they want you to do, then they won't want you to be back," Garrett told me. "If that's the case, then I don't wanna be on this team. . . . But Kyrie is the enigma of the century, so who knows?" KD had just called from Los Angeles, saying not to worry—that everything would work out. Garrett sat down with his family, preparing to switch between CNN and Fox News for the election results, and wondered if everything would.

NOVEMBER 7, 2020 🌚

Brooklyn

SO MUCH REMAINED up in the air. Draft picks and dramatic trade demands. Rapid tests at the arena. Unclaimed bodies in the

freezer trucks still parked outside the practice facility. The vaccine. The damn presidency, of course. And on top of everything,
Steve Nash knew the virus would only start to waft around
again, with the arrival of a New York winter.

After nine weeks in his new job and four extended evenings
of election-result anxiety, however, it was a frolicky Saturday
morning: He could play in a masked-up weekend soccer match,
push one of his five children on the playground swings and still
make it back to his brownstone, just down the block from Kenny
Atkinson's old place, in time for brunch. Nash was also politically aware enough to admit, within hours of being unveiled as
Atkinson's replacement in September, that a system of white
privilege and oppression had, by its very nature, allowed him
to become a first-time NBA head coach at 46 years old, despite
little relevant experience—even though he was, technically, a
former MVP and current Hall of Famer. For a Canadian, Steve
Nash was very, very Brooklyn.

At 11:25 a.m. on that second Saturday in November, Coach
Nash heard the windows of the city open up again. *Woo! Let's
goooooooo!* Spoons banged on pasta strainers, pots on pans and
pans on PlayStation controllers, anything anybody could find
to cheer like they had for the hospital workers and delivery guys
at the height of The Curve, and as they might again cheer for
basketball before too long: An American champion had been
declared.

Nash drove past the Trader Joe's on Atlantic Avenue, where
dozens and then hundreds and soon thousands of Brooklynites
applauded the passengers of every vehicle with a honking horn:
NBA basketball coaches and U.S. mail carriers, the bus drivers
and the garbage dudes, a whole entire city—a whole fractured
nation—could exhale. Not many Americans waiting on line
for a coronavirus test had been truly happy until that morning,

and there hadn't been this many people on the Barclays Center plaza since the system decided not to arrest the cops who killed Breonna Taylor. It was no victory parade, but the end of the nightmare of the tangerine tyrant in Washington was, for the moment at least, enough.

Fans of progress lined the sidewalks outside Barclays straight through the afternoon, until they up and started dancing together in the streets. Chuck Schumer, the Democratic leader in the Senate, rode by in his town car and stopped outside the arena. He held his cell phone out the window.

Woo! Thank you, Joooooooooe! Wooooooooooo!

"You hear that?" asked the senator, to the president-elect on the line.

"Thank *you!*" said Joe Biden.

Schumer extended the phone out toward the Barclays Center crowd one last time, rolled up his window and drove off. "Did you hear that? That's Brooklyn!"

Across the country, Kevin Durant woke up to the Pacific Ocean, a gale-force and altogether heavy morning in Los Angeles, but he saw that the surfers were out on the beach—things couldn't be so bad. The TV networks just called it, his housemates said: Biden and Harris had finally won. There was some rosé on ice, except KD's crew didn't exactly trust the media that the race was over, and, anyhow, he'd been distracted by the entirety of this election year, when the winds of change spun into a vortex.

"There's a cap on what we can do when we just wanna spread awareness, because there's only so much awareness can do," he'd said the other day at a virtual conference series developed for him by his personal brand, since ESPN had cancelled *The Boardroom*. "That's what we need as a country more than anything: It's all about getting to that next person and really impacting somebody's life in a positive way. If we do that, then, you know, things are looking forward. Politics, it feels like it's taken over our world right now, and our world is way bigger than just politics at this point. And if we understand what that is, and still live life, then you'll see things are looking up."

The entourage headed to the gym and got in a weight-lifting session, real quick. They were busy packing up to fly east in a week, for the first time since KD's positive result had shocked the world. He was excited to be headed someplace like home, determined to make history again and again, in Brooklyn, guided by the currents of basketball greatness at his back. It no longer mattered to him if the fans would be shouting; so long as there were nine more hoopers in that arena, there would always be a next season.

KD got on a bicycle. He was still thin enough for the ocean's bluster to knock him sideways, but he pedaled straight ahead to the boardwalk all the same, among the people, and shouted back at a second wind. "Back to the grind," he said. "Time to get back to work!"

APPRECIATIONS

THE ATHLETES WHO SHARED their life stories with me are the real storytellers here, and I hope to have done them justice. Thank you, and sorry about the long-winded questions. You taught me to listen.

I appreciate, too, my three goliath Davids. My mentor at *Esquire*, David Granger, wrote me an email in 2019 with the subject line *Someone should write a book . . .* , and the body copy summoned me: *. . . starting today, about the Nets in the next year. Who is the best writer in New York who gives a fk about basketball?* I was not, but I wanted to be, and what a year to follow, and God bless David Granger, now my agent at Aevitas Creative Management. Dave Finocchio is a believer, and he believed in me at *Bleacher Report* when he didn't have to and when I kept banging down the door. I appreciate David Levy for opening it.

Thank you to my editor at Dey Street Books, Matthew Daddona, for encouraging me to write with purpose in a hurry. Kevin McDonnell, another OG from the Granger days of *Esquire*, fact-checked with calm. Shout-out to Ben Osborne, the most loyal man in sports journalism, for reading every word with expertise and encouragement, and to Ian Blair for doing me the same solid.

"You need to understand that the Nets fall somewhere be-tween the CIA and old KGB when it comes to secrecy," wrote Brian Lewis, the longtime beat writer for *The New York Post*, during the NBA's virus hiatus. "And that's over a hangnail or a sprained pinkie toe, in the best of times." The team's public-relations staff lived up to its reputation, but I appreciate Aaron Harris, Eli Pearlstein, Mitch Heckart and Megan Walsh for putting up with me. Mandy Gutmann from BSE Global put up with me even more. Elle Hagedorn from the NBPA never let me down, and PR staffers from every NBA team deserve a vacation.

Reporting this book was a change for me, from the office life of an editor to a life without offices, and I appreciated the companionship of the Nets beat writers: Brian, Greg Logan of *Newsday*, Kristian Winfield and Stefan Bondy of *The New York Daily News*, Malika Andrews of ESPN, Michael Grady of YES Network, Tom Dowd of NBA.com, Mike Mazzeo, and my guy Alex Schiffer of *The Athletic*. Special thanks to Robert Windrem and Anthony Puccio of NetsDaily, for your large hearts and your journalistic integrity. Local reporting matters.

The NBA's top national writers are better than many Wash-ington reporters, and their work is all over these pages: Adrian Wojnarowski, Shams Charania and Ramona Shelburne, es-pecially, as well as David Aldridge, Chris Ballard, Howard Beck, Tim Bontemps, Nick Friedell, Vincent Goodwill, Chris Haynes, Tim Kawakami, Lee Jenkins, Jason Lloyd, Zach Lowe, Jackie MacMullan, Chris Mannix, Dave McMenamin, Rachel Nichols, Brandon Robinson, Taylor Rooks, Marc Spears, Mar-cus Thompson, Joe Vardon, Brian Windhorst and Royce Young. The Professional Basketball Writers Association welcomed me, and Josh Robbins got my back.

Kindness kept me going in 2020, and a lot of that came from the *B/R Mag* squad: Mirin Fader, consistently, plus Jonathan

Abrams, Lars Anderson, Lance Fresh, Ishaan Mishra, Mark Smoyer, Yaron Weitzman and Dylan MacNamara. Thanks to Jared Diamond, Erik Malinowski and Gabriel Snyder for the early wisdom, to Jake Fischer, Jarod Hector, James Herbert and Michael Pina for the company, to Cindy Li for the international expertise, to Norman Oder for the BK watchdogging, and to Katherine Rowe and Jon Nobil for the L.A. and D.C. hospitality. Attention to detail from Rosy Tahan, Andrea Monagle, Jessica Rozler and Victor Hendrickson for HarperCollins got this project to the printer in time, in one piece. So did the heart of Terrel Seltzer, at the buzzer.

I appreciate, most of all and more than ever, my family. Scarlet and Sienna, you are my favorite team. I love you.

ENDNOTES

1: DECISIONS, DECISIONS

10   looking down the staircase of a penthouse: LeBron James, interview by Rio Ferdinand, *#5 Magazine*, October 2009.

10   "Now there's something else to shoot for": Mark Binelli, "Jay-Z: King of America," *Rolling Stone*, June 24, 2010.

11   asked LeBron to imagine: Brian Windhorst, "Three Days in July: The High-Stakes Maneuvers that Assembled LeBron, Wade and Bosh," ESPN.com, June 29, 2020.

11   the minority owner knew: "Food for Thought: Conversations with Jay-Z," hosted by Harry Allen, Angie Martinez and Stephen A. Smith, aired September 2009, on BET.

11   a well-intentioned effort: *More Than an Athlete*, episode 2, "Decisions, Decisions," directed by Austin Peters, aired November 20, 2018, on ESPN+.

12   "He paved the way": Howard Beck, "Superteam Era May Be Here to Stay After LeBron and KD Changed Free-Agency Game," *B/R Mag*, June 6, 2017.

12   a quiet jet ride: *More Than an Athlete*, episode 2, "Decisions, Decisions," directed by Austin Peters, aired November 20, 2018, on ESPN+.

12   crying: Jackie MacMullan, "Pat Riley: LeBron 'Did the Right Thing' When He Left Miami," ESPN.com, April 9, 2018.

12   "I think that had a lot to do with race at that time": Mark Anthony Green, "The King," *GQ*, November 2017.

13   "was the same system used in the South where the plantation owner owned all the houses that you live in": William C. Rhoden, *Forty Million Dollar Slaves*, (New York: Crown, 2017), 232.

13   "to give every ballplayer a chance to be a human being": *The Curious Case of Curt Flood*, written by Aaron Cohen, aired July 13, 2011, on HBO.

16   like he'd never felt before: GQ Sports, "Kevin Durant on His Legendary Game at Harlem's Rucker Park," GQ.com, November 16, 2017.

18   "It just didn't work": *All the Smoke*, episode 14, "Kevin Durant," hosted by Matt Barnes and Stephen Jackson, aired February 6, 2020, for Showtime.

18   His foot felt slanted: "Kevin Durant Returns," October 22, 2019, in *Knuckleheads with Quentin Richardson and Darius Miles*, podcast, 1:06:25.

20   "this would be cool to do for real": Jackie MacMullan, "For the Culture: KD, Kyrie and What Comes Next for the Nets," ESPN.com, October 28, 2019.

21   "chill, on the low, all-black everything": "Kevin Durant and Rich Kleiman," September 10, 2020, in *The Old Man and the Three*, podcast, 1:36:00.

2: THE CLEAN SWEEP

24   "the garage stage": Steven Bertoni, "Three Point Play: Inside Kevin Durant's Multimillion-Dollar Basketball, Media and Investing Empire," *Forbes*, December 31, 2019.

24   "A championship would be a whole other level": Bertoni, "Three Point Play."

27   "a polarizing star": "Spencer Dinwiddie on the Growth of the Nets," December 9, 2019, in *Winging It with Vince Carter*, podcast, 41:46.

28   "New York might be real fun next year": "Spencer Dinwiddie Goes Inside Relationship with Kyrie Irving," July 17, 2019, *Back to Back with Shams Charania*, podcast, 25:01.

29   "Bro, it's perfect for you": "Spencer Dinwiddie Goes Inside Relationship with Kyrie Irving."

30   "the Nets are owned by a Russian industrialist": Aaron Elstein,

"Prince's Former Manager Londell McMillan Explains Jay-Z's Beef with Him," *Crain's New York*, February 5, 2018.

30 "was the same Barclays that financed the trans-Atlantic slave trade": Norman Oder, "As 40/40 Club Opens the Night before Arena Debuts, a Vigil and March Draws 150 people, James, Montgomery," *Atlantic Yards/Pacific Park Report*, September 28, 2012.

30 "The One Percent that's robbing people and deceiving people": Zadie Smith, "The House That Hova Built," *The New York Times Style Magazine*, September 6, 2012.

32 *I'm the Black Branch Rickey*: Jay-Z, "Brooklyn Go Hard," track 8 on *Notorious: Music from and Inspired by the Original Motion Picture*, Bad Boy Records, 2009.

33 "I must tell you that it was Mr. Rickey's drama and that I was only a principal actor": Jackie Robinson and Alfred Duckett, *I Never Had It Made: An Autobiography of Jackie Robinson* (New York: Ecco, 1972), xxiv.

34 *Scott Boras, you over, baby*: "Crown," featuring Travis Scott, track 8 on Jay-Z, *Magna Carta . . . Holy Grail*, Def Jam, Roc-A-Fella Records, 2013.

36 twelve bathrooms: J. R. Moehringer, "Kevin Durant's New Headspace," *WSJ Magazine*, September 10, 2019.

37 Taurean would brush his teeth in the communal bathroom: "Brooklyn's Taurean Prince," December 11, 2019, in *The Woj Pod*, podcast, 31:33.

38-9 Nearly 75 percent of NBA players identified as Black or African American: Richard E. Lapchick, "The 2020 Racial and Gender Report Card: National Basketball Association," The Institute for Diversity and Ethics in Sport, University of Central Florida, 6.

39 "full-contact living from the time you woke up until the time you hit the pillow": Greg Logan, "For Nets Coach Kenny Atkinson, Competition Was a Family Affair," *Newsday* (NY), November 25, 2017.

40 "I'm not doing it": MacMullan, "For the Culture."

3: FIGHT FOR FREEDOM

50   The NBA had been striking deals: Jim Yardley, "The N.B.A. Is Missing Its Shots in China," *The New York Times Magazine*, February 1, 2012.

50–1   "But at the end of the day": Jack McCallum, "The World According to David Stern," *Sports Illustrated*, November 6, 2006.

51   and to the commissioner's office: Ira Boudway with Qian Ye, "Nets Owner Joe Tsai Is Caught Between Brooklyn and Beijing," *Bloomberg Businessweek*, January 22, 2020.

52   checking the flight-status map: DeAndre Jordan and Spencer Dinwiddie interview, *The Jump*, ESPN, October 8, 2019.

52   gathered at the team hotel: Marc J. Spears, "Inside the Clippers' Final Days with Donald Sterling as Owner," *The Undefeated*, April 24, 2019.

52   to rewatch some game tape: *Blackballed*, episode 2, "The Fish's Head," directed by Mike Jacobs, aired May 18, 2020, on Quibi.

52   "*Nah*": "DeAndre Jordan," February 13, 2020, *R2C2 is UNINTERRUPTED*, podcast, 53:16.

52   But Sterling would shake his hand a little too long: *Blackballed*, episode 4, "Property," directed by Mike Jacobs, aired May 19, 2020, on Quibi.

52   He knew that each year: *Blackballed*, "Property."

53   denied rooms at the team hotel: A. L. Hardman, "Baylor's Refusal to Play Here Brings ABC Protest," *The Charleston Gazette-Mail*, January 18, 1959.

53   "I'm not an animal put in a cage and let out for the show": Mike Whiteford, "In 1959, Elgin Baylor Took a Stand for Dignity at Civic Center," *The Charleston Gazette-Mail*, September 7, 2019.

53   *he didn't just say this shit*: *Blackballed*, "Fish's Head."

54   DeAndre was mad: *Blackballed*, "Property."

54   "What's going on with you, DeAndre? Talk to us": *Blackballed*, "Fish's Head."

54   "I don't want to play": *Blackballed*, "Fish's Head."

54   "I think that's bullshit": "DeAndre Jordan" in *R2C2 is UNINTERRUPTED*.

54   "Yeah, DeAndre, fuck that. I'm not playing either": *Blackballed*, "Fish's Head."

54 several broke down crying: *Blackballed*, "Fish's Head."

54 "OK. My name's Glenn Rivers. I'm from Maywood, Illinois, and I'm Black": Spears, "Inside the Clippers' Final Days with Donald Sterling as Owner."

54 "And if *any* of you think you're more pissed than me, you gotta be fucking kidding": *Blackballed*, episode 6, "The Choice," directed by Mike Jacobs, aired May 21, 2020, on Quibi.

54 If they wanted to make some sort of statement: "DeAndre Jordan" in *R2C2 is UNINTERRUPTED*.

55 considered signing with the Clippers: Brian Windhorst, *LeBron Inc.* (New York: Grand Central Publishing, 2019), 150.

55 The Clippers practiced that weekend at the University of San Francisco's gym: Spears, "Inside the Clippers' Final Days with Donald Sterling as Owner."

56 considered splintering off: "Bigger than Basketball with DeAndre Jordan," May 28, 2020, in *Ledlow & Parker*, podcast, 43:28.

56 "I wasn't being negative or anything, but I was standing for something bigger than myself": Spears, "Inside the Clippers' Final Days with Donald Sterling as Owner."

57 "It's just *us*": "Fallout," Ramona Shelburne, *30 for 30 Podcasts*, Season 5, Episode 4, ESPN, August 20, 2019, 10:57.

57 Doc Rivers was so busy: *Blackballed*, episode 7, "The Protest," directed by Mike Jacobs, aired on May 25, 2020, on Quibi.

57 "It was": Ramona Shelburne, "When the Donald Sterling Saga Rocked the NBA—and Changed It Forever," ESPN.com, August 20, 2019.

57 "Obviously, it wasn't enough": *Blackballed*, "The Protest."

58 Silver appreciated: *Blackballed*, "The Protest."

58 "Black rage personified, Black power in the flesh": John Papanek, "A Different Drummer," *Sports Illustrated*, March 31, 1980.

58 alongside Steve Nash: Shelburne, "When the Donald Sterling Saga Rocked the NBA."

58 But that same day, at the Clippers practice facility: Spears, "Inside the Clippers' Final Days with Donald Sterling as Owner."

58 "Damn": *Blackballed*, episode 9, "Bigger Than Sports," directed by Mike Jacobs, aired May 26, 2020, on Quibi.

62   Tsai had to visit alone: Brian Lewis, "Joe Tsai Opens Up about NBA's Escalating China Controversy," *New York Post*, October 8, 2019.

62   LeBron and the Lakers got word of the cancellations: Dave Mc-Menamin, "Inside LeBron James' and Adam Silver's Make-or-Break Moments in China," ESPN.com, October 15, 2019.

4: A CONSPIRACY OF SILENCE

66   "what you guys stand for": McMenamin, "Inside LeBron James' and Adam Silver's Make-or-Break Moments in China."

66   The young king's $90 million Nike deal required him: Windhorst, *LeBron Inc.*, 101.

67   LeBron claimed: Howard Beck, "Cavalier Seeks Players' Support for Darfur," *The New York Times*, May 16, 2007.

67   Team USA fell silent: Chris Mannix, "Where's the Outrage? Suddenly, Team USA Is Silent on Darfur," *Sports Illustrated*, August 8, 2008.

68   Michael Jordan didn't consider himself an activist: *The Last Dance*, episode V, directed by Jason Hehir, aired May 3, 2020, on ESPN.

68   the story of one fan hit a switch: LeBron James interview, *CNN Tonight*, July 30, 2018.

69   LeBron directed the composition of the photograph: Jody Avirgan, *30 for 30 Podcasts*, Season 2, Episode 1, "Hoodies Up," ESPN, November 14, 2017, 19:54.

69   "Years from now": Jemele Hill, "The Heat's Hoodies as Change Agent," ESPN.com, March 26, 2012.

70   Silver responded that he'd never fined players like LeBron: McMenamin, "Inside LeBron James' and Adam Silver's Make-or-Break Moments in China."

70   said he was in danger of losing lucrative Chinese sponsorship deals: Bill Oram, "What It Was Like to Cover the Lakers in China When the Media Was Shut Out," *The Athletic*, October 12, 2019.

77   "quite sad": Samaria Rice, interview by Roland Martin, NewsOne Now, January 5, 2016.

81   who had several business-school friends involved in Hong Kong: Jackie MacMullan, "Philadelphia 76ers' Daryl Morey was worried

Hong Kong tweet might end NBA career," ESPN.com, December 23, 2020.

5: THE CIRCUIT BOARD

84   he'd only been checking: Moehringer, "Kevin Durant's New Headspace."

85   "They're literally megastars—very, very powerful—so you can't treat your players as employees anymore": Joe Tsai, interview for the Stanford University Entrepreneurial Thought Leaders series, April 29, 2020.

85   "It's kind of a socialist system": "Joe Tsai," May 7, 2019, in *Overtime with Paul Carcaterra*, podcast, 57:32.

86   "ESPN, TNT, they already use all our likeness, and everything we are, in order to build up these characters": "Kyrie Irving (Part 2)," October 1, 2020, *The ETCs with Kevin Durant*, podcast, 1:10:00.

88   KD used to pull up with thirty people to a club: Alex Williams, "How Kevin Durant Became Silicon Valley's Hottest Start-up," *The New York Times*, February 18, 2017.

89   "a bionic foot": Jackie MacMullan, "Why Kevin Durant Sees the World Differently Now," *ESPN The Magazine*, June 1, 2017.

89   "Am I gonna be alone forever?": Zach Baron, "The Flash Forward," *GQ*, March 2015.

90   "It was the same thing with the foot": Lee Jenkins, "Thunder Road," *Sports Illustrated*, May 30, 2016.

90   at around fourteen years old: Marcus Thompson, *KD: Kevin Durant's Relentless Pursuit to Be the Greatest* (New York: Atria Books, 2019), 44.

92   "I gotta get out more": "MacMullan, "Why Kevin Durant Sees the World Differently Now."

93   "As a world, we need to cry with each other. That shows we care": Baron, "Kevin Durant Doesn't Care What You Think of Him."

94   biking around Madrid relatively unnoticed: MacMullan, "Why Kevin Durant Sees the World Differently Now."

94   Jay-Z told KD to keep things simple: "Kevin Durant," February 10, 2017, in *The Bill Simmons Podcast*, podcast, 1:17:00.

95   "We can all do our best to take the heat off of you. But the most important

thing is that *you* have to not give a fuck": Andre Iguodala with Carvell Wallace, *The Sixth Man* (New York: Blue Rider Press, 2019), 199.

95 He called Steve Nash: Tim Kawakami, "Kevin Durant, Steve Nash and a Hall of Fame Friendship That Brought Them Both to the Warriors," *The Mercury News* (CA), January 5, 2017.

95 Nash told him: Kawakami, "Kevin Durant, Steve Nash and a Hall of Fame Friendship That Brought Them Both to the Warriors."

95 "It's not about championships": Zach Lowe, "Kevin Durant Stands Apart Among All-Time Greats," ESPN.com, June 12, 2018.

96 "Fake is what runs the world right now": Darren Rovell, "Inside Kevin Durant's Growing Empire," *ESPN The Magazine*, May 23, 2018.

98 Kleiman and KD drove by the San Francisco office of a food-delivery app called Postmates: Matthew Shaer, "Kevin Durant's Killer Crossover," *Fast Company*, November 2017.

98 "Talk that shit": "Durant Company Partner Rich Kleiman," January 15, 2018, in *A Waste of Time*, podcast, 1:31:09.

101 "I could connect with this man": Kyrie Irving, interview by Michael Grady, aired October 18, 2019, on YES Network.

101 "you want to put that Maserati in a glass case": Kenny Atkinson, interview by Mike Francesca, WFAN, November 1, 2019.

6: RISE OF THE UNDERDOG DISRUPTORS

105 consulted him about a fan giveaway: Nick Friedell, "Bobbleheads Have Become the NBA's Biggest Little Status Symbol," ESPN.com, March 10, 2020.

105 the corporation was not the asset: "New Fan Engagement Models for Athletes and Influencers," May 26, 2020, in *a16z Podcast*, podcast, 19:11.

107 bought a new house as an investment: Leo Sepkowitz, "Has Spencer Dinwiddie Got a Deal for You," *B/R Mag*, October 12, 2018.

109 "If my name was James Harden": Elizabeth Swinton, "A Story Through Sneakers: Spencer Dinwiddie's Big Splash in the Footwear World," SI.com, December 14, 2018.

110 "People don't understand the movement": Ramona Shelburne, "Speak It into Being," *ESPN The Magazine*, May 15, 2017.

112 "often emerge as the biggest winners": Anita Elberse, *Blockbusters: Hit-making, Risk-taking, and the Big Business of Entertainment* (New York: Henry Holt and Co., 2013), 149.

113 "I'm not afraid of it": Swinton, "A Story Through Sneakers."

114 "Is it a power play?": Boardroom, "Spencer Dinwiddie Gives the Breakdown on Shoe Business, Bitcoin Aspirations, NBA/Nets Journey & More," posted December 16, 2019, YouTube video.

116 it didn't go well: Jemele Hill, "Jay-Z Helped the NFL Banish Colin Kaepernick," *The Atlantic*, August 15, 2019.

116 "Something didn't smell right": Ken Belson, "Colin Kaepernick's Workout Derailed by Dispute with N.F.L.," *The New York Times*, November 16, 2019.

116 he predicted Jay-Z's partnership could do no wrong: "Kevin Durant Returns," in *Knuckleheads with Quentin Richardson and Darius Miles*.

117 had a role in the running of secret Twitter accounts that talked shit about his own team's players: Ben Detrick, "The Curious Case of Bryan Colangelo and the Secret Twitter Account," *The Ringer*, May 29, 2018.

118 *I'm not a businessman / I'm a business, man*: "Diamonds from Sierra Leone (Remix)," featuring Jay-Z, track 13 on Kanye West, *Late Registration*, Roc-A-Fella, Def Jam, 2005.

118 "If you look at any great regime, anywhere throughout history, if you're talking about a dynasty": "New Fan Engagement Models for Athletes and Influencers," May 26, 2020, in *a16z Podcast*, podcast, 4:00.

119 We're powerful enough to, if we wanted to, create our own league": Howard Bryant, "The Truth According to Carmelo Anthony," *ESPN The Magazine*, October 18, 2016.

7: IRL

124 found it ironic: Iguodala with Wallace, *The Sixth Man*, 209.

126 "Basketball—this life—it's an illusion": Mike Vorkunov, "From Kobe to Kyrie, How 'The Alchemist' Became the Book to Live by in the NBA," *The Athletic*, October 16, 2019.

128 "a ticking time bomb": "Kyrie Irving: NBA Cleveland Cavaliers," July 19, 2017, in *Short Story Long*, podcast, 1:36:36.

128   *Warriors, boy—that team over there, they some bad boys*: "Kyrie Irving (Part 1)," September 29, 2020, in *The ETCs with Kevin Durant*, podcast, 1:06:11.

129   "Block it out mentally, psychologically": "Kyrie Irving (Part 1)," in *The ETCs with Kevin Durant*.

130   "One thing I learned about leadership": "Kyrie Irving joins *The Vertical Podcast*," January 14, 2016, in *The Woj Pod*, podcast, 38:17.

130   "stop being so fuckin' stubborn and just ask for help when you need it": "Kyrie Irving: NBA Cleveland Cavaliers" in *Short Story Long*.

131   "I will never leave the court without him": Jason Lloyd, *The Blueprint: LeBron James, Cleveland's Deliverance and the Making of the Modern NBA* (New York: Dutton, 2017), 214.

132   Kobe loved the rope-a-dope: Kobe Bryant, *The Mamba Mentality: How I Play* (New York: MCD Books, 2018), 59.

132   Kyrie still felt like he had to isolate: "Kyrie Irving (Part 1)," in *The ETCs with Kevin Durant*.

132   "The war is over? There's no more games?": "Kyrie Irving (Part 1)," in *The ETCs with Kevin Durant*.

132   *Make it happen*: Lee Jenkins, "'I'm Ready': The Text That Started the Warriors' Dynasty," *Sports Illustrated*, June 12, 2017.

133   "To make the trip": Arash Markazi, "Kobe Bryant Has an Idea Why Kawhi Leonard Picked Clippers," *The Los Angeles Times*, October 21, 2019.

133   he'd hardly watched pro basketball: *All the Smoke*, episode 11, "Kobe Bryant," hosted by Matt Barnes and Stephen Jackson, aired January 9, 2020, for Showtime.

133   He did that because the legends who'd come before him: *All the Smoke*, "Kobe Bryant."

139   "I want all of you guys to try and take my spot from me": Alex Schiffer, "'I Just Want to See These Kids Do Extremely Well': Inside a Kyrie Irving–Influenced Practice at the Patrick School," *The Athletic*, January 13, 2020.

140   "Keep your circle small": Adam Zagoria, "Eyeing Return to Court, Kyrie Irving Continues Strong Bond with High School Alma Mater," Forbes.com, January 11, 2020.

141   *They mad they ain't famous / They mad they're still nameless*: Kanye West,

"Famous," featuring Rihanna and Swizz Beatz, track 4 on Kanye West, *The Life of Pablo*, GOOD, Def Jam, 2016.

8: ACTIVISTS WEAR SNEAKERS, TOO

148 "he had to prove it in ways that LeBron didn't": James Herbert, "How Garrett Temple Figured Out Life in the NBA," James Herbert, CBSSports.com, November 1, 2019.

149 Alton Sterling and Philando Castile became the five hundred sixty-eighth and five hundred seventy-second people killed by American law enforcement in that election year: "The Counted: People Killed by Police in the US," *The Guardian*, 2016.

150 "I'm not worried about Muhammad Ali": Bill Russell with Tex Maule, "I'm Not Worried About Ali," *Sports Illustrated*, June 19, 1967.

150 "the new '60s": Bryant, "The Truth According to Carmelo Anthony."

153 "I feel ever since he's got into office, or since he ran for the presidency, our country has been so divided, and it's not a coincidence": Chris Haynes, "Kevin Durant on President Trump: 'I Don't Agree with What He Agrees With,'" ESPN.com, August 17, 2017.

155 "All the gestures have been done, and all the conversations have started": Marc J. Spears, "David West's Anthem Protest May Be Barely Noticeable—but It Speaks Volumes," *The Undefeated*, October 2, 2016.

159 dropped out of DePaul in the middle of class: "Wilson Chandler," April 9, 2019, in *Knuckleheads with Quentin Richardson and Darius Miles*, podcast, 56:45.

164 "because they've always supported me": Ann Killion, "Colin Kaepernick Sits Courtside Next to Warriors, Who 'Always Supported Me,'" *The San Francisco Chronicle*, May 20, 2019.

9: KEEPER OF THE SOUL

167 he'd made $50 million when it sold to Apple: Windhorst, *LeBron Inc*, 127.

169 where LeBron had sensed an irrevocable misalignment: "LeBron

James, Part 2," December 7, 2020, *Road Trippin'*, Uninterrupted, podcast, 34:00.

170   He admired the legacy of The Decision upon control: "Kyrie Irving on Leaving LeBron, Boston's Future, Summer Rumors, and Empowered Players," June 15, 2018, in *The Bill Simmons Podcast*, podcast, 1:27:22.

171   "He's not a dick in the locker room. He's a *solid*-ass teammate. He's not doing too much. He's doing just enough": "Kevin Durant," on *All the Smoke*.

174   "That steady climb, it starts in the summertime and goes throughout the season": "Kyrie Irving on Leaving LeBron, Boston's Future, Summer Rumors, and Empowered Players" in *The Bill Simmons Podcast*.

177   It was a time when Mr. Russell felt very lonely playing a child's game: Bill Russell and Taylor Branch, *Second Wind: The Memoirs of an Opinionated Man* (New York: Random House, 1979), 182.

177   "the white people in Boston liked him": Russell and Branch, *Second Wind*, 183.

177   "I thought of myself as playing for the Celtics, not for Boston": Russell and Branch, *Second Wind*, 202.

177   had been so happy that Kyrie landed with an historic franchise: "Kyrie Irving (Part 1)," in *The ETCs with Kevin Durant*.

178   to become a politically outspoken student-athlete in Boston: Kevin Armstrong, "Kyrie Irving's Dad Survived Wife's Death and 9/11, but Is Just Days from Seeing Son Reach NBA Dreams," *The New York Daily News*, June 18, 2011.

180   "life became way more important than basketball": "Kyrie Irving (Part 1)," in *The ETCs with Kevin Durant*.

182   Kyrie had rehearsed his pitch in the mirror, and though his heart was pounding, he was confident in his craft: "Kyrie Irving (Part 1)," in *The ETCs with Kevin Durant*.

183   "When a party of warriors go on a hunt": Black Elk with Joseph Epes Brown, *The Sacred Pipe: Black Elk's Account of the Seven Rites of the Oglala Sioux* (Norman: University of Oklahoma Press, 1989), 16.

185   He had spoken to LeBron on the morning of the crash: John Branch, Nicholas Bogel-Burroughs, Sarah Mervosh and Miriam Jordan, "'Helicopter Went Down, Flames Seen': Kobe Bryant's Last Flight," *The New York Times*, February 8, 2020.

186 Adam Silver ran into Dr. David Ho: Ramona Shelburne, "How the NBA Moved So Quickly on Coronavirus Testing," ESPN.com, March 19, 2020.

187 it was the same breadcrumb: "Kyrie Irving (Part 1)," in *The ETCs with Kevin Durant*.

10: DISINFECTED

195 "I came in every single day and kept my head down, I didn't say much, I wasn't too excited about much, so my coaches and my teammates thought something was wrong with me": "Kevin Durant," on *All the Smoke*.

196 he'd never bothered returning to the Bay after surgery: Moehringer, "Kevin Durant's New Headspace."

198 "He didn't like what his situation was": *All the Smoke*, episode 14, "Kevin Durant."

198 KD didn't care about being the king of New York: "Kevin Durant and Rich Kleiman," September 10, 2020, in *Old Man and the Three*, podcast, 1:36:41.

199 "And from that point": "Kyrie Irving (Part 1)," in *The ETCs with Kevin Durant*.

200 Atkinson used the solo commute from Downtown Brooklyn to his brownstone in nearby Cobble Hill as a form of therapy, and he tried to take a different path every time: Joe Vardon, "The Boys Are Back in Town: How Nets Coaches and Players Live Among Brooklynites, Like the Dodgers of Old," *The Athletic*, June 10, 2020.

203 the NBA sent a memo to teams: Shelburne, "How the NBA Moved So Quickly on Coronavirus Testing."

203 the league office sent another memo: Adrian Wojnarowski and Zach Lowe, "Fist-Bumps among Short-Term Recommendations as NBA Plots Coronavirus Strategy, Memo Says," ESPN.com, March 2, 2020.

11: TIMEOUT

219   *It was all good just a week ago / Last week I had everything*: "A Week Ago," featuring Too $hort, track 7 on Jay-Z, *Vol. 2 . . . Hard Knock Life*, Def Jam, Roc-A-Fella Records, 1998.

220   "The problem": Ramona Shelburne, "NBPA's Michele Roberts Defends Players, Critical of Government on Virus Testing," ESPN.com, March 18, 2020.

220   "part of the psyche of the country": Adam Silver, interview on *SportsCenter*, ESPN, March 18, 2020.

220   had been advising the league since 2016: Shelburne, "How the NBA Moved So Quickly on Coronavirus Testing."

220   he delivered the owners a bleak picture of infection rates: Adrian Wojnarowski (@wojespn), "Sources: The ex-US surgeon general Vivek Murthy delivered NBA Board of Governors call a message consistent with other credible health organizations on grim potential impact of coronavirus pandemic in U.S., but left owners with hope of re-starting season/playoffs before July," Twitter, March 17, 2020, 6:34 p.m.

220   "rethink spectators": jr. nba, "Teamwork: Staying Connected While Physically Distant with Dr. Vivek Murthy and Candace Parker," posted May 15, 2020, YouTube video.

220   offered a seedling of hope: Adrian Wojnarowski (@wojespn), Twitter, March 17, 2020, 6:34 p.m.

220   "We need to get our social-media influencers out there": Dr. Jerome Adams, interview by George Stephanopoulos, *Good Morning America*, ABC, March 19, 2020.

221   as he did for seven or eight hours a day: "Episode 2—Kevin Durant," August 5, 2020, in *Play for Keeps*, podcast, 54:04.

224   you could be on the moon: Garrett Temple, interview by Michael Grady, YES Network, March 26, 2020.

224   He thought how surreal it had become: "Nets' Garrett Temple: Navigating Covid-19, Players Compensation Unknown, *Tiger King*," in *Tampering*, podcast, 6:30.

225   "Buy a gazillion tests": Peter Hamby, "Baseball? Coachella? Handshakes? Tinder? Anthony Fauci on the New Rules of Living with Coronavirus," VanityFair.com, April 15, 2020.

226 watched that Netflix documentary: "Nets' Garrett Temple: Navigating Covid-19, Players Compensation Unknown, *Tiger King*," in *Tampering*, podcast.

226 "You can't really do that, little man. Not right now": "Nets' Garrett Temple: Navigating Covid-19, Players Compensation Unknown, *Tiger King*," in *Tampering*, podcast, 8:20.

12: THE ROAR OF THE CROWD

239 "If you look at the Los Angeles Lakers or the Milwaukee Bucks, they're in first place when the season got suspended": Joe Tsai interview, interview for the Stanford University Entrepreneurial Thought Leaders series.

240 were beginning to feel comfortable: Adrian Wojnarowski, "NBA Owners, Execs Hopeful for Return after Call with Adam Silver, Sources Say," ESPN.com, May 12, 2020.

240 "The alternative": Adam Silver, interview on *SportsCenter*, ESPN, June 15, 2020.

13: A REVOLUTION ON TOP

244 Brooklyn's accidental new town square: Norman Oder, "Brooklyn's Accidental New Town Square," Bklyner.com, June 10, 2020.

246 "I didn't know how to protest": Malcolm Brogdon, "When Protests Fade, Here's What We Must Focus on as Americans," *USA Today*, June 5, 2020

249 "good with me": Kristian Winfield, "Barclays Center Is at the Heart of NYC Protests, and Joe Tsai Approves," *The New York Daily News*, June 7, 2020.

251 He tried going to therapy: "Kyrie Irving (Part 2)," in *The ETCs with Kevin Durant*; *#SayHerName: Justice for Breonna Taylor*, aired on July 8, 2020, on PlayersTV.

252 "We want to see the level we can get to now, sharing it with a person that we believe in": "Kyrie Irving (Part 1)," in *The ETCs with Kevin Durant*.

254   George Floyd was his family, too: Mirin Fader, "'This Is So Much Bigger,'" *B/R Mag*, August 24, 2020.

256   "more of an impact on this issue than almost any organization in the world": Adam Silver, interview on *Inside the NBA*, TNT, June 4, 2020.

257   "There's so many issues that you wanna tackle—that *I* wanna tackle," "Kyrie Irving (Part 2)," in *The ETCs with Kevin Durant*.

257   was gut-wrenched to hear: *#SayHerName: Justice for Breonna Taylor*.

257   "Black lives matter, but this is more than a movement—this is a revolution that has been underground, and now it's on top": *#SayHerName: Justice for Breonna Taylor*.

260   *We reach out to you because we want all of your voices to be heard*: Sam Amick, "Why LeBron James Wasn't on Friday's NBA Player Call about Orlando Concerns," *The Athletic*, June 12, 2020.

260   The host was a user named Ky Birving: Amick, "Why LeBron James Wasn't on Friday's NBA Player Call about Orlando Concerns."

264   for franchises to hire more diversely in front offices and coaching staffs, to partner with Black-owned arena vendors and local businesses, to donate a lot more money: Malika Andrews and Adrian Wojnarowski, "Avery Bradley: Coalition Wants NBA's Plan for Black Causes Before Restart," ESPN.com, June 16, 2020.

265   "We run the industry": "Kyrie Irving (Part 2)," in *The ETCs with Kevin Durant*.

266   Kyrie believed NBA players could start their own league someday: Stefan Bondy, "For the NBA Players, Canceling the Season Could Devastate the Salary Structure for Now and the Future," *The New York Daily News*, June 16, 2020.

267   "I'm pulling out your chair at the table and I'm pushing it in": Chantel Jennings, "This Week in the W: Natasha Cloud and Kyrie Irving, rookies and triple-doubles," *The Athletic*, August 10, 2020.

268   "I *haven't* done the job that I've wanted to do in my responsibility to speak up on these things, but now that I do, I'm here in full force to *be* that voice, to *be* that platform": *#SayHerName: Justice for Breonna Taylor*.

14: THE TOOTHPASTE IS OUT OF THE TUBE

270   "It's like a dorm room": *The Bridge*, season 2, episode 7, aired July 31, 2020, on NBA.com

272   "The week after that": Jacque Vaughn, interview by Michael Grady, YES Network, June 17, 2020.

273   he'd purchased across the street from Barclays Center: Joe Vardon and Alex Schiffer, "A Bubble and Bamboo: How Jacque Vaughn Hopes to Coach Kyrie Irving and Kevin Durant," *The Athletic*, July 28, 2020.

274   "Anyone who suggests that the players should be intending to create revolutionaries out of their fans—that's an incredibly naive assumption": David Aldridge, "'I Think Basketball Is Secondary': On the Restart, and Keeping the Message Alive," *The Athletic*, July 28, 2020.

277   "They're not protesting the game": "Kings: Garrett Temple and Doug Christie on Social Activism," March 25, 2018, *Purple Talk: A Sacramento Kings Podcast*, podcast, 41:57.

281   "Why are they here again?": Chris Ballard, "'These Tragedies Have to Stop.' Inside the Kings' Decision to Stand Up for Stephon Clark," *Sports Illustrated*, March 29, 2018.

281   *You ain't seeing no game tonight*: Dale Kasler, Tony Bizjak, Nashelly Chavez and Hudson Sangree, "Protesters Block Golden 1 Center, Again, after Disrupting Council Meeting on Shooting of Stephon Clark," *The Sacramento Bee*, March 27, 2018.

290   "that guy": Astead W. Herndon, "LeBron James on Black Voter Participation, Misinformation and Trump," *The New York Times*, October 21, 2020.

292   George Hill took his coaches on the Milwaukee Bucks to breakfast: Taylor Rooks, "The Most Magical Place on Earth," *GQ*, December/January 2021.

292   Sterling still thought it was bullshit: Marc J. Spears, "Milwaukee Bucks Guard Sterling Brown Reflects on His Team's Demonstration," *The Undefeated*, August 31, 2020.

293   "We can't just not play this game and then go back to our room": Kyle Korver, panel at Creighton University, Omaha, Nebraska, October 25, 2020.

293   Ownership helped get the lieutenant governor of Wisconsin on speakerphone: Ramona Shelburne, Marc J. Spears, Adrian Wojnarowski,

Malika Andrews and Zach Lowe, "Inside the Hectic Hours around a Historic NBA Boycott," ESPN.com, August 27, 2020.

294   "We don't know exactly what the future holds": Kyle Korver, panel at Creighton University.

296   "We're out": Chris Haynes, "Inside the Emotional 48 hours That Saved the NBA's Bubble," Yahoo! Sports, August 28, 2020.

296   "They'd be crucified": "Protests in the Bubble and Kobe's Legacy, With Kent Bazemore," August 27, 2020, in *Winging It with Vince Carter and Annie Finberg*, podcast, 1:11:01.

296   That's why you couldn't skip steps like this strike: "Protests in the Bubble and Kobe's Legacy, With Kent Bazemore," in *Winging It with Vince Carter and Annie Feinberg*.

297   "And the younger generation that we have to teach": "Protests in the Bubble and Kobe's Legacy, With Kent Bazemore," in *Winging It with Vince Carter and Annie Feinberg*.

297   "Y'all need to set up a more permanent structure": *The Shop*, Episode 8, "Barack Obama," directed by Robert Alexander, October 30, 2020, on HBO.

297   "It's not going to be solved overnight": *The Shop*, Episode 8, "Barack Obama."

298   "a suspension of activism": *The Shop*, Episode 8, "Barack Obama."

298   he'd been disappointed when Jordan, consumed by living up to his own image, joked about Republicans buying sneakers, too: *The Last Dance*, episode V, directed by Jason Hehir, aired May 3, 2020, on ESPN.

298   "And that," Obama would conclude, "is the next evolution: translating this not just from protest but then also understanding how they can use their *power*, which is significant—formidable, more than it was probably twenty or thirty years ago": "The Future of Sports with Barack Obama and Bakari Sellers. Plus, Million Dollar Picks Week 15," December 17, 2020, in *The Bill Simmons Podcast*, podcast, 11:08.

298   Basketball players especially, he later reminded LeBron, had set a new tone for young people: *The Shop*, Episode 8, "Barack Obama."

ENCORE

302-3 "Our stories is the *same* thing—it's pushing the culture forward in another way": Jay-Z, interview with Elliott Wilson, *The Truth with Elliott Wilson*, Life+Times, July 24, 2013.

303 "turned their back on social responsibility": Alexandra Zawia, "Harry Belafonte on Capitalism, Media Moguls and His Disappointment with Jay-Z and Beyoncé," HollywoodReporter.com, August 7, 2012.

303 "This is going to sound arrogant, but my *presence* is charity": Jay-Z, interview with Elliott Wilson.

304 a majority of Americans finally supported athletes kneeling during the anthem: Rick Maese and Emily Guskin, "Most Americans Support Athletes Speaking Out, Say Anthem Protests Are Appropriate, *Post* Poll Finds," *The Washington Post*, September 9, 2020.

306 "a legislative agenda": Adam Silver interview, ESPN, November 18, 2020.

307 "Go ahead": Anthony Slater, "Kevin Durant on James Harden's inevitable MVP chase: 'It's his turn,'" *The Athletic*, April 2, 2018.

307 But in 2020 he was willing to forgo a contract extension of $50 million a year: Adrian Wojnarowski, "Sources: James Harden rejects Rockets extension; focus on trade to Nets," ESPN.com, November 16, 2020.

308-9 Unclaimed bodies in the freezer trucks still parked outside the practice facility: Paul Berger, "NYC Dead Stay in Freezer Trucks Set Up During Spring Covid-19 Surge," *The Wall Street Journal*, November 22, 2020.

310 "There's a cap on what we can do when we just wanna spread awareness, because there's only so much awareness can do": "Young CEO Experience," presented by Overtime and *The Boardroom*, October 27, 2020.

ABOUT THE AUTHOR

MATT SULLIVAN has been an editor at *The New York Times*, *The Guardian*, *The Atlantic*, *Esquire* and *Bleacher Report*. His work in sports, celebrity and investigative journalism has been honored more than a dozen times by *The Best American Sports Writing*, the National Magazine Awards and the Edward R. Murrow Awards. A native New Yorker and graduate of Duke University, Matt lives with his wife, their daughter and their French bulldog.